To Mr. Linda
Sims

with Best
Regards

Chikara Higashi
Oct. 22, 1987
at Tokyo

The Internationalization Of The Japanese Economy

THE INTERNATIONALIZATION OF THE JAPANESE ECONOMY

CHIKARA HIGASHI
Member, House of Representatives, Tokyo, and
President, Temple University, Japan

G. PETER LAUTER
School of Government and Business Administration
The George Washington University
Washington, D.C. 20052
USA

KLUWER ACADEMIC PUBLISHERS
Boston, MA

Distributors

for the United States and Canada: Kluwer Academic Publishers, 101 Philip Drive, Assinippi Park, Norwell, MA, 02061, USA

for the UK and Ireland: Kluwer Academic Publishers, MTP Press Limited,
Falcon House, Queen Square, Lancaster LA1 1RN, UK

for all other countries: Kluwer Academic Publishers Group, Distribution
Centre, P.O. Box 322, 3300 AH Dordrecht, The Netherlands

Library of Congress Cataloging in Publication Data

Higashi, Chikara.
  The internationalization of the Japanese economy.
  Bibliography: p.
  Includes index.
  1. Japan — Economic conditions — 1945–
2. Japan — Economic policy — 1945–   . 3. Japan–
Foreign economic relations. I. Lauter, Geza P.
(Geza Peter) II. Title.
HC462.9.H45 1987   337.52 87-3893
ISBN 0-89838-199-1

Copyright

Contents

List of Tables and Figures

TABLES

FIGURES

Acknowledgments

Much of the information and insight presented in this book was obtained through personal interviews particularly with Japanese and, to a lesser extent, American government officials and business executives in Tokyo and Washington, D.C. While they are too numerous to mention individually, their willingness to take time out of their busy schedules is very much appreciated.

Michaela Siren of Washington, D.C., provided invaluable support not only in the editing and preparing of the manuscript but also in her contribution to writing two sections of the book. Karen Ball, a graduate student of The George Washington University, gave additional assistance.

Foreword

The internationalization of the Japanese economy, or the shift from an export-led to a domestic demand-led growth, is one of the important current developments in the world-economy. It involves the interaction of a variety of economic, social and cultural factors which many observers outside of Japan need to appreciate in order to understand what the process entails.

Drs. Higashi and Lauter have written a book which is providing detailed insight into the policy alternatives which the Japanese government has chosen to achieve the objectives of the internationalization process. Moreover, they have also analyzed the potential problems which surround the implementation of the complex policies.

I believe that their book is a valuable addition to both the academic and the general literature on Japan's efforts to change its role in the world economy and to contribute to the well-being of people everywhere.

Michio Watanabe
Tokyo, March 1987

Minister of International Trade and
Industry
December 1985—July 1986

Minister of Finance
July 1980—November 1982

The Internationalization Of The Japanese Economy

1 THE PATH TO ECONOMIC POWER

Japan, known around the world as a small, resource-poor island country, has experienced a greater than tenfold increase in its gross national product (GNP) in real terms since 1950. Annual growth rates ranging from 10 percent during the 1960s to approximately 3–4 percent in the early 1980s have not only resulted in continually increasing world GNP shares but will also enable Japan to match the Soviet Union as the second largest economy behind the United States by the beginning of the twenty-first century.

The statistics on United States–Japan bilateral trade reported in this book were obtained from both American and Japanese sources. Any discrepancy between the two sets of data is the result of the differing calculating methods used.

The U.S. Department of Commerce reports imports (Japanese exports) on a CIF (cost, insurance, and freight) basis, whereas Japan reports its custom-cleared exports on an FOB (free on board) basis, which excludes insurance and freight costs.

The fluctuating yen–dollar exchange rate caused additional data distortions. Yen amounts reported between 1981–1985 were converted at an average exchange rate of Y 230 to the U.S. dollar, while yen amounts in 1986 were converted at Y 165.

TABLE 1−1.   World GNP shares of selected countries and regions: 1960−2000 (in percentages)

Country	World GNP share		
	1960	1980	2000
Japan	3	10	12
USA	33	22	20
Other OECD countries	26	31	26
Industrial countries	62	63	58
NICs*	3	4	7
LDCs	11	11	13
Developing countries	14	15	20
USSR	15	13	12
Eastern Europe	4	5	5
China	5	4	5
Communist Bloc	24	22	22
World, total	100	100	100

* NICs = Newly industrializing countries (Republic of Korea, Hong Kong, Singapore, Brazil, Mexico, and Taiwan).

Source: *Japan 1986: An International Comparison* (Tokyo: Keizai Koho Center, 1986), p. 8.

Table 1−1 shows the past and projected world GNP shares between 1960 and the year 2000.

This remarkable growth in Japan's economy was characterized by a rapid increase in export activity. In 1965 Japan's world export share was approximately 5 percent, and by 1985 its share exceeded 10 percent; during the same 20 year period, the United States' share decreased from 16 percent to approximately 11 percent. Japanese exporters established major world market shares while global economic growth decreased in real terms from 4.4 percent during 1970−1975, to 3.9 percent between 1975−1980, to approximately 3 percent from 1980. Japanese exports increased significantly as a percentage of imports by all Organization for Economic Cooperation and Development (OECD) countries between 1978 and 1983 particularly in advanced products as shown in table 1−2. It is noteworthy that these years were marked by generally low growth rates in most member countries.

As Japan's export market shares increased, current and trade account surpluses began to emerge during the second half of the 1960s, then became persistent and grew rapidly, particularly during the early 1980s.

TABLE 1−2.   Japanese exports of advanced products as a percentage of
OECD imports: 1978 and 1983

Product	Year	
	1978	*1983*
Computers	5.2	18.0
Office machines	43.8	58.3
Telecommunications equipment	26.5	41.8
Stereos, televisions, VCRs, etc.	50.6	99.3

Source: *OECD Commodity and Trade Statistics* (Paris: Organization for Economic Cooperation and Development, issues 1975 through 1984).

The Japanese current account surplus reached $24.2 billion in FY 1983, $37
billion in FY 1984, and $50 billion in FY 1985 which represented 3.7
percent of GNP, and was, thus, larger than the Federal Republic of
Germany's postwar high of 2.7 percent achieved in 1974, and matched the
U.S. record of 3.7 percent set in 1947, shortly after World War II when the
United States dominated the world economy.[1]

Not surprisingly, such a performance generated a proliferation of literature attempting to explain this economic phenomenon. One extreme of
this literature is represented by such an adulatory work as *Japan as
Number One,* whereas the opposite extreme is represented by a book as
hostile as *The Japanese Conspiracy.*[2] Between these two extremes is a
mixed bag of mostly adulatory publications dealing with the sociocultural
and managerial dimensions of the Japanese success story. While most of
these publications provide some interesting insights, the authors' extreme
or limited positions make it difficult to obtain a reasonable and comprehensive understanding of the Japanese experience.

There are, however, two recent books with differing but complementary
approaches that represent the best of the genre to date. *The Competition:
Dealing With Japan* by Pepper, Janow, and Wheeler, of the Hudson
Institute, examines the macroeconomic issues surrounding Japan's growth,
while *Kaisha: The Japanese Corporation* by James C. Abegglen and
George Stalk, Jr., analyzes the microeconomic aspects of Japan's post-
World War II economic performance.[3] Here, the authors avoid extreme
positions and support their arguments with sound evidence. Together these
two books provide the most convincing analysis of Japan's evolution into
an economic power.

Objectives of This Book

During 1985–1986 important developments took place in Japan. Partially in response to external pressures generated by the persistent current account surpluses, and partially as a result of self-initiated soul-searching aimed at a redefinition of the country's role in the twenty-first century, these two years have generated much debate about the nation's future. New "visions" of the future, programs and reports, such as the 1985 market opening Action Program, the 1986 Maekawa Commission Report, and a number of other studies identified the basic issues in need of consideration and resolution. Although responsible politicians, government officials, business leaders, and academicians, all of whom are so-called internationalists, agree that Japan's new status as an economic power calls for a revised global role, many Japanese do not yet fully appreciate their country's impact on the world economy. They still see Japan as somewhat vulnerable and unique, and believe that it should be treated as a special case among the world's nations. Others believe that Japan alone is asked to endure painful economic changes to please other nations which suffer from symptoms of "advanced industrial nation's disease" such as the lack of international competitiveness due to low productivity, high wages, prodigious spending habits, and a craving for comfort rather than a willingness to work hard. Some express resentment over the fact that other nations never seem to consult Japan on anything except trade issues, and then only to lecture the Japanese about their "unfairness" or what they need to do in order to satisfy the demands of others. Despite international and domestic claims of rapidly rising affluence, Japanese complaints about economic constraints, such as heavy mortgage repayments, rising tax and social security contributions, and increasing education costs are becoming more frequent and noticeable. This is particularly true among those who see themselves as members of the middle class with annual incomes of up to approximately 10 million or about $60,000 in 1986. Therefore, there is disagreement within Japan not only concerning the necessity to redefine the nation's international role but also with regard to the ability to do so.

Most people, however, agree that something needs to be done. In a poll conducted by the New York Times, CBS news, and the Tokyo Broadcasting System in the spring of 1986, 62 percent of the Japanese agreed that their country is now a world economic power with international responsibilities; only 31 percent disagreed.[4] Informed people also understand that past attempts of pursuing only a balance between domestic demand and exports to reduce the huge current account surpluses are not realistic, because given the income elasticity of Japanese exports (1.7) and that of imports (0.7), such a policy would require domestic economic growth three of four times that of the world economy over extended periods of time to generate enough imports to balance the surpluses. Thus, in addition to the establishment of more stable and realistic exchange rates through the coordination of national economic policies by the major industrial nations, Japan needs to achieve a balanced combination of higher imports, increased foreign investment and aid, as well as growth of domestic demand to reduce the surpluses and to develop a new international role.

The objective of this book is to explore the key issues surrounding the domestic and international policy options the Japanese have chosen to internationalize the economy.[5] The 1985 Action Program, the 1986 Maekawa Plan and the related "visions" of the future published in 1985–1986 are used as the basis of discussion. The program, the report, and the visions were selected because they represent the different aspects of the internationalization process as it is emerging. The 1985 Action Program was import-oriented, and it was formulated primarily in response to strong foreign, particularly American, pressures. The 1986 Maekawa Commission Report was the result of both external pressures and a genuine, comprehensive, domestic soul-searching process initiated by the internationalists under the leadership of Prime Minister Nakasone. The visions, such as the 1986 Ministry of International Trade and Industry (MITI) report on "Japan in the Global Community: Its Role and Contribution on the Eve of the Twenty-First Century," were produced to stimulate additional ideas in the emerging society-wide debate.

In addition, the major events in Japan and the United States that have led to the 1985–1986 developments are also explored, as are the domestic controversies surrounding the internationalization process. The focus of this book is on Japan, but because the United States is its most important trading partner and the guarantor of its national security, the evolution of U.S.–Japan trade relations as they have led to a variety of recent American demands upon Japan to change its economic ways are also included in this discussion.

It is, however, not within the purview of this book to identify "winners" and "losers" in the international trade arena of the future. While intellectually stimulating, such prognostications do not contribute to a better understanding of the policy options Japan has selected to redefine its international role. According to a 1986 survey of the *Nihon Keizai Shimbun* (The Japan Economic Journal), most people in the United States and Western Europe see Japan as an economic threat, although they think that the Japanese are a friendly people.[6] Given a list of 30 countries from which to choose international competitors posing an economic threat to their nations, respondents in the United States, the United Kingdom, France, and the Federal Republic of Germany chose Japan as the country that most concerns them. Japan was seen as the number 2 and 3 economic threat, respectively, in Canada and Italy. Over 70 percent of the respondents in all the participating countries believed that Japan unreasonably restricts imports. While one can argue the validity of data reported in international surveys, the fact remains that Japan's economic success is perceived as a threat by many people throughout the world. Thus, a better appreciation of Japan's domestic and international policy options in redefining its global role is more helpful than predictions of who is going to be *Ichiban* (Number One) at the turn of the century. Undoubtedly, international economic competition will get tougher in the future, and in numerous industries Japan will be in the forefront of this competition. However, what the world needs is not economic domination by a single nation but more effective multilateral cooperation.

As indicated previously, the internationalization process will be controversial. Quick and easy changes should not be expected. The process will extend over a number of years and will be marked by debates, marginal changes, trial and error, and probably even some retreats. Many of the proposed policy options touch on fundamental values and call for wrenching adjustments within the Japanese society. Moreover, the rapid appreciation of the yen during 1985–1986 has unleashed economic forces that are contributing to the internationalization process, but at the same time are also creating a new set of domestic problems, such as unemployment, which need to be considered. To minimize these problems or to see the uneven progress as a clever plot either to delay the inevitable or perhaps not change anything at all, underestimates the difficulties associated with altering deeply ingrained habits and addressing new socioeconomic problems anywhere, let alone in a strongly tradition-bound society such as Japan.

The views expressed within some American and Western European political and business circles, that Japan's internationalization process represents fancy windowdressing since it will not quickly eliminate Japan's large current account and trade surpluses, are based on unrealistic expectations. The objective of the internationalization process is not to eliminate such imbalances *per se*, but to establish a more balanced multilateral trade environment in which both the benefits and the burdens of free trade are more equitably shared by all participants, including Japan. In such an environment, excessive long-term current account and trade imbalances will be less likely, and whenever they occur, they will be addressed through a more rational discourse than is presently the case. This, of course, assumes that the new Uruguay round of GATT (General Agreement on Tariffs and Trade) negotiations will result in a strengthening of the global trade system.

The Evolution of the Japanese Economy

To discuss the domestic and international policy options chosen by the Japanese to internationalize the economy, it is first necessary to provide an overview of the evolution of Japan's post-World War II economy.

Japan entered its era of rapid economic growth at a time when the mass-production methods in a number of key industries, such as automobiles and consumer durables, began to mature, and worldwide demand for such products was strong. At the same time, the establishment of the General Agreement on Tariffs and Trade provided an environment in which nations could practice free trade. This was made possible by the enlightened economic leadership of the United States which, partially out of self-interest and partially out of the recognition that a 1930s-type protectionist environment could easily result in another economic disaster, convinced most nations of the noncommunist world that free trade benefits everyone.

Two countries that made the most of the new international economic environment were the Federal Republic of Germany and Japan. Free of any big politico-military ambitions and protected by U.S. military power in the ensuing East–West cold war, both nations devoted their considerable talents and energies to rebuilding their economies and continual development.[7] In a relatively short period of time, Germany and then Japan became formidable international competitors. For the former, this essentially meant the re-establishment of a pre-World World II position, but for Japan, it meant breaking new ground.

While for a long time it was fashionable to explain the rapid growth and continually improving international competitiveness of the postwar Japanese economy through the "Japan Inc." concept, recent analyses have revealed that more complex forces have been at work.[8] Undoubtedly, Japan did have a national strategy to develop its economy; this strategy consisted of goals, ideas on how to accomplish those goals, and specific policies and institutions needed to implement the ideas. However, as indicated in an insightful study of international competitiveness, "...key differences in strategies do not appear to be between those that are more coherent and those that are less so, but between those that are growth/productivity/opportunity oriented on the one hand and those that are distribution/security/resources oriented on the other".[9] In other words, while close and systematic cooperation between business and government was important, the key elements in Japan's economic success were the strong growth and productivity orientation of both government and business. The validity of this argument can be demonstrated by simply considering the large number of nations whose close government—business relations did not produce the same results as occurred in Japan, because the growth-productivity orientation was absent. Abegglen and Stalk make the same point at the micro level.[10] According to them, it was the growth orientation of the *kaisha* nurtured by strong domestic competition, that made the Japanese corporations such formidable international competitors, and not their supposed "unfair" competitive practices.

This growth-productivity orientation was based on what Scott calls "the dynamic (revised) theory of comparative advantage" which the Japanese introduced, and which today is followed by a number of the newly industrializing countries (NICs), such as South Korea and Brazil.[11] According to the classical notion of comparative advantage, a country's resources are given, change very slowly over time, and once fully used, lead to increasing costs. Not subscribing to such a static view of the world economy, the Japanese decided to alter their "given" comparative advantage, labor. By creating other critical resources, such as technology, and by fully exploiting the benefits of the learning curve and the economies of scale of production, they quickly became internationally competitive in a number of selected industries. Simply stated, the Japanese did not accept the proposition that more than 100 million able and highly motivated people subscribing to a common set of values should be limited to the exploration of their "given" comparative advantage. The Japanese envisioned more for their country than simply specializing in labor-intensive products for the indefinite future. They did not accept the low standard of living and the chronic balance of payment deficits which the classical theory of comparative advantage ordains for those nations less fortunately endowed with resources.

Altering the "given" comparative advantage and enhancing the growth-productivity orientation called for an active government policy role. Growth areas needed to be identified, capital allocated, technology obtained, various means of increasing productivity had to be developed, and markets needed to be secured. This was done through a variety of measures that collectively became known as industrial policies. The following is an outline of these policies as they were applied in Japan from the early 1950s until the late 1960s.

Industrial Policies

Japan's postwar industrial policies have long been a topic of controversy. Those who subscribe to the conspiracy explanation of Japan's economic success consider such policies irrefutable proof of powerful government agencies, such as MITI, the Economic Planning Agency (EPA), and the Ministry of Finance (MOF), organizing and successfully managing a systematic economic assault on the rest of the unsuspecting world. In their view, most industrial policies violated international trading rules (GATT), thus providing Japan with unfair competitive advantages. Others, basing their analyses on the classical or "static" notion of comparative advantage, argued that the Japanese strategy did not involve anything new or very unusual.[12] As is the case with such controversies, the most reasonable explanation lies somewhere between the two extremes.

There can be no question that the Japanese introduced a more effective strategy for industrializing in general, and for achieving international competitiveness in particular. They had no choice, because rapid economic growth and increasing productivity and exports were needed to cope with the shortage of resources, the chronic balance of payment problems, and the low standard of living during the immediate postwar years. The homogeneous nature of the society and its tradition of discipline and goal orientation provided an environment in which industrial policies could be effectively developed and applied within a relatively short period of time.

A discussion of industrial policies immediately introduces a problem of definition. Equating such policies with "targeting," the practice of selecting winners and losers in the international marketplace, too narrowly defines these policies. The argument that all government economic policies somehow impact the economy and, therefore, are industrial policy, renders this concept analytically useless. The diversity of economic policies available and the multiple, broad impact of their combined applications make it difficult, if not impossible, to measure their effectiveness. So, while the Japanese undoubtedly developed and applied a new strategy, and while this strategy was successful, generalizations about its precise effectiveness, fairness, or unfairness are questionable at best, misleading at worst. The most that can be convincingly said is that within a relatively short period of time, Japan managed to create the critical resources necessary to becoming competitive in today's global economy.

Japan's example is inspiring. While most developing countries do not possess the societal characteristics needed to imitate Japan's success, many will at least try.[13] Few developing-country governments can afford to accept indefinitely the second-class economic citizenship that the traditional methods of industrialization confer. Thus, to avoid acrimonious trade conflicts, the international community needs to adjust current trade rules to accomodate the new industrialization strategies which reflect the political and economic realities of the world as they exist, not as they ought to be according to some idealized notion of the past. While the concept of free trade should continue to play a central role, it should not be allowed to degenerate into a static article of faith to which nations pay lipservice but do not abide because it has little or no relevance to reality. Every nation knows that industrialization and trade are dynamic activitites, and that domestic political necessities often override the principles of free trade as they are embodied in the current set of GATT rules.

If the Japanese experience is properly evaluated, a general understanding about the legitimacy of the various dynamic, industrial policy measures might be reached. The emotional and often meaningless debates about fairness and unfairness could be replaced by a more useful discourse on how to provide for a more effective industrialization process on the basis of a dynamic concept of free trade and competition. This, of course, is not an easy task, and it may take many years to achieve. However, considering the alternative, it is worth a try. While not on the agenda of the new Uruguay round of GATT talks, it can only be hoped that the participating nations will pay some attention to these issues during the discussions scheduled through 1990.

In the meanwhile, no generally accepted definition or interpretation of industrial policies as applied by Japan is available. Perhaps one of the most insightful explanations was given by Abegglen and Stalk who argued that

> . . . the principal role of the government of Japan at the operating, business level of industrial change and growth has been to facilitate and accelerate the workings of the market, to speed the process of reduction of declining sectors, and to work clear the way for market forces to have full play in emerging growth sectors. At the broader level of national policy, the government of Japan has been a critical force in providing the social infrastructure, in providing supportive fiscal and monetary policy, and in providing general directions for the business community.[14]

Abegglen and Stalk see the industrial-policy and macroeconomic-policy combination provided by the Japanese government as a forceful guiding mechanism that paved the way for the economy to become internationally competitive. To this, one should add that until the mid-1960s, as in all developing countries, protection of infant industries was a centerpiece of this mechanism, and that the resulting protectionist attitudes were carried

over by some government and business circles into later years. Protectionism, however, was not only used to promote the development of emerging
industries but was also meant to deal with the difficulties of an overvalued
yen.[15] Japan was committed to a fixed exchange rate set under the Bretton
Woods system in 1949, resulting in chronic balance of payment deficits
until the mid-1960s. Japan responded to this problem with strong foreign
exchange controls, including severe limitations on foreign investment both
at home and abroad, import quotas, high tariffs, and a variety of tax and
other incentives for exports. The balance of payments difficulties naturally
promoted import substitution.

The industrial-policy and macroeconomic-policy combination used was
neither routine nor a sophisticated conspiracy violating international trade
rules; it was a well-conceived, uniquely Japanese way of accomplishing
challenging objectives in the shortest possible time. It is worth noting that
protectionism during the 1950s and 1960s did not necessarily violate
international trade rules, because under the Bretton Woods system, nations with balance of payment problems were expected to reduce trade
deficits and thereby protect the exchange value of their currencies.

The uniqueness of the Japanese strategy was not so much in its policy
measures but in the combinations of those measures and in the societal
framework within which the policies were applied. The homogeneous and
well-educated population could be called upon to devote its considerable
energies to the achievement of the growth-productivity objectives, to
sacrifice consumption for savings, and consequently, to accept a lower
standard of living than could have been realized. Such human qualities
were harnessed by the elite bureaucracy and business leaders who were
respected, trusted, and could provide the necessary leadership.

The theoretical foundations of Japan's industrial policies were developed by two different generations of economists.[16] The first generation
was educated before or during World War II, and its influence was very
noticeable between the early 1950s through approximately 1965, during
which time MITI played a dominant role in developing and implementing
industrial policies. This generation was dedicated to the transformation of
a defeated, underdeveloped nation into a modern, developed state through
the creation of an industrial base hidden behind protective barriers. These
economists were influenced by the highly centralized planning systems
emerging throughout the world in the late 1940s and early 1950s. They
believed that the government must not only formulate development plans
but also regulate the activities of the private sector. Competition did not
play an important role in their deliberations for the postwar economy.

During the 1950s and 1960s when Japan became a member of various international organizations, such as the GATT, this generation viewed the resulting external demands for economic liberalization not as an opportunity to participate in the emerging free trade system but as a cost that the nation, albeit grudgingly, had to pay to once again become a full member of the international community. During the mid-1960s when this first generation of economists was gradually replaced by the next generation, its influence did not suddenly disappear but was carried over into subsequent years.

The next generation of economists was educated mostly in the West, and came home with ideas that were largely unknown in Japan at the time. They subscribed to the general equilibrium theory of microeconomics, as well as the welfare, economic, and industrial organization concepts developed mainly in the United States. They argued that a competitive market mechanism was the only way to allocate resources efficiently, and that industrial policies were needed to upgrade industries when, for some reason, the market mechanism performed inadequately. Not surprisingly, the second generation clashed with the first, and in general, displayed a much less cooperative attitude toward government agencies and industrial policies. Second generation members were particularly critical of the formation of the Nippon Steel Corporation through the merger of two major steel companies, and supported the Fair Trade Commission (FTC), which had very little influence during the 1960s and early 1970s.

Private sector economists of both generations were regularly consulted by the bureaucracy and its economists during the policy formulation process. They played an important role in the various councils established to advise government agencies. The most important of these, the Industrial Structure Council established by MITI, generated various medium-term and long-term policy reports called "visions" which the Japanese government published. While the recommendations of the council were not binding, they were reflected in the specific policies formulated by the administrative branch and approved by the Diet. After the mid-1960s, however, the two different generations of economists working in both the private and public sector began clashing over policy options. So, except for the first two decades following the war, industrial policy formulation was not free of conflicts; in fact, it was marked by diverse arguments during the lengthy consensus formulation process which preceded final decisions.

From the outset, MITI led the development and implementation of industrial policies.[17] Its name and organizational structure reflected the indivisibility of production and international trade as national objectives, and its highly qualified staff orchestrated the various activities needed to achieve the aims. Supported by other government institutions, such as the

Economic Planning Agency (EPA), the Japan Development Bank (JDB), and the Export-Import Bank, MITI also maintained a cooperative relationship with the powerful Ministry of Finance (MOF) as well as other key ministries. However, behind the support and cooperation that eventually emerged once a consensus was reached were long and acrimonious disagreements and debates, and it was not always the views of MITI that characterized the emerging policy. More often than not, it was the powerful Ministry of Finance in charge of the purse strings that had the last word on important issues.

The industrial policies reflected consensus concerning the growth objectives which were based on an assumed set of domestic and international economic conditions.[18] Continuous improvements in productivity and international competitiveness in a "targeted" group of industries were the foremost considerations in deciding on the appropriate combination of policies. The specific instruments included infant industry protection and import substitution, as well as tax incentives to promote savings for investments. For example, no tax was levied on income from small savings acounts (*maruyu*), postal savings accounts, and central government bonds. Double taxation of corporate income was minimized, special depreciation measures were established for certain assets, tax-free reserve funds for a variety of purposes were allowed, and selected service export tax credits were given. In general, the tax measures were aimed at improving the financial situation of companies and at promoting exports.

Supportive tax policies were backed by direct government lending at favorable terms. The Fiscal Investment and Loan Program, administered by a special bureau of the Ministry of Finance, was the major program used. The key institution, the Japan Development Bank, provided long-term, low-interest loans primarily for capital investment in emerging industries, but researh and development efforts generating innovations based on technologies originating elsewhere were also supported. The primary advantages of such loans over loans made by private banks were lower interest rates, longer life, and the absence of compensating balance requirements. Pepper and associates cite a U.S. International Trade Commission study, according to which only about 1.6–2.0 percent of the value of individual loans offered through such programs could be considered a subsidy.[19] They also found that as a percentage of all loans, lending by the Japan Development Bank was relatively insignificant.

Another important policy measure was the exemption of certain types of cartels from the Anti-Monopoly Law, which was introduced after World War II and based on the American antitrust laws. The Japanese have always been very pragmatic about their laws and have never elevated any

of them to the position of sacred covenants. If the antimonopoly requirements were not conducive to economic growth and the continuous improvement of productivity, they were willing to make exceptions as needed.
Thus, already during the mid-1950s, recession and rationalization cartels
became legal subject to case-by-case approval by the Fair Trade Commission. Rules on interlocking directorates were changed, and the limits on
bank ownership of corporate stock were raised. In addition, MITI sponsored a number of special industry laws, some of which exempted various
types of joint economic behaviour from the antitrust laws. The total
number of authorized cartels increased from 53 in 1953 to 1,079 in 1966,
and then gradually declined to 886 in 1970, and 422 in 1986.[20]

Beginning in the mid-1960s when direct government control over many
aspects of the economy was relaxed or eliminated, MITI and some of the
other agencies continued to exert their influence through administrative
guidance. Japanese laws and directives were written in a general language
so as to allow the bureaucracy to interpret their intent according to the
special circumstances prevailing at the time of their application. Due to the
respect and trust that the elite bureaucrats enjoyed, administrative guidance, although informal and not legally enforceable, was usually followed
by those who received it.

The decline of industrial policies as major economic management tools
continued without interruption throughout the 1960s and 1970s, and was
over by the early 1980s. Changes in both the international economic
environment and in the domestic economy, the increasing plurality of
Japanese society, and various external pressures all contributed to this
process. Following MITI's loss of control over foreign exchange allocations
during the 1960s, steps were taken to liberalize technology imports, foreign
exchange controls, and import quotas. Tariffs were lowered, virtually all
export promotion programs (except for a tax-break allowed for small and
medium size firms) were eliminated, and because of the increasingly larger
fiscal deficits, the Ministry of Finance granted fewer favourable tax treat-
ments. The financing role of the Japan Development Bank was substantially reduced, and the number of cartel exemptions was also curtailed.
Foreign investment controls were gradually eliminated, and a number of
different market opening measures were introduced.

By the early 1980s, the goals of the Japanese economic policy became
much broader than they had been in the past. Less emphasis was put on
growth and more placed on environmental problems, social welfare, small
business, and the macroeconomic problems associated with large budget
deficits. The reduction in the size, cost, and influence of government
through "administrative reform" also moved to the forefront. Business was

doing well on its own; the private sector was successful, and it did not want much government contact. Certain applications of industrial policy did continue, such as aid to structurally depressed industries, support to small-sized and medium-sized enterprises, development of visions, promotion of research and development (R&D), and administrative guidance; however, for the most part by the early 1980s the Japanese economy was not functioning much differently than that of the United States or Western Europe. This was noted by a number of American experts on Japan during a series of congressional hearings.[21] Some even implied that the only major difference between the Japanese economy and others was its continuing strong growth and productivity orientation.

By most standards, the Japanese economy of the early 1980s was quite different from that of the 1960s and 1970s. Nevertheless, within certain American and European political and business circles Japan continued to be viewed in terms which, in some cases, would even have been an exaggeration 25 years earlier. These circles ignored the liberalization efforts which took place and clung to an outdated, static picture of a dynamic economy that was undergoing constant changes. Impressed by the achievements of *kaishas* like Toyota or Sony, they perpetuated the myth that the Japanese economy was a fiercely efficient steamroller which, under the single-minded and often "unfair" leadership of MITI, was about to roll over the world and wipe out all of its competitors. Notwithstanding the accomplishments of the Japanese economy in general and the *kaisha* in particular, these views were erroneous in several respects.

When judged by growth and productivity standards over a 25−year to 30−year period, the Japanese economy performed consistently better than the American or European economies, yet MITI, EPA, and the other agencies did not possess any mystical powers to achieve that performance. For example, as table 1−3 shows, during the era of rapid worldwide growth (1956−1971), Japanese government forecasters regularly under-estimated the growth of the domestic economy. At a time of relative international stability, such performance was hardly an indication of infallible leadership.

Economic forecasting is a difficult task. It is limited by numerous factors which cannot be predicted. Thus, the performance of the Japanese government forecasters should not be considered unusual. American and European forecasters were plagued by similar problems in trying to predict the courses of their economies. The illustration should nevertheless help destroy the myth that the Japanese government agencies had some sort of supernatural hold over the economy and, consequently, could manipulate it according to their will.

TABLE 1–3. Long-term economic forecasts and actual results: 1956–1971

Name:	Five-year plan for economic self-support	New long-range economic plan	Doubling national income plan	Medium-term economic plan	Economic and social development plan
Period:	1956–1960	1958–1962	1961–1970	1964–1968	1967–1971
Cabinet:	Hatoyama	Kishi	Ikeda	Sato	Sato
GNP growth forecast:	5.0%	6.5%	7.8%	8.1%	8.2%
Actual:	8.7%	9.9%	10.7%	10.6%	10.9%

Source: *Japan's Industrial Policies* (Washington, D.C.: The Japan Economic Institute, 1984), p. 13.

TABLE 1–4. Long-term economic forecasts and actual results: 1970–1990

Name:	New economic and social development plan	Basic economic and social plan	Economic plan for the second half of the 1970s	New economic and social seven-year plan	Outlook and guidelines for economic society in the 1980s
Period:	1970–1975	1973–1977	1976–1980	1979–1985	1983–1990
Cabinet:	Sato	Tanaka	Miki	Ohira	Nakasone
GNP growth					
forecast:	10.6%	9.4%	6%+	5.7%	4%
Actual:	5.9%	4.2%	5.7%	4.2%	—

Source: *Japan's Industrial Policies* (Washington, D.C.: The Japan Economic Institute, 1984), p. 13; and *Japan 1986: An International Comparison* (Tokyo: Keizai Koho Center, 1986), p. 12.

Table 1−4 shows that government forecasts for the 1970−1990 period were approximately of the same quality as those for the previous era, except that in a period of slower global growth, officials consistently overestimated the potential of the Japanese economy. As a result of the deflationary effects of the 1985−1986 yen appreciation, the overall 4 percent growth rate projected for the 1983−1990 period is not likely to be reached either.

Government agencies made errors in more areas than forecasting. The automobile industry is a classic example of the problems MITI faced when picking its winners and losers. In the early days of the automobile industry, MITI strongly objected to that industry's plans to export, because the officials did not believe that there was a market for Japanese automobiles. Although by 1962 MITI was willing to support these exports, its officials insisted on certain structural changes, demanding that manufacturers merge, thus creating a dominant Japanese automobile *kaisha*. Only three small mergers took place, and simultaneously, against MITI's objections, several new producers entered the industry. When MITI finally left the industry alone around 1969, the individual manufacturers took off on the road to international success. Television, stereo equipment, camera equipment, and other types of manufacturers were not high on MITI's list of deserving industries, either. Nevertheleses, through their own efforts, they also successfully penetrated world markets. Today these industries not only hold major market shares but they are also the technological leaders in their fields.

The Key Role of Productivity and Savings

While infant industry protection together with the macroeconomic-industrial policy combination played a major role in the rapid growth of the postwar Japanese economy, focusing only on these measures provides an incomplete picture. It was the growth-productivity orientation of the Japanese government and business that made the impressive results possible, particularly as it was reflected in the continual increase of manufacturing productivity and net household savings rates. International comparisons of these two key factors show why the Japanese economy developed so much faster than its competitors. Table 1−5 shows the growth trends in manufacturing productivity in the major industrialized countries over a period of nearly 30 years.

The data clearly show that except for the 1973−1979 period when the first oil shock and its aftermath caused manufacturing productivity to

TABLE 1–5. International comparison of manufacturing productivity growth trends: 1950–1979 (in percentages)

Country	Time periods					
	1950–1979	1950–1967	1967–1973	1973–1979	1977–1978	1978–1979
United States	2.4	2.6	2.9	2.2	0.5	1.5
Japan	8.5	9.5	10.0	4.2	7.9	8.3
Canada	3.9	4.1	5.1	4.8	4.7	0.8
France	5.2	4.9	6.1	5.1	4.9	5.4
West Germany	5.7	6.1	5.3	5.0	3.4	5.2
Italy	6.0	6.4	7.2	3.3	3.0	2.2
United Kingdom	2.7	3.0	4.2	0.6	1.2	2.2

Source: *Report of the Japan-United States Economic Relations Group* (Washington, D.C., 1981), p. 41.

TABLE 1−6. Productivity differences in the manufacturing sector according to plant size: 1981 (in percentages)

Number of employees	30−49	50−99	100−199	200−299	300−499	500−999	1000 or more
Productivity	46.1	48.6	58.8	67.7	78.2	88.0	100.0

Source: *Useful Labor Statistics* (Tokyo: Japan Productivity Center, 1984), p. 16.
Note: Firms with more than 1,000 employees represent 100 percent productivity.

decline, for most of the 1950−1979 period Japan was well ahead of the other nations. However, when considering the Japanese performance, it must be noted that there were significant differences between the aggregate productivity levels and the productivity of individual industries or firms. Table 1−6 demonstrates the productivity differences according to plant size during the early 1980s. The productivity of companies with fewer than 300 employees, the small-sized to medium-sized firms, was just more than half that of companies with 1,000 or more employees.

So, it was the large *kaisha* that were in the forefront of continuous productivity improvements. These companies carried the improvements into the international marketplace through what Abegglen and Stalk call the "winners competitive cycle."[22] This is based on the proposition that for a company to succeed in a highly competitive environment, it must grow faster than others. A company can do this by increasing market share through the efficient manufacture and aggressive marketing of high quality products. The *kanban* (just-in-time) inventory system, aggressive price cutting through cost reduction based on the learning curve, or continuous new product introduction are some of the means to such an end. The funds generated through growing market shares are reinvested to finance the repetition of the cycle. Abegglen and Stalk also point out that the process is more effective in high-growth as opposed to low-growth economies. Thus, for many years the large Japanese *kaisha* had better opportunities to exploit this cycle than their American or European competitors.

The other major factor in the growth-productivity orientation that differentiated Japan from the rest of the industralized world was the high rate of personal savings. Once postwar inflation was brought under control in 1951 and real income began to rise, savings increased steadily throughout the years. While expected to level off once the economy stabilized in the 1960s, savings continued to grow, although at a slower pace. Table 1−7 provides an international comparison of net savings trends as a percentage

TABLE 1−7. A comparison of net household savings in selected countries:
1960−1981 (as a percentage of disposable income)

Countries	Years		
	1960−1966	1967−1973	1974−1981
Japan	17.2	18.1	21.4
United States	7.2	8.4	7.4
Federal Republic of Germany	16.0	16.1	12.2
France	12.2	12.8	13.1
United Kingdom	5.6	5.7	9.2
Italy	17.5	19.2	21.8

Source: *OECD Economic Outlook, Historical Statistics, 1960−81* (Paris: Organization for Economic Cooperation and Development, 1983), pp. 69−70.

of disposable household income over a 20−year period.

The *maruyu* (tax-exempt small savings) arrangements played a major role in the postwar savings system. Through the *maruyu*, small savers could exempt interest earned on deposits and make tax-free investments in government bonds and certain pension plans. While a number of different institutions offered savings opportunities, one of the most important of these was the postal system established in 1875 and managed by the Postal Savings Bureau of the Ministry of Posts and Telecommunications (MPT). By channelling the small deposits into government and industry, the postal savings system provided a substantial part of the capital needed to finance postwar growth. In the early 1980s, this accounted for more than 30 percent of individual savings deposits, worth approximately $500 billion.[23]

External Trade

As mentioned earlier, Japan needed rapid economic growth and constantly increasing exports to cope with the shortage of resources, the low standard of living, and the chronic balance of payment problems of the immediate postwar years. Promoted through infant industry protection and macro-economic-industrial policy combinations, external trade began to grow rapidly around 1960. Table 1−8 shows the evolution of Japan's global trade over a period of more than 30 years until 1983. Except for the stagnation due to the first oil price increase and its after-math in the mid-1970s, Japan's external trade grew at a rapid pace until the early 1980s

TABLE 1−8. Japanese exports-imports and their share in world totals: 1950−1983

	Exports		Imports	
	Value ($ million)	Share of world total (%)	Value ($ million)	Share of world total (%)
1950	820	1.4	974	1.6
1955	2,011	2.3	2,471	2.7
1960	4,055	3.4	4,491	3.6
1965	8,452	5.0	8,169	4.5
1970	19,318	6.7	18,881	6.3
1975	55,753	6.9	57,863	7.0
1980	129,807	6.9	140,528	7.3
1981	152,030	8.2	143,290	7.5
1982	138,381	8.1	131,931	7.4
1983	146,927	8.8	126,393	7.3

Source: *Facts and Figures of Japan* (Tokyo: Foreign Press Center, 1985), p. 45.

when it slowed again. As table 1−8 illustrates, the growth of exports gradually outstripped that of imports in the early 1960s, and by 1965 the trade balance showed a surplus which, except for the mid-1970s, lasted into the 1980s.

In 1968 the current account balance also turned positive, and with the exception of the first and second oil shock years, it remained in surplus thereafter. Table 1−9 shows the evolution of the current account balances over a period of 20 years.

The chronic balance of payment problems of the postwar years initially required tight government controls over all external trade and foreign exchange activities. Consequently, until the early 1960s, all such transactions were monitored by the government. However, in June 1960 the General Principles of Liberalization Plans of Trade and Foreign Exchange were adopted, and Japan decided to increase the liberalization ratio of imports from 40 to 80 percent within three years. The plan was advanced in the fall of 1961, and a decision was made to increase the liberalization ratio to 90 percent by September 1962. In February 1963 Japan joined the GATT and, consequently, could no longer restrict imports on the basis of international payment difficulties. Additionally, in 1964 Japan ratified Article 8 of the International Monetary Fund (IMF). The gradual removal of control over foreign exchange transactions culminated in the Foreign Exchange and Foreign Trade Control Law introduced

TABLE 1–9.   Japanese current account balances:
1961–1982 (in $ millions)

Year	Balance
1961	−982
1962	−48
1963	−780
1964	−480
1965	932
1966	1,254
1967	−190
1968	1,048
1969	2,119
1970	1,970
1971	5,797
1972	6,624
1973	−136
1974	−4,693
1975	−682
1976	3,680
1977	10,918
1978	16,534
1979	−8,754
1980	−10,746
1981	4,770
1982	6,850

Source: Various editions of annual *International Financial Statistics* (Washington, D.C.: International Monetary Fund).

in December 1980. Under this law, all restrictions were removed, although the Ministry of Finance retained some authority to reimpose capital controls if necessary.

Liberalization of trade, foreign exchange, and the oil price shocks were probably the major external factors that played an important role in changing Japan's export structure over the years. Until the mid-1950s, exports consisted mainly of textiles, apparel, toys, china, and other light industrial products. However, as the industrial structure was gradually upgraded, exports increasingly shifted toward higher value-added items. In the 1960s, textiles and other light industrial products began to lose their international competitiveness, because domestic wage levels rose and a number of developing countries established light and labor-intensive industries, just as Japan had done in the late nineteenth century. By the 1960s, steel, shipbuilding, petro-chemical, machine, and precision industries were becoming intenationally competitive. In the 1970s, these industries continued to gain strength, although the shipbuilding industry had to operate at under-capacity because of a decline in worldwide demand. The automobile industry became competitive in the early 1970s, and established itself as one of the world leaders by the mid-1970s primarily through the fuel efficiency and high quality of its cars. Electronics, telecommunications, and other high technology industries broke into world markets during the late 1970s and early 1980s.

Japan's most important trading partner is the United States. The importance of America as a market for Japanese exports began in the early 1950s and has continued into the 1980s. Table 1–10 shows the evolution of Japanese trade with the United States between 1960 and 1983, including the share of this bilateral trade in total exports and imports. As the data show, the percentage of Japanese exports going to the United States has increased over time while the percentage of imports from America has decreased. Not surprisingly, the sharp growth in exports during the early 1980s, and the only slight increase in imports were harbingers of serious bilateral trade conflicts.

Japan's merchandise trade balance with the United States was negative until 1965. The United States experienced an annual trade surplus of $200–300 million except in 1961, when the surplus grew to more than $700 million.[24] Table 1–11 shows the evolution of bilateral trade balances

TABLE 1–10. Japanese exports to and imports from the United States: 1960–1983 (in $ millions)

Year	Exports		Imports	
	To USA	% of total	From USA	% of total
1960	1,102	27.2	1,554	34.6
1970	5,940	30.7	5,560	29.4
1975	11,149	20.0	11,608	20.1
1980	31,367	24.2	24,408	17.4
1982	36,330	26.2	24,179	18.3
1983	42,829	29.1	24,647	19.5

Source: *Nippon: A Chartered Survey of Japan 1985–1986* (Tokyo: Kokusei-Sha, 1985), p. 89.

TABLE 1–11.   Japan's merchandise trade balance with the United States:
1973–1983 (in $ millions)

	Exports	Imports	Balance
1973	9,449	9,270	179
1974	12,799	12,682	117
1975	11,149	11,608	−459
1976	15,690	11,809	3,881
1977	19,717	12,396	7,321
1978	24,915	14,790	10,125
1979	26,403	20,431	5,972
1980	31,367	24,408	6,959
1981	38,609	25,297	13,312
1982	36,330	24,179	12,151
1983	42,829	24,647	18,182

Source: *Japan 1986: An International Comparison* (Tokyo: Keizai Koho Center, 1986),
p. 36.

during the second half of the 1970s when the Japanese surpluses became
increasingly larger.

During these 10 critical years, the composition of goods flowing from
Japan to the United States was quite different from that which moved in
the opposite direction. Japan's exports included only small amounts of
agricultural products, crude materials, mineral fuels, or chemicals. The
overwhelming majority of goods sent to the United States consisted of a
wide range of manufactured items, including machinery, telecommunications equipment, transportation equipment, and other products, such as
watches, toys, and sporting goods.

In contrast, American exports of manufactured goods and equipment in
the same categories accounted for less than one-third of annual shipments
to Japan. The majority of American exports were agricultural commodities, crude materials, and mineral fuels, including coal. While the United
States also exported high-technology products to Japan, some observers
likened the structure of trade between the two nations to trade between a
developing and an industrialized nation. Such comparisons, although sim-
plistic insofar as they ignore the resource endowments and structural
differences between the two countries, were an indication of the emotional
and often superficial nature of the debate that eventually engulfed U.S.
Japanese trade relations.

The Evolution of U.S.–Japan Trade Conflicts

Japan's international trade conflicts in general, and with the United States in particular, began during the late 1960s and early 1970s. Until then its increasingly competitive stance in the world markets and growing trade and current account surpluses were accepted. World trade was still increasing at a satisfactory pace; economic growth, although interrupted by periodic recessions, was still strong enough in the major industrial countries to mask the gradual loss of international competitiveness by certain American and European industries, and unemployment levels still fluctuated within politically tolerable limits. Bilateral disagreements over trade issues were usually short-lived and settled in a reasonably amicable manner.

Beginning with the 1969–1971 textile conflict with the United States, however, the frequency, nature, and duration of the trade disagreements began to change. There were multiple reasons, some of which were inherent in the political-economic development process of the competing nations while others were primarily attributable to domestic and international economic policy choices made by the governments. One of the most significant political-economic developments was the change in the role of the United States. Specifically, the relative decline in America's economic and political power in the 1960s and thereafter made it difficult for the United States to maintain its traditionally liberal and paternalistic trade policies toward Europe, Japan, and the developing countries. The beginning of this new era was marked by the first U.S. global trade deficit in 78 years, a deficit of just over $2 billion in 1971. This, combined with Japan's emergence as a major international competitor, created trade conflicts which were conducted in an increasingly acrimonious fashion over longer periods of time.

In addition to the 1969–1971 textile conflicts, two other periods stand out during the 1970s and early 1980s.[25] The years 1976–1978 and 1981–1984 were marked by acrimonious and emotionally charged disagreements between Japan and the United States. These periods correspond with the years when Japan had large current and trade account surpluses, the United States and some Western European trading partners had large current and trade account deficits. With respect to the U.S.–Japan trade conflicts, the data show the following:[26] from 1967 through 1972, America's current account shifted from a surplus of over $2 billion to a deficit of approximately $6 billion. During the same time, the Japanese current account swung from a small deficit to a surplus of approximately $7 billion. From 1975 through 1978, the U.S. current account moved from a surplus of more than $18 billion to a deficit of approximately $14 billion; at the same time, Japan moved from a small deficit to a surplus greater than $16 billion. In terms of the bilateral trade balances, in the 1966–1972 period, America's bilateral trade deficit rose from an annual average of $0.5 billion to over $3.5 billion. Following a dip during 1973–1975, the U.S. deficit jumped to more than $8 billion in 1976–78. In 1981 the deficit reached about $16 billion, and it continued to increase, reaching $20 billion in 1983. In the same year the United States experienced a current account deficit of $40.8 billion, whereas Japan's current account surplus jumped to $21 billion from $6.8 billion in the previous year.

The U.S.–Japan trade conflicts had several major dimensions.[27] The first category consisted of national trade policies involving market access, the fairness vs. unfairness debate, and the various nontariff barriers. Also included here was the question of the low level of Japanese manufactured imports. The conflicts usually emerged over either the sharp increase in Japanese exports of textiles, steel, color televisions, and automobiles, or the inability of American exporters to expand their sales of agricultural, telecommunications, and related high-technology equipment in Japan.

Macroeconomic issues and monetary policy comprised another dimension, particularly the implications of America's increasing budget deficits and Japan's efforts to control its budget in line with the administrative and fiscal reform policy. As Bergsten and Cline pointed out, the opposing trends of the national budgets had important implications for the bilateral trade balances and conflicts.

The structural differences of the two economies represented the last major dimension. The differences in household savings, Japan's traditionally close supplier relations (*keiretsu*), its complex distribution system, the American exporters lack of savvy and drive to penetrate the Japanese markets, the short-term orientation of U.S. corporate managers, the price, quality, and competitiveness of American products, and related matters were the issues raised most often. Naturally, throughout the course of the debates and the ensuing negotiations, issues frequently overlapped; the nature of the Japanese distribution and supplier systems, for example, were included in the discussions on market access in general, and on nontariff barriers in particular.

The most heatedly debated issues concerned trade policy. Specifically, market access and alleged unfair trade practices have dominated U.S.–Japan trade conflicts since the mid-1970s. As a number of American industries lost their international competitiveness, local unemployment became a problem; and as the U.S. bilateral trade deficits with Japan increased, more and more industries sought help in Washington. Members of Congress, understandably sensitive to pressures from their constituents, responded by lashing out at the Japanese, the most visible competitors making inroads into the U.S. markets. Concerns in other categories, such as monetary and macroeconomic policies, received less attention, because other than the experts, most people and the press on both sides of the Pacific did not fully understand the complex issues involved. So, other than discussions at the highest level, relatively little attention was paid to these other matters. Another relevant issue, the internationalization of the Japanese economy as envisioned during the second half of the 1980s, was not sufficiently discussed by the two governments either, although matters of domestic economic growth generated some heated debates in 1978. Moreover, little time was spent on the discussion of structural problems in the American economy or the trade implications of the increasing budgetary deficits. The Japanese tried to approach these matters jointly, but the United States found it more expedient to focus on other points of disagreement.

This is not to say that international trade experts have not tried to assess realistically the causes of the huge U.S. trade account deficits. Some have argued that there were many causes with deep roots on both sides of the Pacific. They believed that these causes should be addressed through broad negotiations and coordinated multilateral actions, involving not only the United States and Japan but also the European Community and other nations.[28] On the American political scene, however, circumstances made it difficult, if not impossible, for even the most enlightened member of Congress to pursue such ideas. Pressures from single issue interest groups, a less orderly structure of Congress due to the demise of the once omnipotent committee chairman system, and the reduced influence of the White House after Watergate all combined with the uneven performance of the American economy to preclude a broader approach. Thus, members of Congress were conditioned to respond to specific pressures. The result was an increasingly assertive and protectionist Capitol Hill that paid more attention to trade policy issues than at any time since the mid-1930s, working against a free trade-oriented but hard-pressed Administration that tried to achieve a balance between the domestic pressures and America's international obligations.

Many members of Congress also believed that a clear and simple line could be drawn between fair and unfair trade practices. Ignoring the complex relationship between trade, macroeconomic, and structural policies as determinants of a nation's international competitiveness, they considered Japan's continuing bilateral trade surpluses as prima facie evidence of unfair Japanese trade practicese. A congressional axiom arose whereby the higher the bilateral trade imbalances became, the more unfair the Japanese actions had to be. Thus, by the late 1970s, the size of the annual bilateral trade imbalances dominated congressional debates on trade to the exclusion of most other relevant issues. This is not to argue that the bilateral imbalances were economically sustainable or politically acceptable over the long run, because clearly, something had to be done; however, focusing on the bilateral imbalance and using the amorphous notion of unfair trade practices as the single most important explanation for what was happening was an erroneous domestic political strategy at best, and a denial of reality at worst.[29]

From the beginning of the bilateral trade conflicts, the Japanese also adhered to some questionable views and practices. Perhaps the most basic of these was the inability, or in some cases the unwillingness, of the responsible leaders, such as the politicans and government officials, to publicly recognize the nation's transition from a weakling to an economic power during the second half of the 1970s. Consequently, at every level of society, the Japanese continued to exhibit the "small country" mentality which had been rooted in the nation's long history of isolation, lack of natural resources, and economic uncertainty. Inward-looking, uncertain about the economic future, and passive in international relations, the Japanese presented a two-sided Janus face to the world. The country's gradually emerging economic power and its aggressive international trade competitiveness contrasted the self-effacing and passive behavior exhibited by Japanese representatives in the international arena. The "little brother" attitude of military, political, and economic dependency toward the United States, the wait-and-see approach marked by defensiveness in international negotiations in general and in the trade conflict with America in particular, was a reflection of the unresolved clash between long-held self-perceptions and the sudden economic reality.

During the 1970s, only the Japan experts appreciated the nature of the clash between perception and reality taking place in Japan. Most others considered the contrasting behaviour patterns as convincing proof of duplicity. Some Japanese politicans and government officials may not have wanted to publicly admit the transition in order to continue benefitting from the "small and dependent" posture. It was, however, disingenuous to consider the inability of a people to quickly revise its self-perception under rapidly changing conditions as a single-minded, society-wide conspiracy, particularly since these changes did not equally benefit every sector of the economy.[30] The reverberations of the two oil-price shocks also dampened the enthusiasm of many Japanese to see their country as an emerging economic power. Finally, it is important to understand that during the 1970s and also the 1980s, the fruits of hard work and increasing international competitiveness manifested by the current account surpluses were not translated into a generally improved quality of life. While the standard of living as measured by the traditional economic indicators, such as per capita income, was getting better every day,[31] quality of life measures, such as leisure time, housing conditions, and other similar socioeconomic considerations, did not reflect the enormous wealth the nation was accumulating. Thus, the average Japanese did not personally experience the country's transition into a world economic power.

Japan's limited international orientation also complicated the bilateral trade conflicts. Strange as it may seem in light of the country's international competitiveness and the remarkable individual successes of its major corporations, the Japanese were not adroit in dealing with the outside world. For historical reasons, such as the long, self-imposed isolation under the shoguns, it took some time to develop and hone the skills needed to deal with the international community, some of whose members have on occasion taken advantage of the Japanese. Thus, partly by choice and partly out of necessity, the Japanese were passive observers rather than active participants in the international organizations and diplomatic deliberations.

Manufacturing high quality products and aggressively marketing them throughout the world is one thing; however, negotiating political and economic matters in international fora in a foreign language is quite another matter. Until Yasuhiro Nakasone assumed the premiership in the early 1980s, Japan never had a prime minister of international stature who could speak to world leaders in English and deal with them as an equal. Previously, Japan had had a succession of prime ministers who had possessed strong domestic political bases but lacked broad international experience. Most members of the Diet had similarly limited backgrounds and qualifications. Only a few spoke foreign languages and had extensive international contacts. Among government career officials, with the exception of the staff of the Ministry of Foreign Affairs and to a lesser degree MITI, there were only a handful of influential officials who possessed the necessary skills and experience to effectively represent the nation's interests. In most other ministries a prolonged international involvement was seen as risking a promising career.

The Japanese generally believed that because they depended on the United States in a number of important ways, such as defense and markets, the Americans should be more understanding and supportive. They also resented the unequal relationship and resulting feeling of dependency because they believed that America had chosen Japan as its scapegoat in order to vent its frustrations about the declining international competitiveness of its industries. Most Japanese saw America as a big bully who wanted to pressure the small, defenseless Japan into unquestionably following its commands. There was a tendency to regard the American trade laws and trade policy actions as specifically directed at Japan. The Japanese did not recognise that the trade laws in principle were directed at a certain type of economic behavior based on American values, and not against any individual country *per se* no matter how acrimonious its disagreements with the United States might have been. They listened to the Congressional rhetroic, and viewed the trade laws as instruments of intimidation. The aggressive American approach and the way in which Japanese politicians and government officials often used the "American pressure" argument to obtain political and interministerial consensus, of course, did not help matters.[32] Suffice it to say that in the Japanese society, form has always been considered at least as important as substance, and thus, America's habit of exerting strong pressure may have received more attention than it needed.

The Japanese political decision-making process, based on a lengthy consensus-seeking approach, often involved intricate interministerial turf battles which led to long delayed responses to American trade negotiation demands.[33] While on occasion the Japanese side used the delays as a negotiation ploy, in most cases the delays could not be avoided. The American side, however, suspected that most of the time delays were planned and used as an excuse for inaction.

Thus, by the late 1970s, U.S.–Japan trade relations assumed the format of tiresome morality plays with predictable outcomes.[34] Undoubtedly, the domestic political realities in both America and Japan foreordained much of the routine process and results; nonetheless, it is regrettable that the leaders of both nations failed to acknowledge the futility and muster the political courage to address the trade imbalance question more realistically.[35]

Notes

1. The Japanese fiscal year (FY) begins on April 1 of each year and ends on the following March 31.
2. Ezra F.Vogel, *Japan as Number One* (Cambridge: Harvard University Press, 1979); Marvin Wolf, *The Japanese Conspiracy* (New York: Empire Books, 1983).
3. Thomas Pepper, Merit E. Janow, and Jimmy W. Wheeler, *The Competition: Dealing With Japan* (New York: Praeger Publishers, 1985); James C. Abegglen and George Stalk, Jr., *Kaishu: The Japanese Corporation* (New York: Basic Books, Inc., 1985).
4. *The New York Times* (May 3, 1986), p. 1.

5. While both "restructuring" and "internationalization" are used to refer to the changes expected in Japan, hereafter the term internationalization will be used because it is more comprehensive and better conveys the intent of the changes.

6. *The Japan Economic Journal* (May 3, 1986), p. 4.

7. For a more detailed exposition of this theme, see Richard Rosecrance, *The Rise of the Trading State* (New York: Basic Books, Inc., 1986).

8. The term "Japan Inc." was used sarcastically to characterize the close and systematic cooperation between the Japanese government and business community that prevailed for many years.

9. Bruce R. Scott, "National Strategies: Key to International Competition," *U.S. Competitiveness in the World Economy*, Bruce R. Scott and George C. Lodge, eds.(Boston: Harvard Business School Press, 1985), p. 72.

10. Abegglen and Stalk, *Kaisha: The Japanese Corporation, op.cit.*, pp. 5—6.

11. Scott, *"National Strategies," op.cit.*, p. 93.

12. Scott, *Ibid.*, p. 96.

13. A case in point is Brazil. In 1984 it passed a law that prohibits the import of small computers for eight years, and then it supplemented this action with an industry development plan. This United States responded with a Section 301 (unfair trade practices) action in the fall of 1985. The Brazilians, however, maintain that domestic law is sovereign and cannot be changed under foreign pressure.

14. Abegglen and Stalk, *Kaisha: The Japanese Corporation, op. cit.*, pp. 33—34

15. Beginning in the mid-1960s, the yen was undervalued until 1971. During the following years, it was periodically undervalued to various degrees.

16. Ryutaro Komiya, "Industrial Policy's Generation Gap," *Economic Eye*, March 1986, pp. 22—24.

17. For a detailed discussion of MITI and its role, see Chalmers Johnson, *MITI and the Japanese Miracle* (Stanford, CA: Standford University Press, 1982).

18. For a detailed discussion of the various policy measures and their application over time, see chapter III in Pepper et al., *The Competition, op.cit.*

19. *Ibid.*, p. 117. Other important public financing institutions were the Industrial Bank of Japan and the Long-Term Credit Bank of Japan.

20. Figures received during personal interviews with Fair Trade Commission officials in Tokyo, May 1986. For current list of exceptions, see appendix A.

21. U.S. Congress, Joint Economic Committee, *Industrial Policy Movement in the United States: Is It the Answer?* (Washington, D.C.: U.S. Government Printing Office, 1984), pp. 44—47.

22. For a detailed discussion of how the *kaisha* continually increased productivity and how the "winner's competitive cycle" develops, see Abegglen and Stalk, *Kaisha: The Japanese Corporation*, op. *cit.*, chapter 4, 5, and 3, respectively.

23. *The Wall Street Journal* (December 13, 1985), p. 34.

24. Annual statistical summaries of Japan by the Keizai Koho Center.

25. For a detailed discussion of the specific issues involved in these conflicts and of their resolution, see I.M. Destler, Haruhiro Fukui, and Hideo Sato, *The Textile Wrangle: Conflicts in Japanese-American Relations 1969—1971* (Ithaca, N.Y.: Cornell University Press, 1979), and I.M. Destler and Hideo Sato, *Coping with U.S.-Japanese Economic Conflicts* (Lexington, MA: D.C. Heath, 1982).

26. The following data were obtained from the various annual issues of the *International Financial Statistics* of the International Monetary Fund and U.S. Department of Commerce publications.

27. For a detailed discussion of these issues, see C. Fred Bergsten and William R. Cline, *The United States-Japan Economic Problem* (Washington, D.C.,: Institute for International Economics, 1985), pp. 3–13.
28. See, for example, C. Fred Bergsten "What to Do About the U.S.–Japan Economic Conflict," *Foreign Affairs* (Summer 1982), pp. 1059–1075; and Gary R. Saxonhouse, "The Micro- and Macroeconomics of Foreign Sales to Japan," in *Trade Policy in the 1980s*, edited by William R. Cline (Washington, D.C.: Institute for International Economics, 1983), pp. 259–304.
29. There were, of course, voices of reason as well. A good example is the General Accounting Office, which in its 1979 report on *United States-Japan Trade: Issues and Problems* (Washington, D.C.: General Accounting Office, 1979) presented a measured appraisal of U.S.–Japan trade relations to Congress.
30. See previous discussion regarding slower growth of the agriculture, textiles and ship-building industries.
31. See, for example, *1983 World Bank Atlas* (Washington, D.C.: The World Bank, 1983).
32. See, for example, Kazuo Ogura, *U.S.–Japan Economic Conflict* (Tokyo: Nihon Keizai Shimbun, 1982).
33. For a detailed discussion of the process, see Chikara Higashi, *Japanese Trade Policy Formulation* (New York: Praeger Publishers, 1983).
34. The repetitive pattern is discussed in appendix B.
35. Prior to the mid-1980s, the only major agreement that tried to address some of the fundamental causes of the bilateral trade imbalances was the Strauss-Ushiba communique of 1978. The agreement committed both the United States and Japan to take certain measures and to work together on others designed to achieve high levels of noninflationary growth, improve their respective balance of payments position, bring the MTN negotiations to a successful conclusion, and to increase assistance to developing countries.

2 THE ORIGINS OF INTERNATIONALIZATION

The years 1981–1984 were characterized by the interaction of a number of events in both in the United States and Japan which le to a head-on collision over trade matters between the two nations. Foremost among these events was the rapid increase of Japan's global trade surpluses while the global balances of the United States deteriorated year by year. Table 2–1 shows these trends.

TABLE 2–1.   Japanese and United States global trade balances: 1981–1984 (in $ millions)

Year	Country	
	Japan	*United States*
1981	19,967	− 27,978
1982	18,079	− 36,444
1983	31,454	− 67,216
1984	44,257	−114,107

Source: *Japan 1986· An International Comparison* (Tokyo. Keizai Koho Center, 1986), p. 33.

Concurrently, Japan's bilateral trade surpluses with the United States also grew at a rapid pace. Exports to America increased by about 55 percent between 1981 and 1984, whereas imports from the United States showed only a 4 percent increase over the same period, as shown in table 2−2.

Predictably, the aforementioned trade statistics caused concern around the world, particularly in Tokyo and Washington. The Japanese knew that the rapidly growing global and bilateral trade surpluses would intensify the already critical attitudes of the European Community (E.C.) and the United States. Japanese politicians and government officals braced themselves as best as they could against the new round of "unfair trade practices" charges. Since it was generally acknowledged that Japan's average tariff on industrial imports would be 2.9 percent versus 4.3 percent in the United States and 4.7 percent in the European Community when the Tokyo Round Tariff reductions are completed in 1987, it was inevitable that the critics would point to nontariff barriers as the means through which the Japanese kept their markets "closed." Thus, during the early 1980s, the various traditional trade arrangements and practices of Japan came under increasing scrutiny and criticism particularly in the United States and Western Europe.

Trade Myths and Realities

The vehement criticism of Japan by American and European government and business circles was frequently based on incomplete or outdated information. The resulting erroneous views spread around the world, and were used even by politicians and businessmen who had access to more accurate information. Although in most cases the criticisms did include an

TABLE 2−2.   Japanese exports to and imports from the United States:
1981−1984 (in $ millions)

Year	Exports	Imports	Balance
1981	38,609	25,297	13,312
1982	36,330	24,179	12,151
1983	42,829	24,647	18,182
1984	59,937	26,862	33,075

Source: *Japan 1986: An International Comparison* (Tokyo: Keizai Koho Center, 1985), p. 36.

element of truth, there was a great reluctance among the critics to change their well-entrenched views once events in Japan or throughout the world invalidated them. The result was a combustible mix of trade myths and realities which tended to confuse, rather than clarify, economic relations between Japan and the rest of the world, particularly the United States.

The Closed Nature of the Japanese Market

Scholarly studies and the annual Organization for Economic Cooperation and Development (OECD) country surveys which presented analyses of the possible reasons for Japan's huge global and bilateral trade surpluses arrived at different conclusions than most American and European politicians and businessmen.[1] Bergsten and Cline, for example, found that over the 1980−1984 period, Japan's bilateral trade surplus with the United States as a percentage of total bilateral trade turnover increased by 18 percent. However, during the same period of time, 17 of America's 25 most important trading partners did better than Japan; the median increase for their bilateral surpluses was 29 percent. Explaining the reasons for the Japanese surplus, Bergsten and Cline emphasize the differences in private sector saving rates, and the overvalued dollar during the years studied. As they point out, the Japanese did not become more protectionist in this time, and consequently, market barriers could not have been the major cause of the growing trade imbalances between 1980 and 1984. They argue that by international standards, Japan's import/GNP ratio is not unusual, and that the relatively low share of manufactured goods in total imports reflects the country's comparative disadvantage in natural resources rather than a concerted effort to keep foreign products out. On the basis of structural considerations Bergsten and Cline conclude that Japan is likely to maintain a long-term global current account surplus of about 1−1.5 percent of GNP, and an annual bilateral trade surplus with America of approximately $20−25 billion, even if it immediately met all U.S. trade demands.

Other studies and the OECD country surveys also cite the different export and import structure of Japan as compared to the rest of the world, the decrease in oil prices, reduction in the use of raw materials due to major changes in the structure of output, and the general decline in the raw material intensity of various industries, as reasons for the increasing global surpluses.[2] The U.S.−Japan bilateral trade imbalances were explained by the differing business cycles of the two nations and the overvalued dollar caused by the huge American fiscal deficits of the early 1980s.

While dispelling the popular belief that the closed Japanese marketplace is the major cause of the global and bilateral surpluses, the authors of these studies and country surveys nevertheless mention nontariff barriers such as distribution system (OECD study), and the *keiretsu* or industrial conglomerate arrangements (Bergstein and Cline) as possible import constraints. They emphasize, however, that the arguments supporting such views are mostly anecdotal, and that even if such arrangements reduced imports, their impact could not readily be measured. Other sources cited Japanese product standards, certification processes, and consumer behaviour as import constraints.

The Distribution System

The 1984 OECD country survey points out that the Japanese distribution system may be a particularly difficult import obstacle, because the institutional network has several more layers than exist in other industrialized countries, and because intermediaries may not buy foreign products just because they are less expensive than comparable domestic products. Undoubtedly the Japanese primary, secondary, and even tertiary wholesalers are engaged in an unusually complex relationship with retailers, and provide other services not offered in other countries. According to the Economic Planning Agency (EPA), there are about 14 retail shops in the country for every 1,000 people.[3] This compares with 11 in France, 6 in the United Kingdom, 6 in the United States, and 5 in the Federal Republic of Germany. On the average, the distribution channels are also three times longer than those in other industrialized countries, which slows down the flow of goods and substantially increases the final price to consumers.

The wholesalers provide an array of services, including *henpin* (the return of unsold merchandise for reimbursement), and a variety of rebates whose amount is determined by the wholesaler's representative on a case-by-case basis. Presently, various government agencies are evaluating such Japanese distribution practices and their potential impact on imports. For example, in 1985 Japan's Fair Trade Commission (FTC) asked for a study of the distribution system. The authors of this report, published in the summer of 1986, concluded that the distribution arrangements and practices could make it difficult for foreign companies to enter the Japanese marketplace.[4] They recommended that the FTC consider measures that would eliminate or at least change some of the more burdensome features of the existing system.

Such recommendations, however, would be difficult to implement. Small Japanese distributors have a great deal of political influence; they are numerous and well known in their communities. Furthermore, small retailers are currently protected by the Large-Scale Retail Store Law, which gives the "mom and pop" neighbourhood stores veto power over proposed new stores larger than 27,000 square feet, as well as over expansion of large retail chains. Thus, importers are forced to sell their products through more expensive, smaller outlets.

With this type of local clout, most politicians are reluctant to propose major changes in the existing distribution system that could provoke resentment. The political weight of small distribution intermediaries is illustrated by the EPA data which show that approximately 20 percent of Japan's working population is engaged in distribution, with 1 out of 4 nonmanufacturing businesses being a wholesaler; in the United States, this ratio is 1 out of 10; and in the Federal Republic of Germany, it is 1 out of 9. The political power of distribution intermediaries, however, is not unique to Japan; in France, for example, they have a virtual veto over any major change in the distribution system so that no French politician would dare to ignore their views, and in the Federal Republic of Germany, small retailers have repeatedly repelled consumer group demands for longer business hours.

Thus, the Japanese distribution system is unusual only with respect to certain traditions and practices. It is difficult to penetrate but equally difficult for the Japanese government to change. Contrary to some views expressed in the United States and Europe, it is not a system created by MITI or other government agencies to keep foregin products out, nor is it illogical; given Japanese circumstances the system has its internal logic. However unusual and irritating this logic may be, the distribution system is a reflection of the historical evolution of the Japanese society and economy. Most of the traditions and practices are so well entrenched that even new Japanese companies find it quite difficult to get into the distribution systems. Consequently, it is erroneous to decry the system as a nontariff barrier that must be speedily dismantled. Such demands are unrealistic and cannot be met within the foreseeable future, if ever. Instead of asking the Japanese government to intervene, foreign companies should learn to function within the system, and help change it from the inside as market conditions and consumer behaviour allow and promote changes over time. The sharp appreciation of the yen during 1985–1986, for example, has already set some forces in motion which are likely to induce changes in the near future.

The Keiretsu Arrangements

The alleged restraining effects of the *keiretsu* system on imports has also received a great deal of attention outside Japan. Over the years, the governments and business circles of the United States and Western Europe have often charged that *keiretsu* companies reject business with firms outside the group whenever the goods and services offered directly compete with those provided by the *keiretsu* members. Moreover, they claim, this is true even if goods and services offered by the non-*keiretsu* companies are better in quality and/or price.

Historically, the major reason for the evolution of the *keiretsu* system aside from financing was the desire for continuity of supplies and orders. Japanese businesses, just like Americans or Europeans, have always preferred certain suppliers over others for reasons of continuity as long as the price, quality, and other critical transaction considerations were within acceptable ranges. Thus, it is possible that restrictive intragroup practices occur even today. However, to argue that such practices are institutionalized through the *keiretsu* system regardless of the variations in transaction considerations ignores the highly competitive nature of the Japanese marketplace, and the aggressive growth and cost reduction orientation (i.e., price competitiveness) of the Japanese companies, as discussed in chapter 1. No Japanese company could consistently afford to violate basic economic considerations and still remain domestically and internationally competitive over the long-run, particularly after the yen appreciation.

The importance of the *keiretsu* system in the Japanese economy is also exaggerated abroad. According to a 1986 survey by the FTC, industrial corporations belonging to the six largest *keiretsu* (Mitsubishi, Mitsui, Sumitomo, Fuyo, Sanwa, and Dai-Ichi-Kangyo) accounted for only 4.6 percent of all employees, 15 percent of total assets, 16.5 percent of total sales, and 17.5 percent of total net profits of the Japanese industrial sector in 1984.[5]

Even if loyalty influences business decisions, the magnititude of the *keiretsu* buying and selling transactions does not seem large enough to act as a major nontariff barrier as alleged. In 1984, the FTC reported, the six largest trading companies, each belonging to a different *keiretsu*, on the average obtained 11.5 percent of total purchases and made 4.6 percent of their total sales to other members of the group.[6] For the manufacturing companies of the same *keiretsu*, the proportions were 12.4 and 20.4 percent, respectively. Thus, even if the 11.5 and 12.4 percent of total purchases of trading and manufacturing companies, and the 4.6 and 20.4 percent of all of their sales were made entirely on the basis of group loyalty

— an assumption that can neither be sustained nor challenged — the overwhelming majority of all purchases and of all sales by the trading and manufacturing *keiretsu* members were with nongroup companies.

According to the same FTC study, the intragroup transactions involved a number of broad product categories as shown in table 2−3. Except for machines and equipment, the percentages of intragroup deals in the other categories are rather low.

TABLE 2−3. Proportion of major product categories in the intragroup transactions of the six major *Keiretsu*: 1984

Product categories	Purchases	Sales
Textiles and apparel	3.1%	1.2%
Food and agricultural products	0.5%	0.6%
Mining, metal materials, and chemicals	9.9%	6.7%
Machines and equipment	21.1%	2.8%

Source: Internal reference papers (Tokyo: Fair Trade Commission, and the Economic Planning Agency, 1986).

At the present time it is not clear what the future holds for the *keiretsu*. The gradual structural changes in the economy, the appreciation of the yen during 1985−1986, and some possible future FTC measures may challenge their existence or merely alter some of their practices. A case in point is the liberalization of the Japanese financial markets. Traditionally, the big city banks stood at the center of the *keiretsu* and provided for all the financial needs of the member companies. Presently, however, many manufacturing firms are becoming independent of the banks and are relying on their own newly created financial expertise. Numerous corporations in need of funds are floating stocks or convertible bond issues in Japan and abroad instead of borrowing from the banks as they did in the past.

Product Standards and Consumer Behavior

In addition to singling out the distribution and *keiretsu* systems, critics of Japan have argued that Japanese product standards and consumer behavior also significantly limit imports. It is true that historically, the Japanese have always used a different system of establishing and enforcing product standards. In most industrialized nations, if a product fails or injures someone, the aggrieved users sue the manufacturer or distributor.

In Japan, the public expects the government to establish and strictly enforce product standards and certification systems to protect the consumer, who very rarely sues the producer if anything goes wrong. Thus, Japan's comprehensive product standards and certification systems were developed to protect and satisfy the Japanese public, and not to keep foreign products out of the marketplace.

This is not to say that the complex standards and other requirements did not create problems for foreign companies trying to enter the Japanese marketplace. Their restrictive impact was reinforced by the Japanese legal system which was different from that of the rest of the world, particularly the United States. The absence of clearly written laws and recognizable underlying legal principles, together with the traditional administrative guidance, made it difficult for foreign companies to obtain the insight they needed to function within the Japanese regulatory system. This, and the the lack of transparency in the governmental decision-making process which, compared to that of the United States, was subject to more cultural nuances reflected in the practice of administrative guidance, frustrated and irritated Americans and other nationalities dealing with Japanese government agencies in charge of product standards and certification.

Therefore, product standards and related requirements need to be reviewed and changed to conform to international practices. It is, however, very difficult to obtain estimates of the impact of the standards and other requirements on Japan's trade balances with the rest of the world, and with the United States in particular. Nevertheless, Bergesten and Cline tried, and claim that about $5−8 billion in American exports may have been negatively affected by the Japanese practices.[7]

As a signatory of the products standards code of the 1979 MTN Agreement (Tokyo round), the Japanese obligated themselves to remedy the situation during the early 1980s. As part of a set of measures, they established the Office of the Trade Ombudsman (OTO) in 1982 to provide a central clearinghouse for complaints concerning the various standards, certification requirements, approval procedures, and other nontariff barriers. Eventually, changes were introduced and new measures were taken to increase the transparency of the standards formulation process. Thus, while remnants of the traditional arrangements still hindered foreign companies prior to the 1985 Action Program, product standards and certification systems were no longer as restrictive as in the past.

The discriminatory attitudes of Japanese consumers against foreign products have allegedly also contributed to Japan's trade surpluses. Unquestionably, Japanese consumers are very demanding and are especially quality-conscious. They are difficult to satisfy, and hold the providers of

TABLE 2-4.   Japanese consumer attitudes toward fforeign and domestic products: 1983

Consumers	Percentages
Do not differentiate between foreign and domestic products	66.3
Prefer domestic products	26.4
Prefer foreign products	2.3
Don't know	5.0

Source: *Analysis of and Proposals Concerning the Japanese Distribution System, Commercial Practices, and Other Corporate Behavior* (Tokyo: Manufactured Imports Promotion Committee, 1983), p. 12.

products and services to the highest standards of production and marketing. Consumers also exhibit strong loyalty to products which they have found to be satisfactory, and do not readily switch to substitutes, domestic or foreign, unless the substitutes are superior in every respect. Such consumer behavior, to some extent, reflects the Japanese sense of loyalty and is not the result of conspiracy against foreign products. The findings of a consumer attitude survey published in 1983, and shown in table 2-4, support this conclusion.

As the data show, while many Japanese consumers do prefer domestic products (26 percent), the majority (66 percent) do not differentiate among products on the basis of origin, but on the basis of total value provided. In this respect, the Japanese are like Americans, Germans, French, or any other nationality. However, due to the complex, multi-layered distribution system, most foreign products are more expensive than domestic ones, and price is seen by Japannese consumers as a major disadvantage of imports. The results of a survey conducted by the Prime Minister's office, shown in table 2-5, confirm this conclusion.

Thus, except for highly differentiated luxury imports purchased mostly as gifts which are expected to carry higher price tags than similar domestic products, it appears that the high price rather than the foreign origin is what keeps Japanese consumers from buying more imports. It is also noteworthy that for electrical appliances, which require careful postsales service, price was not the major consideration. Consumers were more concerned about the perceived inability to obtain service and parts on a continuous basis. It will be interesting to see whether consumer preceptions of imports change as a result of the sharp appreciation of the yen,

TABLE 2−5.   Japanese views of the advantages and disadvantages of foreign products: 1984 (multiple response in percentages)

Advantages		Disadvantages	
Food products			
Taste good	50	Expensive	54
Make nice gifts	37	Unsure how to use because of	
Satisfying to eat or drink	36	insufficient instructions in	
Good quality	26	Japanese, etc.	22
Inexpensive	11	Taste bad	6
		Poor quality	3
Clothing			
Good colors, patterns, designs	57	Expensive	56
Satisfying to wear	42	Wrong shapes, sizes	16
Good quality	35	Poor quality	16
Inexpensive	26	Poor colors, patterns, designs	7
Make nice gifts	15		
Electric appliances			
Work well	47	Inadequate after-sales service	53
Durable	36	Expensive	28
Satisfying to use	29	No instructions in Japanese	12
Good quality	22	Wrong shapes, sizes	11
Good colors, patterns, designs	19	Work poorly	9
Make nice gifts	11	Poor colors, patterns, designs	8
Inexpensive	9	Hard to use	5
		Poor quality	5
		Break easily	5

Source: *Imports in Daily Life* (Tokyo: The Prime Minister's Office, 1985).

and what impact such changes may have on the volume of imports over the next few years.

Additional Considerations

A discussion of the trade myths and realities, particularly as they apply to U.S.−Japan bilateral trade relations, would be incomplete without a discussion of two additional considerations. The first is the declining international competitiveness of the U.S. economy. While it is an exaggeration to refer to this process as de-industrialization, it is undeniable that the

American economy is not doing as well internationally as it should to maintain a leading role in the world.

The second consideration involves the use of trade balances as the sole measure of the overall economic relations between nations. Although, as discussed later, there are some limitations to the use of more comprehensive measures, particularly in U.S.–Japan trade, there is increasing evidence that trade balance measures alone are an inadequate basis for international economic policy formulation.

America's International Competitiveness

The measurement of a nation's international competitiveness is a complex and somewhat uncertain undertaking. The traditional standards such as the growing trade imbalances, changing import penetration ratios, or declining export shares in the global marketplace are at best unreliable. Nonetheless, if the standards show negative trends over long periods of time, it is reasonable to suspect that the nation in question can no longer produce goods and services under free market conditions which meet the test of the international marketplace while simultaneusly maintaining and expanding the real income of its citizen.[8] By almost any measure, the American economy appears to have reached this stage in recent years.

A case in point is the U.S. machine tool industry, once the world leader in the manufacture of high quality standardized machine tools. At first the industry decided that it could no longer compete with the Japanese and asked for import quota protection for reasons of national security. Shortly thereafter, it obtained similar protection against the Taiwanese, West German, and Swiss imports. By the fall of 1986, it called for quotas against imports from Spain, Korea, Brazil, and Singapore.

One of the major reasons for the declining international competitiveness of the United States is its poor savings-investment balance during recent years. From the mid-1970s to 1982, the balance averaged out to about zero, but beginning in 1983, the situation changed, and the savings shortfall began to take on serious proportions. It reached 2.4 percent of GNP in 1984, and this unfavorable trend continued into 1985–1986. The savings shortfalls were exacerbated by rapidly increasing federal deficits and the resulting government demand for funds, which necessitated capital inflows from abroad, particularly from Japan where the savings-investment balance was reversed.

Thus, from the late 1970s to the early 1980s, America's low saving rate, together with the growing demand of the federal government for funds, contributed to the growth of the current account deficit. It also generated high real interest rates which made it too costly to invest to maintain international competitiveness. In today's world markets effective competition requires not only low real manufacturing costs but also the production and marketing of modern, high quality products; unfortunately most American industries have not been able to invest sufficiently to meet this requirement. For example, between 1981 and 1984, total business expenditures for new plant and equipment increased from $315 billion to only $354 billion, or about 3 percent annually.[9] During the same period, the internationally competitive high-technology industries, such as electronics, started to source components which they could not competitively manufacture at home, in offshore locations such as South Korea. This "hollowing" of America's manufacturing capacity was accompanied by a reduction of research and development expenditures which, as a percentage of GNP, sunk lower than in Japan and Western Europe.[10] Moreover, military research and development which represented approximately half of the total 1984 outlay of $100 billion, but which was less than in the past, no longer provided industry with new product ideas as it had in the 1950s and 1960s when many of the creative ideas were byproducts of the weapons systems and space exploration efforts.

Limited investments and low capital productivity had negative influence on industrial productivity, the key element of a nation's international competitiveness. Table 2−6 shows a summary of comparative industrial productivity trends published in a 1986 report of the Bureau of Labor Statistics of the U.S. Department of Labor.

TABLE 2−6. Comparison of industrial productivity increases in selected industrialized countries: 1985 and 1973−1985 (in percentages)

Country	1985	1973−1985 (Average annual increase)
Belgium	n.a.	5.7
Federal Republic of Germany	5.7	3.8
France	3.8	4.5
Japan	5.0	5.6
United Kingdom	2.8	2.8
United States	2.8	2.2

Source: *International Comparisons of Manufacturing Productivity and Labor Costs* (Washington, D.C.: Bureau of Labor Statistics, U.S. Department of Labor, 1986), pp. 2 and 6.

It is noteworthy that in 1985, American industry performed reasonably well, although only time will tell whether this signals a turn for the better in the future or is simply a short-term phenomenon. Meanwhile, the relatively low average annual productivity increases during 1973–1985 have seriously damaged America's international competitiveness.

Recent U.S. industrial performance looks even more discouraging if unit labor cost trends are also considered. According to the Department of Labor report, taking into account the strength of the dollar, only one major industralized country besides the United States, Canada, experienced increasing unit labor costs between 1980 and 1985. America's major competitor, Japan, showed a decrease of 2.5 percent, and other countries, such as the Federal Republic of Germany and the United Kingdom, experienced reductions of 7.8 and 7.6 percent, respectively, during the same period.

In a less direct but equally demaging fashion, management practices have also contributed to the declining internationl competitiveness of the United States. While the executives of some major corporations are trying to be growth/productivity/opportunity oriented, the majority of them show a preoccupation with short-term objectives, with financial coups rather than with long-term competitiveness.

A major reason for this is the recent shift in control over corporations from individual to institutional investors, such as pensions funds, insurance companies, trust funds, and banks. Whereas individual investors are chiefly interested in long-term gains, institutional investors demand quick results. If certain stocks do not perform, they are unceremoniously dropped. Thus, corporate executives are at the mercy of such impatient investors and have to produce the quick, steady gains demanded. Under the resulting speculative, short-term-oriented economic conditions, only large multinational corporations can possibly generate enough profits to simultaneously achieve short-term expectations and fulfill the long-term commitments that international competition requires. Understandably, most U.S. corporations cannot simultaneously pursue such diverse objectives, and thus must opt for the domestic short-term goals, particularly since managerial rewards are usually attached to such goals and not to long-term international achievements.

Even today, the American financial community not only favors short-term over long-term results but also considers the reshuffling of existing assets over the creation of new ones a more important management responsibility. Takeovers are praised for the supposed financial benefits they bring to stockholders, and the economic sense they embody True, under pre-1987 tax laws, by marking up asset values and then re-depreciating them, the tax bills of the acquirers could be reduced. Futhermore, financing a transaction with debt achieved similar ends because interest was tax-deductible. Yet, while all of this may have been true, and under the old tax laws some individuals got very rich overnight, the use of management time for such ends, the payment of multimillion dollar fees to takeover specialists, and the provision of "golden parachutes" (although limited by law since 1984) to the executives on the losing side of a takeover battle raise doubts about such claims. The American public still awaits evidence that the takeovers have improved manufacturing capabilities, cost structures, research and development skills, quality and scope of product assortments and marketing ability, or more precisely, the international competitiveness of the firms involved. The 1986–1987 insider-information takeover scandals on Wall Street and the subsequent revelations about the conduct of takeover specialists are likely to further erode the public's confidence in the rationale of such transactions.

To respond to the short-term demands, U.S. managers have also experimented with every management concept that promised a quick fix.[11] The experiments ranged from an uncritical adoption of Japanese management methods through "intrapreneurship" (finding entrepreneurs in the firm) to "demassing" (staff reductions) and "strategic alliances" (joint ventures). There is, of course nothing wrong in experimenting with new ideas. On the contrary, management must keep an open mind. However, the short life-cycle of most of the concepts tried implies that they were fads rather than serious innovations which could solve the problems of low productivity, poor product quality, and low employee motivation, which among others, are the major handicaps of America's industries.

American workers have their own views about these problems. In a New York Times/CBS/Tokyo Broadcasting System poll, more than half of the 1,569 American workers asked agreed that the Japanese work harder.[12] They characterized the Japanese as more determined, disciplined, dedicated, organized, efficient, and conscientious. However, American workers are not inherently less able than the Japanese; properly motivated and equipped, they can work just as hard as the Japanese. But labor productivity is only half of industrial productivity; the other half if made up by the capital that is applied to the production process, and it is the low capital productivity in combination with ineffective management practices which contributed to the decline in overall international competitiveness.

Moreover, America's international competitiveness is also curtailed by its trade policies which are designed to dispense equity to anyone, American or not, who seeks remedies for narrowly defined "injuries." Thus, the broader issues surrounding international trade, such as the improvement of the international competitiveness of the economy or the interests of consumers, are not usually properly considered. As a result, in most cases U.S. trade policy formulators represent the narrowly defined concerns of certain interest groups quite well but cannot adequately protect the economic interests of the nation as a whole. A case in point is the computer chip agreement the United States reached with Japan after a long and acrimonious negotiation in 1986. The American side wanted to protect U.S. manufacturers against low-priced Japanese imports, so, under the agreement, Japanese producers were required to submit cost and price information to MITI and the Department of Commerce. Based on such information, the Department of Commerce established minimum prices for the Japanese chips whereas U.S. manufacturers could sell chips at any price. The ink had hardly dried on the agreement when American computer manufacturers complained to Secretary of Commerce Baldridge and United States Trade Representative Yeutter that since the agreement, prices had skyrocketed, in some instances sevenfold within a month. Thus, what a special interest group had gained, had to be paid for by the computer manufacturers, and ultimately, by the computer users. A September 11, 1986, *Wall Street Journal* editorial called the agreement a "microchip monster" and referred to the U.S. chip manufacturers as the "next steel industry." Not surprisingly, by late September the Commerce Department had no choice but to reduce the initial prices set in July by about 50 percent, at least until the end of 1986. By then it had to lower the minimum price again. The reductions, not as sharp as the 50 percent reduction in September, ranged from 8.3 to 40.9 percent for the various chips. Nonetheless, the competitive situation of the U.S. manufacturers had not improved and by February 1987, a *Wall Street Journal* lead-article referred to the agreement as a protectionist failure and cited industry sources supporting such a conclusion. Moreover, about the same time, the U.S. Department of Defense released a special report according to which the quality of American chip technology was "steadily deteriorating" relative to that of the Japanese manufacturers.

Not surprisingly, the price control agreement also quickly resulted in disagreements over the marketing of Japanese chips in third-country markets from where - the United States charged - the chips find their way into the American market at prices lower than those specified in the agreement. The international transhipment of products under price control in certain markets and sold at competitive prices in other markets is of course, an age-old phenomenon and reflects the impossibility of policing international price control agreements concerning products in excess supply. Nonetheless, under strong American pressure MITI officials in early

1987 asked the six domestic semiconductor manufacturers to look out for and, if possible, to minimize such practices. It is, however, unlikely that such efforts can succeed in an industry marked by a globally active "gray market" created largely by the United States-Japan microchip agreement.

As the military leader of the Western world, the United States must also limit the transfer of sophisticated technology to certain countries. The resulting validated licensing system keeps American producers out of many markets. In the summer of 1986, for example, electronics industry representatives complained to the Reagan Administration that the rules discourage foreign manufacturers from incorporating American computers and microprocessors into their products, thus substantially reducing the sales of one of the most internationally competitive industries.

Finally, the limited international orientation of most U.S. companies must also be mentioned. While there are exceptions to this, and whereas a great deal of the information concerning the problem is unsubstantiated hearsay, there is an undeniable kernel of truth in the allegations. A case in point is a 1986 incident reported in *The Wall Street Journal* which illustrates the difference between American and Japanese companies' attitudes toward global market opportunities.

In 1984 the U.S. Census Bureau reached an agreement with the Central Statistical Office of the People's Republic of China concerning the exchange of data. In late 1985, the Chinese provided the Census Bureau with a great deal of socioeconomic and demographic statistics useful for evaluating Chinese consumer good markets. The bureau's staff analyzed the information, and the Department of Commerce included the results in its "Country Market Profile: The People's Republic of China," and offered it to American firms for $300 per copy. Between December 1985 and the fall of 1986, less than 10 copies were sold.

In early 1986 the Japan External Trade Organization (JETRO) obtained a copy and, because the report was not copyrighted, had it translated and published in book form. JETRO distributed the book at no charge to over 700 Japanese member organizations interested in trade with China, including trading companies, manufacturers, department stores, financial and research institutions, and universities. Following this distribution, JETRO printed another 500 copies which quickly sold at $20 per copy.

As a consequence of the interaction of all these factors, the once dynamic growth/productivity/opportunity oriented U.S. economy changed into a distribution/security/resource oriented economy over the years.[13] While this transition may have been desirable from a political and social point of view, it dramatically reduced the international competitiveness of the American economy, particularly in comparison with Japan where such a transition has not taken place, at least not yet.

The Inadequacy of the Trade Balance Measure

A number of students of U.S.—Japan trade relations and some U.S. government officials have recently indicated that the trade balance measure by itself can result in myopic views and erroneous trade policies.[14] According to this argument, U.S.—Japan relations are more complex than the traditional bilateral trade balance measure implies. For example, the shifting of U.S. manufacturing operations to Japan resulted in about $4—5 billion in annual Japanese exports to the United States which are actually produced by American companies. Furthermore, approximately $15 billion in exports are specifically ordered by American original equipment manufacturers (OEMs), and in 1985 alone, American subsidiaries in Japan manufactured and marketed about $50 billion worth of goods there. Thus, once such transactions are taken into account, bilateral economic relations are not as much in Japan's favor as the trade balance measure alone suggests.

The conventional evaluation of U.S.—Japan trade relations also ignores the export of American services. Contrary to widely held beliefs, services are not provided only by low-paid fast-food restaurant employees but also by banks, insurance, advertising companies, and large, multinational construction companies. Moreover, the United States usually obtains a surplus in its service trade, much of it in the Pacific region, particularly Japan.

Thus, in a world economy that is characterized by global networks of multinational corporations as well as by huge nontrade-related financial flows, reliance on the trade balance measure alone does not accurately reflect the scope of U.S.—Japan economic relations. A new set of more comprehensive measures is therefore long overdue. It is, however, difficult to gain widespread acceptance for this, because U.S.—Japan trade relations are not conducted in a rational economic but in an emotional political context. Members of Congress, for example, are angry about the huge bilateral trade imbalances mostly because of the unemployment implications in their electoral districts. These concerns are not groundless; a recent U.S. Department of Commerce study found that between 1979 and 1985, more than 1.5 million manufacturing jobs had been lost.[15] The authors estimated that while in 1977 exports accounted for a 7.1 percent of employment, imports accounted for a 6 percent loss of jobs. By 1984, export-related employment stood at 6.5 percent whereas imports resulted in a 7.8 percent job loss. In the same year, the net loss of jobs (the difference between jobs created by exports and jobs lost through imports) was 1.1 million, or 1.3 percent of total employment. By estimating that a $1 billion loss of exports reduces employment by approximately 21,000 jobs, the Department of Commerce provided members of Congress with a useful argument against Japan and its closed market. Whereas such evidence is tenuous at best, the argument is politically effective because it can be backed up by the huge bilateral trade imbalances, whatever their causes may have been. This reported trade-employment relationship was welcomed by the Democratic members of Congress who had been looking for an effective political issue to use against the Reagan Administration. They found this combination irresistible because it linked their traditional concern for working men and women with a problem of the 1980s which gained more prominence daily. The Democrats believed that they could finally expose the weaknesses of Reaganomics, at least at they saw them.

The Democratic views were additionally supported by newly formed interpretations of the employment implications of free trade.[16] According to some American scholars, in the second half of the 1980s, trade is not based on comparative advantages but on wage-cutting. Therefore, only through strict limits on imports could the negative effects of lower wages on the American economy in general and on the standard of living in particular be limited. The argument was not specifically directed against Japan, but the recommendation that imports be limited naturally had serious implications for the nation which consistently generated the largest bilateral trade surpluses in the American marketplace.

The 1981–1984 Japanese Market Opening 'Packages'

Since the reasons for the rapidly growing Japanese current and trade account surpluses, particularly with the United States during the late 1970s and early 1980s, were complex, it would have been very important to address the imbalances through cooperative multilateral efforts. However, with the advent of the Reagan administration in 1981, the United States unilaterally focused its trade policy on the "opening" of the Japanese marketplace to the exclusion of all other relevant factors. Through this narrowly conceived approach, the Administration wanted to rapidly reduce the high bilateral trade imbalances.

The major reason for this strategy was the desire to obtain maximum domestic visibility fo the Reagan trade policy. It was simpler to point to a set of unilateral Japanese measures developed in response to U.S. demands to improve market access than to obtain political benefits from complex agreements on mutually binding macroeconomic policies which would have been more efficient but which only experts could have understood. Moreover, through tough sounding demands the Administration hoped to contain the periodic protectionist outbursts on Capitol Hill. The American side also believes that specific demands made it more difficult for the Japanese to equivocate, and that unilaterally exerted pressures made it easier for the United States to evade the necessary but politically painful domestic measures such as curtailment of budgetary deficits through spending cuts or tax increases.

Not surprisingly, the Japanese saw things differently. From their point of view, the market opening measures did not address the fundamentals of the trade imbalances and, consequently, could not lead to a lasting resolution of the trade conflicts. Futhermore, most of the measures were seen as unilateral concessions, and the Japanese government was also being required to prefer one industry over another. This caused political problems as, for example, when Japanese farmers charged that the government was selling them out during the bilateral agricultural negotiations of the late 1970s and early 1980s, to secure the American markets for manufactured exports. Neither did the Japanese approve of the American tendency to use specific cases to symbolize the generally closed nature of the Japanese marketplace. Lastly, the Japanese objected to the excessive politicization of some rather insignificant issues because this unnecessarily exacerbated the overall conflict.

As usual, the United States prevailed, and in response to American demands, the Japanese government developed a series of market opening measures or "packages." They typically included the elimination and/or reduction of tariffs on selected products, the simplification of import procedures, increased transparency in economic decision-making, and other similar measures. The Japanese tried to quickly generate as much goodwill as possible, and thus, usually announced the packages in advance. Often, they anticipated and developed packages to blunt congressional anger or to provide the Prime Minister with a suitable *Miyage* (gift) when visiting Washington.

Since most of the measures were hastily developed in a piecemeal fashion under intense American pressure, the packages did not add up to a systematic approach. As a matter of fact, they usually represented what was politically possible at a time when the state of the bilateral trade relations called for some visible action; which is not to say that they were entirely opportunistic or ineffective. The gradual import procedure changes, the increased transparency in economic decision-making, and other related steps helped American companies to enter the highly competitive Japanese market with less frustration. Such benefits, while not immediately reducing the trade imbalances, were bound to be helpful over the long run.

Moreover, on the Japanese side, the review of procedures, requirements, institutions, and the consideration of the nation's global image prior to reaching a consensus on the packages raised the awareness of politicans, government officials, businessmen, and the general public. They began to realize that decisions concerning the new international role of Japan could not be postponed any longer. While the government's response to American demands was always controversial, the resulting debates paved the way for the 1985 Action Program, the 1986 Maekawa Commission Report, and the other "visions" which gave strong impetus to the internationalization of the economy as envisioned during the second half of the 1980s.

The number of market-opening packages introduced depends upon the interpretation of the measures the Japanese have taken over the years.[17] For example, already prior to 1981, several sets of measures were designed to improve market access. The 1985 report of the Japanese Advisory Committee for External Economic Issues, known as the Okita Committee, identified six different sets of measures introduced between December 1981 and 1984.[18] Although the committee divided the packages into three categories such as external economic measures, market opening measures and the promotion of immediate external economic measures ostensibly to differentiate between those that improved market access and those which increased imports in the short-run vs. the long-run, from a practical point of view this differentiation is unimportant. All the packages were developed to meet the American, as well as the increasingly vocal European Community, demands for the opening of the Japanese market. The specific measures, among others, included the two-year advanced implementation of tariff reductions agreed upon in the Tokyo round (December 1981), the elimination and reduction of tariff rates on 215 items (May 1982), improvement of certification systems (January 1983), import promotion campaigns (October 1983), the submission of bills to the Diet to reform the tobacco monopoly (April 1984), and the increase of industrial imports under the Generalized System of Preference (GSP) from developing countries (December 1984).

International reception of the packages was generally critical. However, while prior to 1981 the criticism had come mostly from the United States and usually consisted of an angry and threatening "too little, too late," this time both the sources and the views were more diversified. The Asian Pacific Region nations such as the Republic of Korea complained that the measures favored America and Western Europe, and the Oceanic countries felt neglected because they were not even considered. The Americans and Western Europeans jointly complained that despite a number of successive packages, the trade imbalances have not improved, and that economic decision-making continued to lack transparency, leaving too much scope for administrative guidance. Complaints were heard about the lack of followthrough of high-level policy decisions by the operational staff, particularly by customs officials processing imports.

Unilateral American criticism turned out to be much harsher, but this was to be expected. Between 1981 and 1984 America's bilateral trade deficit with Japan jumped from a little over $13 billion to over $33 billion, an increase of approximately 250 percent. Furthermore, Japan's share of manufactured imports as a percentage of total imports grew only about 3 percent from 21 to 24 percent, and its manufactured imports from the United Stated increased only marginally from $10.1 billion $11.8 billion, or about 16 percent over the same time period.[19] In the opinion of Washington political circles, the trade statistics proved the closed nature of Japan's market and the ineffectiveness of the 1981–1984 liberalization measures.

The trade imbalances were announced against a backdrop of bilateral negotiations. The topics included, among other things, the level of Japanese car exports, defense contributions, and the increase of beef and citrus imports. The negotiations were made more difficult than usual by the mixed reception of a high-level Liberal Democratic Party (LDP) delegation (the Easki mission) in Washington in 1982, the Hitachi-IBM industrial espionage case in the same year, and the 1983 Congressional debates on industrial policies.

As usual, the Administration was restrained in its response and even praised a couple of the packages (for example, the May 1982 and January 1983 measures) as proper steps in the right direction. While it criticized others, it was not as aggressive as many members of Congress, who were in an angry mood and dismissed the packages; these Congressmen wanted immediate and forceful action to reduce the trade deficit. For example, Senator John Danforth introduced the trade-reciprocity bill in 1982 to "force open Japanese markets." Local content legislation continued to be on the congressional agenda as was the unfair nature of Japanese industrial policies.

More moderate voices, however, were also heard. The Council of Economic Advisors, for example, in its 1983 annual report stated that Japan was not the sole cause of America's overall trade problem even though some import barriers burdened bilateral relationships. The fall 1984 USTR report on five (except the December 1984) packages introduced between 1981 and 1984 identified a series of problems as seen by the Administration but also pointed out that the measures opened up new opportunities for U.S. exporters and investors. It was noteworthy that the report relied on an increase in such opportunities as its evaluation standard and not on the impact of the measures on the trade balances. It was also encouraging that during the Congressional hearings on Japan's industrial policies in 1983 and afterwards, an extensive debate took place on the structure, international competitiveness, monetary, exchange rate, and macroeconomic policies of the United States. As a consequence, the fundamental causes of America's growing global and the bilateral trade deficits were beginning to be recognized in Washington, and, at least temporarily, Japan was no longer viewed as the sole cause of the nation's international economic problems.

The Spring 1985 U.S.–Japan Trade Developments

American-Japanese trade relations were off to a good start in 1985. The "Ron-Yasu" meeting in Los Angeles on January 2 was dominated by the now familiar issue of U.S. access to Japanese markets, and the two leaders came away from the meeting with an agreement concerning a new negotiation format. The "Market-Oriented, Sector-Selective" (MOSS) approach was initially to address specific barriers in specific markets, such as telecommunications, medical equipment and pharmaceuticals, electronics, and forest products. Other industrial sectors were to be added to this list at a later date. The items to be reviewed included production, imports, distribution, demand, laws, restrictive rules, business practices, traditions, and consumer preferences.

The MOSS format was proposed by the American side which was dissatisfied with the effects of the market-opening packages to date. The United States argued that the packages were too general, and were very slowly implemented, if at all. American negotiators believed that focusing on specific markets and issues would provide quicker, and most of all, politically more visible results in the form of increased U.S. market shares, and eventually, improved trade balances.

The Japanese were not enthusiastic about the MOSS negotiations because these, too, were narrowly focused and did not include a review of the underlying causes of the bilateral trade imbalances. While the Japanese did not expect too much, they went along with the negotiations because they knew that as a result of the huge bilateral trade imbalances, U.S.–Japan trade relations would be under tremendous pressure during 1985.

Anger was rising in the United States. According to an early 1985 media poll, almost 9 out 10 Americans regarded the trade problem with Japan as either "very serious" or "somewhat serious."[20] Furthermore, by a margin of 3 to 2, they believed that the President did only a "fair" to "poor" job in gaining access to the Japanese markets. Not surprisingly, many members of Congress exploited the resulting rhetorical opportunities for their own political ends. They called upon the Administration and Japan to introduce more measures through which the trade imbalaces could be reduced. While such behaviour was understandable the protectionist demands created problems for the Administration which tried to maintain its credibility in the world as a champion of free trade.

It was the 1984 trade data showing a $33 billion ($37 billion by U.S. standards) American deficit that set off the spring 1985 trade conflict trade cycle which culminated in the Japanese market opening Action Program in July of the same year. After the release of these figures, members of Congress talked angrily about the "dismantling" of American industries. One senator referred to free-trade as "unilateral disarmament," while others started a flurry of activities which eventually led to the introduction of more than 300 protectionist bills.

Of course, not all of the bills were directed against Japan, but a number of them were introduced with the clear intent of "sending a message to Japan" that America's patience with the trade imbalances and all of the past market opening measures had "worn thin."[21] Amidst a series of hearings on America's trade position in general, and U.S.-Japan trade in particular, the idea of an import-surcharge bill surfaced. Eventually the bill was introduced by a troika of leading Democrats, Senator Bentsen, House Majority Leader Rostenkowski, and Representative Gephart, not with the expection that it would pass, but with the intention to shock the White House and the Japanese into "action." Thus, "Japan bashing" got its start.

The bill was the most protectionist legislation introduced in Congress since the Smoot-Hawley Act of 1930, a measure which had disastrous results not only for the United States but for the entire world. In light of this, the import surcharge bill was widely denounced not only in the United States but also by most of the international community.[22] The White House, the mass media, and trade experts agreed that the bill was a bad idea and that it could only damage the United States and the rest of the world. At the same time, all interested parties acknowledged that it reflected the prevailing anti-Japanese sentiment in Congress as well as in many other parts of the nation.

Two additional events fueled the already aggressive mood of Congress during early 1985. First, on March 28, MITI announced that Japan would maintain and raise car export quota ceilings from 1.85 million to 2.3 million vehicles for the April 1985—March 1986 period. The Japanese were concerned that if quotas were lifted, shipments would quickly increase to approximately 2.7 million units because American consumers would purchase more of the high quality Japanese cars in such high demand. In a sense, this was a no-win situation. Whatever the Japanese government decided, one group or another, such as the American car manufacturers, unions, members of Congress, or the Japanese automobile exporters, would have been upset. Expectedly, in the end, all sides were equally dissatisfied with the decision, including the White House, whose alleged signals concerning the matter had been "misread" by the Japanese.

The MOSS negotiations were not going well either, particularly in the area of telecommunications, where the United States had high hopes for increased sales following the privatization of Nippon Telegraph and Telephone (NTT) in the spring of 1985. The Americans wanted fewer regulations, less stringent technical standards, and the right to sell equipment without any restrictions. As usual, they believed that the Japanese were dragging their feet during the negotiations to continue the protection of the domestic marketplace. Among Japanese government officials, there was widespread resentment of the American demands; they privately complained that the United States behaved as if it were still an occupying power. To resolve the stalemate, and to forestall the import-surcharge bill, President Reagan sent a special emmisary to Prime Minister Nakasone to ask for some action which would convince Congress that progress was being made toward the reduction of the trade deficits. Thus, pressure on the Japanese steadily increased.

A tense situation resulted which was complicated by the inability of most Japanese, including responsible government officials, politicans, and the mass media, to understand the nuances of the American political system. They did not sufficiently appreciate the constitutional principle of the separation of power which shaped U.S. trade policy through the interaction between the Executive Branch and Congress. Most Japanese accepted the views put forth by their mass media, particularly the newspapers, tha the protectionist sentiments expresssed in Congress, chiefly for domestic political reasons, represented America's trade policy towards Japan. They did not realized that U.S. trade policy is formulated through the iterative relationship of Congress and the White House, not by Congress alone. They failed to see that the final outcome is always a much more moderate policy than the Congressional statements and debates usually imply.

The Japanese Debate on Demand Stimulation

In a bid to contain the mushrooming bilateral trade conflict, Prime Minister Nakasone appointed State Minister Komoto in March 1985 to formulate a set of specific trade measures based on the the the recommendations of the Committee on External Economic Relations (the Okita Committee), concerning the trade problem. The Prime Minister was anxious to make an advance announcement on April 9 of what was later to become the Action Program because he wanted to fend off criticism of Japan at the April 11–12 OECD meeting in Paris, and hoped to defuse the anti-Japanese sentiments on Capitol Hill.

Such advance announcement of trade measures is done regularly by the Japanese, who after a slow process of consensus building, are always in a hurry to assure the rest of the world, especially the United States, that they are anxious to satisfy satisfy the various demands put upon them. By doing so, however, they raise expectations to such high levels that the formal measures eventually announced always fall short of expectations abroad. Consequently, international response is always negative, and the unrealized expectations reinforce an image of Japan as the insincere trading partner who cannot be trusted. This was part of the reason behind the "Japan-bashing" frenzy which engulfed Washington in the spring and summer of 1985.

Prime Minister Nakasone held his intended press conference on April 9 in which he outlined the proposed market opening measures. The White House received the announcement in a friendly, but guarded manner; Capitol Hill and American business circles reacted cooly and skeptically. Key members of Congress stated that the measures could not deflect oncoming retaliatory legislation. Others, not aware of the gradual shift of power from the bureaucrats to the politicians, argued that while the Prime Minister probably meant what he said, the Japanese bureaucracy would not accept the proposals. Western European reactions, by and large, echoed U.S. sentiments, and at the April OECD meeting in Paris, Japan was severely criticised; Foreign Minister Abe declared afterwards that the conference was one of the most difficult he had ever attended.

To help resolve the increasing trade conflicts, the Okita committee recomended a reconsideration of Japan's traditional savings and consumption patterns, and the stimulation of domestic demand to increase imports. This recommendation initiated a spirited political fight among top LDP politicians, with a hidden agenda from Nakasone's opponents, in the spring of 1985 [23] This argument was not over the desireability of demand stimulation; almost everyone agreed that it was necessary. Rather, the clash seemed to be about how to do it. Prime Minister Nakasone opposed demand stimulation through increased public spending because of his firm commitment to fiscal austerity. He wanted a new, comprehensive set of market access measures and a revitalized private sector to stimulate demand. The Prime Minister was supported by Minister of Finance Takeshita and Minister of Foreign Affairs Abe.

The opposition was led by LDP Vice President Nikaido and the Chairman of the LDP General Counsel, Miyazawa, who wanted fiscal stimuli. They argued that fiscal policy was unnecessarily austere, and that because there was a large surplus of domestic savings over investment, public borrowing would not crowd out private investment and reignite inflation, among other things. Thus, an expansionary fiscal policy would encourage investments without any negative consequences, and would also raise import demand. Although to the outside world the debate appeared to be over economic policy, in reality Nikaido and Miyazawa tried to use the disagreement to engineer an early removal of Nakasone. They both wanted to be Prime Minister, and believed that the debate over demand stimulation provided them with the right issue to realize their aspiration.

In the midst of the increasingly vocal debate, U.S. Secretary of State Shultz gave a speech at Princeton on April 11. Addressing the problems of the world economy, Shultz reviewed the current economic policies of America and of the other industrialized nations, including Japan. He pointed out that for the sake of global prosperity, each nation had to make individual as well as multilateral efforts to moderate trade imbalances. Not mincing words about the U.S. fiscal deficits and their impact on the dollar exchange rate, and thus on trade, the Secretary also discussed Japan's high savings rate and the necessity of domestic demand stimulation without, however, suggesting the fiscal means to do so.

Nevertheless, true to form, the Japanese mass media ignored those aspects of the speech which did not fit their preconceived notions, and declared that America demanded immediate domestic demand stimulation through fiscal means. Such manipulation of Shultz's speech and the appearance of foreign pressure were welcomed by Nikaido and Miyazawa, who capitalized on the distortions to further their hidden agenda. Although the misinterpretation of Shultz's speech was eventually rectified through a personal meeting between Shultz and Minister of Foreign Affairs Abe, bilteral relations were burdened by the unwarranted exaggerations of the Japanese media.

Other interested parties also joined the debate.[24] The president of the influential Keidanren explained in a press conference on April 17 that he was against domestic demand stimulation because the Japanese economy was already plagued by excess capacity. Instead, he argued , Japan should develop an "export adjustment" (restraint) policy to pacify foreign critics. The Chairman of the LDP Policy Affairs Research Council and the Chairman of the LDP Tax System Research Commission concurred. Others, such as the head of the Keizai Doyukai and president of Nissan, and the vice president of Keidanren and president of Toyota, disagreed; they wanted additional market access measures and the expansion of domestic demand through the revitalization of the private sector. While the latter views had merit, the previous arguments in favor of export adjustment reflected a curiously short-sighted view of the interests of the Japanese economy. A substantial curtailment of the exports of Japan's internationally most successful industries would have meant giving up hard-earned competitive advantages just to assuage nations whose industries did not keep pace with the world-market developments.

Throughout the debate Prime Minister Nakasone remained firm on his position. He rejected demand stimulation through fiscal means, and instructed the various ministries and government agencies to prepare a broad set of economic measures which focused on market access and increased imports, which he eventually presented to the world as the Action Program of July 1985.

In retrospect, it is noteworthy that during the entire debate underlying the development of the 1985 Action Program, none of the participants ever justified increasing domestic demand to raise the living standards of the Japanese people. The focus of the debate was always on how foreign demands, particularly those coming from the United States, could best be satisfied regardless of how this affected the Japanese themselves. Such a reactive, as opposed to proactive, stance has long been characteristic of Japanese international economic policy formulation to the detriment of the nation's long-term economic interests.

Notes

1. See, for example, the Saxonhouse study cited in chapter 1; the Federal Reserve Board of New York, "Japan's Intangile Barriers to Trade in Manufactures," *Quarterly Review* (Winter 1985–86), pp. 11–18, and the most comprehensive current examination of the issue by C. Fred Bergsten and William R. Cline, *op. cit.* Also, *Japan* (Paris: Organization for Economic Cooperation and Development, 1985), particularly pp. 39–54.
2. Japan shows high export and low import income elasticity relative to the rest of the world. High income elasticity for exports has resulted from Japan's concentration, in commodities and areas that have high demand growth rates. The low income elasticity of imports is

caused by Japan's industrial structure which is geared toward high value added products designed to save resources and reduce imports of raw materials, particularly fuel. Consequently, the percentage of manufactured goods in relation to total imports is low.

3. All EPA data reported were obtained through personal interviews and from internal working papers in Tokyo, in March and May 1986.

4. *The Japan Economic Journal* (July 5, 1986), p. 7.

5. FTC and EPA internal working papers obtained during personal interviews at these agencies in Tokyo, in March and May 1986.

6. *Ibid.*

7. Bergsten and Cline, *The United-States-Japan Economic Problem, op.cit.* p. 124. For a discussion of these issues, see also *Progress Report: 1984* (Tokyo: U.S.-Japan Trade Study Group, 1984).

8. From the definition of international competitiveness by the President's Commission on Industrial Competitiveness.

9. *Economic Report of the President* (Washington, D.C.: Government Printing Office, 1986), p. 311.

10. For a detailed discussion of this trend, see "The Hollow Corporation," *Business Week* (March 3, 1986), pp. 57–81.

11. For a detailed discussion see "Business Fads: What's In and Out," *Business Week* (January 20, 1986), pp. 52–61.

12. *The New York Times* (September 1, 1985), p. 36.

13. While in some ways the European economies have done a little better in terms of productivity, most of the observations made about the United States can equally be applied to Western Europe.

14. See, for example, John M. Cline, "Inter-MNC Arrangements; Shaping the Options for U.S. Trade Policy," *The Washington Quarterly* (Fall 1985), pp. 57–71; Jane Sneddon Little, "Intra-Firm Trade and U.S. Protectionism: Thoughts Based on a Small Survey," *New England Economic Review* (January/February 1986); and Kenichi Ohmae, "Rising Yen But No Falling Trade Gap," *The Wall Street Journal* (July 1, 1986), p. 26. In April 1986, Allen Wallis, Undersecretary of State for Economic Affairs reportedly said of this subject: ". . . If we base our trade policy toward Japan — and indeed, our attitude toward that country and its people — on one number, we will have a bad policy and provoke results that are not in our interest." From *Asahi Evening News* (April 25, 1986), p. 9.

15. Office of Business Analysis, *Trade Ripples Across U. S. Industries*, a working paper (Washington, D.C.: U.S. Department of Commerce, 1986).

16. John M. Culbertson, "Free Trade is Impoverishing the West," and "Control Imports Through Bilateral Pacts"; "Importing a Lower Standard of Living," in *The New York Times* (July 28, and August 11, 1985, and August 17, 1986), pp. F3, F3, and F3, respectively.

17. For a detailed chronological discussion of all the various economic measures introduced through 1983, see the successive yearbooks on U.S.-Japan economic relations published by the Japan Economic Institute of America, now known as the Japan Economic Institute.

18. "Report of the Advisory Committee for External Economic Issues" (Tokyo, April 9, 1985). The establishment of the Office of Trade Ombudsman in 1982 was also part of the first package. For details of the measures see Appendix C.

19. *Japan 1985, An International Comparison* (Tokyo: Keizai Koho Center, 1985), p.36 and "The Japanese Government, External Economic Measures: The U.S. Government's Assessment of Their Implementation and Impact," (Washington, D.C.: Office of the

United States Trade Representative, 1984), p.2.

20. *Business Week* (April 8, 1985), p. 53.

21. For a select list of the bills addressing U.S.-Japanese trade relations, see appendix D.

22. Staff Working Paper, "The Effects of Targeted Import Surcharges" (Washington, D.C.: Congressional Budget Office, 1985); and "Costs and Benefits of Protection" (Paris: Organization for Economic Cooperation and Development, 1985).

23. This debate had its roots in the past because Japan's experience with Keynsian demand stimulation methods during the late 1970s was controversial. In response to U.S. pressure, the government adopted the "locomotive" thesis of economic growth, and set a real growth target of 7 percent in 1978. Prime Minister Fukuda encouraged "provisional and exceptional fiscal policies for positive expansion" in order to implement a proposal to help end the world recession caused by increased oil prices. The result was a dramatic increase in Japan's annual fiscal deficits, from 7 trillion yen to 14 trillion yen in one year. By FY 1985, Japan's ratio of outstanding long-term debt to GNP was 48.8 percent, and the debt service absorbed about 20 percent of the annual budget (in FY 1984, the U.S. public debt/GNP was 33.8 percent. See Takuji Matsuzawa, "Keidanren's Viewpoint on Government Spending and Future Administrative & Fiscal Reform, *Keidanren Review* (October 1985), p. 3.

24. The Keidanren (Japan Federation of Economic Organizations) is a private, nonprofit organization representing all branches of economic activity in Japan. It influences national policy formulation. The Keizai Doyukai is an economic organization for national policy studies. It is also a private, nonprofit organization, and is financed entirely through subscriptions; it, too, is quite influential.

3 THE ACTION PROGRAM AND ONGOING U.S.–JAPAN TRADE CONFLICTS

In his April 9, 1985, nationally televised speech Prime Minister Nakasone was surrounded by line-charts and bar-charts, and used a schoolmaster's pointer to urge his countrymen to increase their purchase of foreign products. Moreover, he also explained the economic rationale for his request, but did not dwell on the more subtle motives. The Prime Minister wanted to achieve several objectives with his bold and unusual move. First, he wanted to demonstrate to the United States, particularly to members of Congress, that his government understood the dangerous state of U.S.– Japanese trade relations. At the same time, he also wanted to show sensitivity to the general international economic situation, marked by huge Japanese current and trade account surpluses, and convince a skeptical world that Japan would do its share to reduce the imbalances.

Prime Minister Nakasone also wanted to reestablish his policy priorities domestically, particularly among the LDP politicians who attacked him during the debate on demand stimulation. Thus, what to many critics appeared to be a unique but superficial public relations move by Japanese political standards, was in fact a carefully planned political strategy designed to impress domestic and international friends and foes alike. In taking his case to the people through television, Nakasone not only demonstrated his unique political style but also tried to obtain much needed public support for the measures which eventually became known as the Action Program of July 1985.

At the same time, by making an early announcement, Nakasone raised expectations abroad to a level that, in its final form, the Action Program could not fulfill. Moreover, according to some cynical Japanese and foreign observers, through his television plea for more imports, he unintentionally strengthened the perception abroad that the Japanese discriminated against foreign products. Finally, others have pointed out that by choosing such a dramatic method to address the trade balance problem, particularly in relation to the United States, Nakasone may have also created the impression that his government was succumbing to the relentless American pressures. However, while the strategy was controversial, there was no disagreement that the Prime Minister's unique personal leadership style influenced the development of the Action Program and of the other measures which were aimed at the internationalization of the Japanese economy. Furthermore, his style was well received abroad, particularly in the United States.

Prime Minister Nakasone's Leadership Style

When Yasuhiro Nakasone became Prime Minister in 1982, most Japanese were skeptical, and some even expressed a dislike for the new head of government. Among his critics, Nakasone had an image of a calculating wheeler-dealer who always followed the political winds. A number of domestic political pundits called him a "weathervane" and gave him little more than six months in office.

However, Nakasone proved his detractors wrong, and by the summer of 1986, when he dissolved the Lower House and called elections for both the Lower and Upper Houses on the same day, he had been Prime Minister for three and one-half years, with consistently high public poll approval ratings (over 50 percent), outlasting the tenure of his three predecessors. After the overwhelming electoral victory of the LDP on July 6, 1986, the party leadership decided that he would continue in office at least one year beyond October 1986, when his term as LDP President should have ended and, according to party rules, he should have been replaced as Prime Minister.

He achieved this against great odds, particularly after the May 1986 Tokyo summit went awry. Many of his domestic critics, particularly a couple of influential leaders of the LDP who wanted to take over as Prime

Minister, considered the summit a failure for Japan in general and for Nakasone in particular. The summit achieved as much as could be realistically expected, but his critics judged it only for one outcome: the inability of Nakasone to convince the other participants that the steep appreciation of the yen had gone far enough. Only Chancellor Kohl of the Federal Republic of Germany paid any attention to the Prime Minister's concern; the others said that a strong yen was long overdue to correct the trade imbalances. Even President Reagan could not support Nakasone, because the growing U.S. trade imbalances and the upcoming fall 1986 congressional elections made this politically impossible. Nonetheless, critics seized the opportunity and declared that the much publicized "Ron-Yasu" relationship had no substance to it. By mid-May, the Prime Minister's opponents declared that the was in no position to call double elections, and even if he did, he could not possibly lead his party to a margin of victory that would enable him to stay in power beyond October 1986.

However, the critics again underestimated Nakasone's political savvy. He engineered the overwhelming LDP electoral victory, and as a result, he was seen as a forceful leader both at home and abroad; in this, he surpassed former Prime Minister Tanaka, who for many years was the acknowledged strongman of Japanese politics. While many of Nakasone's critics continue to view him as a crafty politician, most Japanese have learned to like his political manner which combines traditional Japanese philosophy and respect for old values with an appreciation of the Western world. The result is a unique leadership style which is characterized by flair and a degree of publicity consciousness never seen before in a nation where reticence remains a virtue.

Nakasone aspired to the prime ministership for a long time, and in the interim developed his policy priorities so that when the day arrived, he was ready to move forward with his plans. His domestic program is based on the desire to "settle all outstanding accounts in postwar politics." By this he means a restructuring of the broad socioeconomic and educational framework within which the nation's political parties have operated since the 1950s. This framework is the legacy of the LDP which monopolized power for 30 years, and whose policies began to flounder when Nakasone began his rise in the early 1980s. At that time, while the government reached the outer limits of its financial capabilities, expenditures were still mounting, and the ratio of budget deficits to GNP not only reached new heights but also significantly surpassed those of America and of the Western European nations, except Italy. Abroad, Japanese prime ministers were the "odd-man-out" in international conferences; at home, most politicans, government officials, and the general public were still prisoners

of the *shimaguni konjo* (insular, small-country mentality) which was becoming increasingly incongruous with the nation's mounting economic
power.

Nakasone began implementing his domestic program while he was still
director general of the Administrative Management Agency in 1980. To
reduce the size of government and to revitalize the private sector, he
recommended the formation of a special reform council to Prime Minister
Suzuki. The recommendation was accepted, and by 1981, administrative
and financial reforms without tax increases were under way.

Nakasone has a strong sense of history and of patriotism. To bolster the
nation's self-respect, in 1985 he made an official visit to the Yasukuni
Shrine, which is the spiritual home of Japan's war dead; he was the first
post-World War II prime minister to make this visit.[1] Undaunted by the
resulting domestic and foreign criticism, he continued to express his strong
personal conviction that the Japanese must re-enter the world as a confident people if they are to accept new international responsibilities. He
believes that in addition to knowledge and modern technology, this can be
accomplished only through a renewed respect for old values and traditions
which have shaped the nation throughout its long history.

Nakasone also has a global perspective of Japan's role. From his first
day in office, he had made internationalism a major theme of his government. This global orientation and his vision of Japan's future as an
economic power, in combination with his leadership style, has earned him
the respect of world leaders which past Japanese prime ministers lacked.
When Nakasone meets with the heads of other Western nations, he
displays an aggressive sense of self-confidence which was missing in his
predecessors, who never managed to act as equals among their peers.

While Nakasone is well liked and respected outside Japan, and many of
his countrymen have come to appreciate his style, his personality and
nontraditional leadership occasionally creates problems in the LDP and
the government. Articulate and telegenic, he shows authoritarian ten-
dencies which most of the top LDP politicians and the bureaucrats resent.
Critics overwhelmed by the range of Nakasone's ideas and his leadership
style refer to him as a "presidential prime minister" who makes decisions
by himself in a "top-down" as opposed to the traditional "bottom-up"
manner. While Nakasone respects traditional Japanese practices, he believes that because the world is complex and changes rapidly, the top-down
decision-making process is often more effective. Undoubtedly, this individualistic, Western style leadership and his relative negligence to engage in
the extensive *nemawashi* so important in Japan, as well as his lukewarm
support of those who have helped him in the past, are not in accordance

with traditional Japanese political behavior.[2] This, and his heavy reliance on "brain trusts," or private advisory committees, in the policy formulation process is seen by many politicians and bureaucrats as an attempt to undermine their influence. Most senior politicians believe that he is not relying enough on their advice, does not seek their agreement in time, and uses the brain trusts to endorse his views, thereby gaining public acceptance for, as well as overcoming intraparty resistance to, his policy plans. This criticism has some merit because in contrast to past prime ministers, Nakasone does not view himself as an organizer-coordinator of routine matters but rather as an originator-executer of ideas which he also wants to realize in his own fashion. Examples of this include his views on the controversial tax and educational reforms and the internationalization of the Japanese economy as set forth in the 1986 Maekawa Commission Report prepared by one of his brain trusts.

Some critics fault Nakasone for realizing his political program at the expense of the weaker social groups such as the aged, who have been hit the hardest by his insistence on fiscal austerity. Although he has inherited the various economic and social problems, such as the increases in medical costs and the inadequate support system for the elderly, the critics charge that his fiscal policies magnified the problems and have led to a loss of "warmth" in the relationship between government and the people, which is an important aspect of Japanese political life. Other critics consider Nakasone's tendency to seclude himself at times instead of informally socializing with other politicians as more proof of his "aloofness" and lack of warmth. It is noteworthy, however, that the same public which Nakasone's critics believe is alienated from him has consistently rewarded him with high public poll ratings and gave the LDP their sweeping electoral victory in July 1986.

The views put forth by a small group of young Dietmen in their May 1986 newsletter typifies the criticism of Nakasone within the LDP. These parliamentarians, none of whom belong to the Prime Minister's faction, accused Nakasone of not developing appropriate economic policies which led to the dramatic appreciation of the yen against the dollar. They called the MOSS negotiations and the 1985 Action Program stopgap measures which cannot resolve the basic underlying problems, and disapproved of the Prime Minister's management of U.S.-Japanese relations. In their view, close personal ties with the President resulted in Japan's uncritical acceptance of American demands. Furthermore, they claimed, Nakasone's "showmanship" has changed the LDP tradition of carrying out policies without posturing, and they called on him to exhibit some warmth and address the problems associated with daily life. The group also objected to the extensive use of brain trusts because the substitution of private advisory groups for political parties and elected representatives endangers the established political process.

The Changing Policy Formulation Process

While frequently criticized at home, Nakasone's global orientation and leadership style is well received in Washington where he is personally liked, and where his statements are taken at face value. Thus, when he runs into domestic resistance and cannot deliver all that the Americans believe he has promised, the White House, members of Congress, and the mass media blame it on the faceless Kasumigaseki bureaucrats, who, in their view, do not want to lose their influence over policy formulation.[3] Such views, however, are erroneous because they are based on outdated notions of the Japanese policy formulation process which underwent some gradual but significant changes during the late 1970s and early 1980s. While this process has not yet ended and will probably continue in the future, certain fundamental trends have already been established, as discussed in the following section.

The Declining Influence of the Bureaucracy

Historically, Japan's highly efficient bureaucracy dominated the policy formulation process. Well educated by the nation's top universities and selected through a demanding examination system, these bureaucrats represented the best talent that the country had to offer. Bound together by a common educational background, but divided by loyalty to their ministries, they nevertheless developed unified policies which served the country well through a long consensus-seeking process. Respected and well informed, they advised and influenced politicians in the Diet and the cabinet. At the same time, politicians could satisfy their constituencies' wishes by simply following the policies developed by the bureaucrats because the economy was rapidly growing and government finances were in good shape. When the time came to look for a postretirement career, many a select group of bureaucrats ran for a seat in the Diet. While those who eventually were elected represented a relatively small percentage of all bureaucrats, they made up a large part of the Diet membership. So, it is not an exaggeration to say that for many years the bureaucrats governed Japan.

This governmental process was so characteristically Japanese and lasted for such a long time that the outside world, and even many Japanese, failed to notice the evolution of historical changes during the 1970s. Gradually and against its will, the bureaucracy was forced to share its nearly exclusive control over policy formulation with the politicians. This is not to say that bureaucrats no longer exert influence; they continue to play a major role in the resolution of routine matters, and throughout the entire nonroutine policy formulation process, politicians, still listen carefully to their views. However, bureaucrats no longer enjoy a unique status, and to exert their influence, they must now form alliances with group of well-placed politicians.

A case in point is a spring 1985 incident in which the chairman of the LDP policy-formulating body asked the once omnipotent Ministry of Finance (MOF) to take certain steps with regard to the delayed FY 1986 budget. The MOF denied the request, so the chairman arranged for a meeting with the officials, lectured them on how "petty bureaucrats should not create petty arguments," and then told them to stay away from his office in the future. Although eventually the disagreement was resolved, the incident illustrates how times have changed. In the past, the elite bureaucracy of MOF would not have gotten into such embarrassing situations with the frequency it does these days.

The bureaucrats themselves agree that they no longer have exclusive control over the policy formulation process. According to the results of a survey published in the March 12, 1986, edition of the *Mainichi Shimbum*, 60.3 percent of the officials polled in 18 different ministries agreed that postwar prosperity was the result of their leadership. However, only 20 percent claimed that the Japanese economy is still led by bureaucrats in the second half of the 1980s.

Bureaucrats gradually lost their exclusive control over policy formulation for a number of reasons. First, over the years a U.S. style political democracy based on elected representatives as opposed to appointed government officials has evolved. Furthermore, by the early 1980s the government was no longer in a position to expand its budgets freely, and politicians would have lost their constituencies' support if they had simply continued to follow the bureaucracy's advice which was no longer supported by generous funding. Moreover, a number of Diet members who have specialized in areas such as education or tax matters for 10 to 20 years have obtained a much better grasp of issues than the officials who are frequently rotated through the various sections of the ministries. Consequently, over the years the politicians 'and bureaucrats' visions began to diverge, and politicians as a group have become much more knowledgeable. Thus, in contrast to past years when more than 90 percent of the legislation was written by bureaucrats and after closed-door (LDP) committee meetings, rubber-stamped by the Diet, in recent years as much as 25 to 50 percent of the submitted legislation was written by the Diet members themselves. Bureaucrats nonetheless still provided valuable expertise throughout the process.

This trend has been accelerated by the increasing number of bureaucrats entering political life at a younger age than their predecessors. Currently, more bureaucrats are leaving in their thirties and forties to run for office than in the past, when officials stood for election in their late forties or fifties after having obtained a considerable amount of seniority in their ministries or agencies. The present day bureaucrats move into politics earlier for a couple of reasons. First, as a general rule, LDP Diet members must have won at least five or more elections, meaning that they must have spent at least 10−15 years in the Diet before they can be considered for cabinet appointments. Thus, bureaucrats entering the political arena after the age of 50 cannot obtain the necessary two or three cabinet appointments to become influential senior politicians. Furthermore, retiring bureaucrats have recently seen their options reduced as the nature of traditional *amakudari* management positions in large corporations usually offered to them has changed.[4] With the gradual deregulation of the economy, corporations are now more independent and, thus, consider it less useful to employ retiring officials. These officials can, of course, still find jobs as advisors,[5] but the road to the top of large corporations is no longer as open as in previous years. This is true throughout the entire private sector, including the recently privatized public corporations, such as Nippon Telegraph and Telephone.

Changes Within the Liberal Democratic Party

The gradual shift of policy formulation from the bureaucrats to the politicians has been accompanied by changes within the LDP itself.[6] Whereas in the past, policy formulation within the party was the domain of the different factions who hammered out an agreement concerning the bureaucracy's policy proposals behind closed doors, in time the Policy Affairs Research Council and its divisions (*bukai*), transcending factions in accordance with policy issues, became the focal point of the process. The number of Council meetings steadily increased over the years, peaked in the mid 1960s, and then gradually declined until the early 1980s, when their frequency again increased to slightly over 1,200 per year, where the number is now stabilizing.[7]

The divisions or *bukai* combine specialized knowledge with political authority within the framework of smaller and therefore more manageable organizational units than the full Policy Affairs Research Council. They are organized along policy, that is, ministry or agency lines and cover the spectrum of government. There are, for example, agricultural and forestry, postal, highway, telecommunications, finance, construction, and aviation divisions, among others. Membership is open to all Dietmen who are interested; each may be a registered member of up to three divisions. However, nonmembers may freely attend divisional meetings of their choice and participate in the discussions.

The heads of divisions are experts in their fields, who have served at least three to five terms in the Diet. They have long-standing associations with the various interest groups formed around the divisions and may have seen years of administrative service as cabinet members, parliament vice ministers, or Diet committee chairmen. The divisional heads manage the relationships between the divisions, administrative organs such as the ministries, and outside interest groups.

The evolution of the divisions as influential, deliberative bodies is illustrated by the number of organizations lobbying the tax division for favors between 1966 and 1986, particularly after 1983 when the pressures for tax reform were beginning to mount. As figure 3–1 shows, in 1968 there were 48 organizations, and just two years later in 1970, this figure nearly doubled, reaching 95. In the 1970–1976 period, there was a steady increase although less rapid, of 35 more organizations, bringing the total number to 130 in 1976. The next three years saw another dramatic increase when 54 more organizations became active. While these numerical increases were great at the time, the largest increase occurred between 1983 and 1986, from 198 to 358 groups. This represents an increase of 80.8 percent between 1983 and 1986, and 732.6 percent between 1966 and 1986, the year in which tax reform was considered.

A critical role in the policy formulation process is played by the *zoku giin*, or political cliques/tribes. These informal groups have evolved along the lines of the specialized divisions but sometimes transcend both factional and divisional lines. There is no limit to the number of *zokus* Dietmen may join. Thus, the *zoku* unite LDP Diet members of varying backgrounds and seniority under the banner of certain special interests. Leadership is in the hands of influential senior politicians ("bosses") who wield a great deal of politial power. Membership continually changes

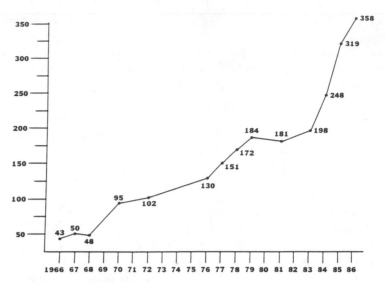

FIGURE 3–1.   Number of Organizations Lobbying For Tax Reform with the Tax System Research Commission of the LDP Policy Affairs Research Council: 1966–1986.

Source: Seizaburo Sato and Tetsuhisa Matsuzaki, *Jiminto Seiken*, (LDP Regime), originally published by Chuokoron-Sha, Inc. (Tokyo, 1986), p. 113. Courtesy of authors and Chuokoron-Sha, Inc.

according to the issues at hand and over time, and may include active cabinet members as well as first-term representatives who get equal opportunity to present their views at the *zoku* meetings.[8]

The *zokus'* ability to prevent the acceptance of a policy contrary to their perceived interest is based on traditional political practice. Throughout the policy formulation process, politicians whose interests are not directly affected usually do not comment on the views expressed by those whose interests are directly involved. As a consequence, the ultimately agreed upon policies always strongly reflect the views of the most affected *zoku* members even though they may be in a minority and some other members of the LDP may have reservations about the overall wisdom of these policies.

A case in point is the agricultural *zoku*. Although it is no longer as dominant as in the past, it continues to be one of the most important political interest groups in the Diet. In spite of its disagreements with industrial interest groups as, for example, the *Keidanren* which challenges the protectionist agricultural policies, the agricultural *zoku* continues to collect large sums of money, obtain blocks of electoral votes, and in general, influence Japanese political life. Its considerable strength is rooted in the importance of the farm vote for the LDP. Moreover, most of the LDP's senior politicians have rural backgrounds; for example, all nine prime ministers who held office since 1960 began their political careers in rural prefectures.

Opposition to the Action Program

Due to the *zokus'* powerful membership, access to information, and strong ties to interest groups (including the relevant bureaucracy), no policy can be formulated and no legislation can be passed into law in Japan today without the support of the relevant *zoku*. Therefore, it is no longer the bureaucracy, but the special interest *zoku* which can make it difficult or even impossible for a Prime Minister to be an effective leader. Whereas the officials of the various ministries can deliberately sabotage the Prime Minister's orders through delaying tactics or other means, they cannot openly challenge him. Only the *zoku* can do that, and this is what happened during the preparation of the Action Program.

While the outside world watched with fascination what it believed to be a struggle between Prime Minister Nakasone and the bureaucracy over the specifics of the program, in reality the Prime Minister had to do battle with the various *zoku* which protected the special interests they represented. Armed with the necessary information from the bureaucrats and support from the special interests groups, they were, thus, in a position to prevent the necessary consensus on any issue they opposed.

One area of particular contention centered on the tariff schedules for agricultural and marine products. While the government proposed a flat tariff rate decrease on these products, the agricultural-forestry *zoku* rejected the idea and agreed to other features of the program only after difficult negotiations. When the Prime Minister tried to reduce plywood tariffs, he had to postpone the move because the *zoku* again resisted. He had to provide an extra budget allocation of more than $1 billion to help the industry modernize before the *zoku* members were willing to agree to the tariff reductions, which, even then, would take effect three years from the date of the discussions.

To expedite the formulation of the Action Program, Nakasone, in an unusual demonstration of his resolve while negotiating with the *zoku*, also pressured the bureaucracy. He invited the vice ministers and bureau chiefs of the various ministries to his office to convince them of his intentions to increase imports. This was unusual because traditionally Japanese prime ministers talk to cabinet ministers first, who tell bureaucrats what they should do. Not surprisingly, a number of officials disagreed with the Prime Minister's approach and plans. An official of the domestically oriented Ministry of Posts and Telecommunications, for example, was quoted as saying that "... Prime Minister Nakasone does not have the power to enforce his personal choice, so it's risky to put your life in the hands of such a man. You never can tell when you will be betrayed."[9]

To increase the effectiveness of the planned measures, to obtain international publicity, and to pressure the bureaucracy, Prime Minister Nakasone also urged foreign participation in the rescheduling of tariffs, simplification of product standars, and import certification procedures because "the world is watching for this as the key to realizing a free market in Japan through the Action Program."[10] Thus, at a meeting of the Director Generals of 22 ministries and agencies, seven guests from the United States, European Community and Pacific region countries were given an opportunity to provide input for the program. The United States promptly submitted a request for market opening measures in 13 areas including the right for U.S. lawyers to practice in Japan, and the expansion of imports of American automobiles, shoes, and wine, among other things; the other foreign representatives also submitted requests, equally detailed, on behalf of their special trade concerns.

Scope of the Program

The Japanese Government-Ruling Parties Joint Headquarters for the Promotion of External Economic Measures, headed by Prime Minister Nakasone, officially announced on July 30, 1985, the Action Program for Improved Market Access, to be implemented over a three-year period. The Program included three basic principles broadly outlining Japan's intentions for increased participation in world economic affairs and aimed specifically at creating wider access in six areas of the Japanese marketplace. The plan further sought to promote international participation in this market-opening process through a new round of multilateral trade negotiations. Herein, Japan declared itself a full-fledged member of the international economic community, willing to accept its status and responsibility as a major economic power.

The underlying premise of the Action Program is stated as a willingness on the part of the Japanese to achieve a market openess "greatly exceeding that of the international level." With this in mind, the plan sets out the following principles:

1. From the basic standpoint of "freedom-in-principle, restrictions only as exception," government intervention would be reduced to a minimum so as to leave the choice and responsibility to consumers.
2. A positive attitude, as befitting Japan's position, will be taken in promoting the new round of GATT negotiations.
3. Special considerations in plan provisions will be given so that the Action Program can help promote the economic growth of developing nations.

These basic principles signal a shift in the Japanese world position from a small country to an economic power, and indicate a restructuring of not only the traditional relationships between Japan and the outside world but also of domestic economic practices and relations between the Japanese government and its citizens.

Selected Areas

The opening of the Japanese market outlined in the Action Program included measures in six areas, which were tariff schedules, import quotas, standards and certification of imports, government procurement, financial and capital markets, and services and import promotion measures. Tariff rates on 1,853 items, including products from the Generalized System of Preferences, were to be eliminated beginning in 1986; tariffs on other products were to be reduced by 20 percent starting the same time, and other products, such as wine, would remain on the same schedules until April 1, 1987. With respect to import quotas, action on the remaining quantitative restrictions, would be taken in consultations and negotiations at GATT talks and other meetings of interested parties.

The Japanese government hoped that revisions of the certification system, traditionally under its strict control, would help alleviate foreign criticism of the system as a nontariff barrier and facilitate market access for imports. The new program envisioned that the number of import items subject to self-certification be expanded to include 14 new products such as carbonated beverages and some electrical appliances. Another measure proposed that test data on imported products obtained in laboratories abroad be accepted by Japanese authorities "to the extent possible."

With respect to import procedures, the Japanese also addressed the issue of "transparency" in the policy-formulating process. The program states that foreign representatives would be allowed to participate in advisory councils, subcommittees, and other policy-formulating bodies to express their views. The Japanese wanted to reflect the opinions of foreign interests in the drafting or revision of standards.

This section also announced an effort to simplify the administrative procedures associated with imports. Measures, such as the publication of schedules for import approvals, were designed to reduce the time involved in these procedures. Other measures reduced the import notification requirements at points of entry and increased authority of customs officials to handle point-of-entry problems.

The program also included a section providing for additional "transparency" in government procurement. The measures promised better access to information concerning the tendering of bids. Among other provisions proposed in this section, bid times would be extended from 30 to 40 days to increase foreign competitiveness on government contracts, and delivery times would be extended "as far as possible." Lastly, while the GATT Agreement on Government Procurement (Tokyo round, 1979) is applicable to 45 government organizations, Japan proposed to apply the agreement to another 16 government-related organizations likely to request foreign contract bidding.

Efforts to liberalize Japan's financial and capital markets had been underway long before the Action Program was drafted, but the Action Program formalized Japan's commitment to market opening measures in this area. The major provisions of this section included a relaxation and ultimate removal of interest rate ceilings on large denomination deposits by the spring of 1987. They also promoted liberalization of interest rate ceilings on small denomination deposits provided that necessary provisions were established to protect depositors. Another feature of this section authorized nine eligible foreign banks to participate in trust banking business. One last provision, which related to the opening of financial markets, liberalized the issurance of floating rate Euroyen notes.

The final area affected by the Action Program was services and import promotion. Many of the Japanese service industries had been sharply criticized by foreigners for maintaining nontariff barriers, particularly in distribution, legal, and insurance services. This section proposed to allow foreigners to participate in these service areas to a limited extent. For example, new legislation was drafted to amend the Lawyers Law to enable foreign lawyers to practice in Japan. With regard to insurance, National Health Insurance, previously provided only to Japanese citizens, would be made available to all foreign residents of Japan. The government further proposed to formulate an international framework for trade in services as another facet of the planned new round of multilateral trade negotiations.

Import promotion fell into several categories. First, in order to encourage private industries' efforts to increase imports, the interest rate of the Export-Import Bank of Japan for import credit on manufactured goods and government procurement would be lowered, and direct investment by foreign firms would be encouraged. Next, the government proposed to enhance the public's "awareness of the importance of imports" through officially sponsored promotions, particularly large-scale import fairs organized by the Japan External Trade Organization (JETRO). In conjunction with this, it also proposed to encourage its citizens to travel abroad to generate demand for imports. Finally, the program also addressed two key foreign concerns: the elimination of counterfeiting and improved distribution.

Counterfeiting of popular trademarks and brand name items of consumer goods has become a serious problem all over the world, but especially in Japan where consumers are particularly brand-conscious, and the manufacturing skills necessary to produce high quality copies are available. Here the Japanese government proposed to actively enforce laws by establishing anticounterfeiting agencies and prosecuting counter feiters. With regard to the distribution system, the government proposed to conduct a fact-finding study on the distribution paths of imported goods and provide the results to consumers. Also, the function of the Office of Trade and Investment Ombudsman was to be strengthened to settle foreign complaints concerning market access.

While the program sets out specific timetables and implementation plans for its measures, it contains certain caveats. For instance, the Economic Planning Agency proposed eliminating or reducing tariffs on 1,853 products starting in March 1986; however, some products such as wine remained on their original schedules for an additional year as a political concession to the agricultural interests. Moreover, the very sensitive product issues were relegated to the area of "future consultations with interested parties." Tariff rates on industrial products would be reduced by 20 percent in principle, unless injuries to Japan's "domestic industries are caused to the extent by import surges or other circumstances due to this measure" in which case "suspension of the measure on related products may be introduced."[11] In other sections, such as the measures related to import quotas, the program does not ignore the politically sensitive issues, but neither does it take concrete steps toward their resolution. With respect to import quotas on beef, citrus fruit, and other agricultural products, for example, the Japanese promise to observe existing arrangements "in good faith." The program proposes that upon the expiration of the present arrangements, Japan will start new "consultations . . . and shall take appropriate actions with sincerity."[12]

Import Campaigns

To raise public awareness of the trade problem and to urge consumers to buy more foreign products, the government in cooperation with the private sector also staged an import campaign in October and November 1985. Some 100 leading figures from the art, sports, and entertainment world were enlisted to help. Import fairs were organized at more than 1,000 sites across the country; Prime Minister Nakasone himself made a much publicized appearance at the Tokyo Fair.

The Japanese government knew that the program could not succeed without the full support of the large private-sector companies. Consequently, already on April 22, 1985, MITI called in the executives of the 60 leading export-oriented corporations and trading companies, asking them to develop their own "action programs." By the end of May, MITI announced that the 60 companies planned to import goods worth more than $96 billion during FY 1985, an increase of $5 billion or 5.5 percent over FY 1984.

On August 23, MITI asked another 74 companies to join the import promotion effort, and by early 1986 projected that the total of 134 corporations intended to import goods worth $104.6 billion in FY 1985, an increase of 7.5 percent from the previous year. Some of the increase was expected from the *sogo-shosha* (trading companies), electronics and machinery manufacturers, department stores, supermarket chains, and energy companies. Most of it, however, was to be generated by the car manufacturing industry that pledged to procure from foreign sources whenever possible. Imports by all companies affiliated with the Toyota group, for example, were expected to reach $917 million in FY 1985, an increase of 9 percent over FY 1984. The parts and components to be imported included tires, windshields, machine tools, and aluminum wheels. Other car manufacturers, such as Nissan and Mazda, expressed similar intentions.

Among the *sogo-shosha*, Marubeni Corp., Sumitomo Corp., C.Itoh & Co., and Nissho Iwai Corp. were the most active. They instituted import incentive systems and other measures to motivate employees to obtain more products from abroad. According to a MITI survey, the combined imports of the top 13 *sogo-shosha* in FY 1985 were expected to increase by $5.9 billion, or 6.7 percent over FY 1984.

Reactions Abroad

Reactions to the Action Program abroad ranged from a wait-and-see attitude to dejected deja vu to outright hostility. As usual, the early announcement of these measures on April 9 raised expectations to a level that could not be met by a program that was shaped through the traditional consensus-formulation process. Furthermore, like all the previous market-access packages, the Action Program was a unilateral response to strong foreign pressures for specific measures within a short period of time. Thus, the program could not address the fundamental issues of the current and trade account surpluses that Japan was amassing. Such a move would have necessitated a broad, coordinated multilateral effort which neither the American nor West European nor most developing country governments were prepared to undertake. A joint effort would have forced these governments to alter many domestic economic policies, which would have been politically unacceptable.

Criticism was immediately widespread. In the developing world, for example, the South Korean press criticized Japan for not directly respond-ing to Korean expectations, while Singapore newspapers argued that the entire program was developed to pacify the United States. Others, such as the Thai and Malaysian press, were less negative and looked forward to some improvement in their trade with Japan. Among the industrialized countries, official circles and the media in Britain expressed scepticism about the entire effort, while the French had doubts about Nakasone's ability to implement the program over the objections of all the vested interests. The Federal Republic of Germany and Australia, on the other hand, were somewhat more positive, and speculated that a fully implemen-ted Action Program might be beneficial.

American Criticism and the Japanese Response

From the Japanese point of view, America's reaction was the most impor-tant. Unfortunately, the official announcement of the program came on the same day as the U.S. Department of Commerce published its monthly trade statistics showing that in June the United States had incurred its second highest monthly trade deficit of all time ($13.4 billion), 34 percent or $4.6 billion of which was with Japan. Thus, when Tokyo made its announcement, the anti-Japanese mood in Washington, particularly on Capitol Hill, was intensifying.

The White House reaction was cool, and although it referred to some parts of the program as "promising," it suggested that the three-year implementation schedule should be enacted "in a more timely fashion." This contrasted the warm praise that the Administration gave the initial announcement in April, and was part of a strategy to dampen the protectionist forces in Congress while keeping pressure on the Japanese. Some U.S. government officials greeted the program with guarded praise; staff members of the U.S. Embassy in Tokyo, for example, said that it would probably help the sales of some foreign products in Japan, such as cosmetics, processed foods, and appliances. Others in Washington noted that the program made no provisions for the removal of agricultural quotas, and that it did not seem to clearly address the admission of foreign lawyers, nor did it include steps to dismantle the structural import restraints such as the distribution system.

Reactions in Congress were uniformly hostile. Leading proponents of the protectionist movement, which by the summer of 1985 overwhelmed both the House and Senate with over 300 bills, expressed scepticism about not only the effectiveness of the Action Program but also the sincerity of the Japanese government.[13] The resulting "Japan-bashing" involved a great deal of "bureaucracy-bashing" because even members of Congress did not realize the shift of policy-formulating power from the bureaucracy to the LDP *zoku* and, thus, vented their anger at the government officials.

One of the key sponsors of the import surcharge bill, Senator Lloyd Bentsen (D-Texas) was reported to have said that while he has not had a chance to look at the program, he was skeptical from past experience because the Japanese bureaucracy "is a master of the hidden trade barriers." Senator John Danforth (R-Missouri), chairman of the Senate International Trade Subcommittee, stated that the Japanese announcement of the program was just another set of fine-sounding words which probably would not lead to any concrete results. Senator John Heinz (R-Pennsylvania) went even further, he called U.S.–Japanese negotiations a con-game in which the United States was the willing dupe. The Japanese, Sen. Heinz added, would not open up their marketplace because they knew that the United States would not take any strong actions against them.[14]

On the other side of the Pacific, the Japanese mass media conveyed the U.S. reactions in their usual style. The reporters did not differentiate between the White House and Congressional views, nor did they explain the motivation behind the Administration's strategy to respond in a guarded manner. Above all, they emphasized the statement made by the various members of Congress, and provided details of some of the 300 protectionist bills pending at that time. Most reporters paid little attention to the American domestic political situation which was the major reason that members of Congress, who were already thinking ahead to the next elections, tried to outdo each other's protectionist rhetoric.

Not surprisingly, such exaggerated reports stoked the fires of resentment in Tokyo. The Japanese could not understand what it was the Americans wanted when, given their domestic political circumstances, they had done as much as possible. They were frustrated by the expectation that they should rapidly change long-standing arrangements and practices, and consequently, they fell back on the only explanation that seemed reasonable. The Japanese believed that America was inefficient and unwilling to take the painful but necessary steps to put its economic house in order, and found it easier to blame Japan for its problems.

Such views, although containing some truth, were as oversimplified as the often repeated American charge that the root of all bilateral trade problems was the closed nature of the Japanese marketplace. While Japan no longer maintained the protectionist barriers of an era past, traditional arrangements and practices, such as product standards, continued to hamper market access.

The Action Program was designed to eliminate these constraints as quickly as possible and thereby improve market access. It was unfortunate that the emotional responses on both sides of the Pacific clouded the introduction of the program. A less emotional examination would have shown that the program was neither a quick and easy way to fix the trade imbalances nor a cynical public relations exercise. It would have revealed the simple truth that the program was a unilateral move in the right direction with possible future benefits for Japan and the rest of the world.

The 1985–1986 MOSS Negotiation Results

The Japanese government published its official report on the first-year implementation results of the Action Program on August 1, 1986. However, already earlier in the year, in January, the American and Japanese governments released a joint communique on the achievements of the Market-Oriented Sector-Selective (MOSS) negotiations, which overlapped with the program in that they also dealt with questions of market access, albeit only in selected industries.[15]

The MOSS talks begin in the spring of 1985, and addressed the Japanese telecommunications, medical equipment, pharmaceutical, electronics, and forestry markets. Both governments agreed to pinpoint and reduce regulatory, tariff, and other existing import barriers in these markets. While officially termed successful in the end, the negotiations had their ups and downs; in some of the highly technical discussions, ill-informed American negotiators were lectured by Japanese bureaucrats on their lack of understanding, which led to frustrations on both sides. Moreover, in late 1985 a disagreement concerning forestry products nearly led to a breakdown; Foreign Minister Abe had to personally intervene to save the situation at the last minute.

In their joint communique, Secretary of State Shultz and Foreign Minister Abe praised the talks. In his individual statement to the press, Abe cited unilateral tariff cuts, a sharp rise in the yen, and substantial changes in the regulation of the telecommunications, medical equipment, pharmaceutical, and electronics markets as positive developments. Secretary Shultz supported Abe's remarks but emphasized that little progress was made toward resolution of the disagreement over forestry products.

While the agreement was noteworthy, the major reason for the optimism and satisfaction expressed in the joint statement was the desire to dampen protectionist sentiments on Capitol Hill, where another cycle of Japan-bashing was expected to begin in the spring of 1986. Nonetheless, representatives of the telecommunications, medical equipment, pharmaceutical, and electronic industries believed that the MOSS agreements would make it easier for their firms to enter the Japanese marketplace.

The First Year of the Action Program

Following the conclusion of the MOSS talks, the Japanese government, later in the year, announced in its first year Action Program report that Japan had made good on most of its promises to reduce tariffs and to eliminate remaining nontariff barriers.[16] The exception was the slow progress in the expansion of agricultural import quotas and the government procurement of foreign products.[17]

While the government's report of the first-year Action Program implementation results was upbeat, the trade data for FY 1985, ending on March 31, 1986, were much less encouraging. According to the customs statistics published by the Ministry of Finance, while total exports increased by 3.3 percent, imports were down by 5.1 percent.

The import decline was mainly caused by the stagnating demand for food, crude oil, coal, and liquefied gas, items which represent more than 40 percent of Japan's annual imports. Also, the total figures reported in U.S. dollars were affected by the unexpectedly rapid decline in the price of some of these items.

In the midst of these discouraging data, there was, however, one ray of hope. Manufactured imports showed a more than expected increase and reached a 31 percent share in total imports, including fuels, an all-time high since World War II and substantially higher than the preceeding year's 20 percent. This positive trend was reinforced by JETRO's August 1986 report which announced that during the first six months of 1986, manufactured imports grew by 23.7 percent to $24.7 billion, representing a 38 percent share in total imports.[18] According to JETRO, the first six-month data indicated that by the end of FY 1986 manufactured imports could surpass the FY 1985 high of 31 percent.

The first-year private sector action program results were also modest. According to MITI data, by the end of FY 1985 the 134 participating corporations reported only a slight 3 percent increase in the value of imports over the previous fiscal year.[19]

To meet their commitments in the future, some of the 134 corporations planned to increase their manufactured goods imports during FY 1986. The 26 member Hitachi group, for example, set an overall goal of $980 million, an increase of 13 percent over FY 1985. Of this amount, Hitachi planned to spend $400 million in the United States, an increase of 12 percent over the previous year.

The results were disappointing, but it was unrealistic to have expected that the Action Program could greatly increase overall imports within a single year, particularly with conditions of stagnating demand in the major import markets. Most knowledgeable observers knew this, and also understood that long-established buying patterns and habits could not be changed overnight, regardless of concentrated import promotion efforts. As one Japanese government official explained, "The aim (of import promotion) is not to make them (the Japanese) buy — the amount is negligible — but to stop them from opposing the idea of increasing imports."[20] The chairman of Marubeni Corporation stated that ". . . import expansion calls are similar to Buddhist chants, constants recitation eventually enables them to seep into one's mind."[21]

One of the reasons that the import promotion campaigns were not very effective was that in addition to the strong loyalty and high quality expectations of Japanese consumers in general, industrial buyers have their own loyalties and very selective standards.[22] Most original equipment manufacturers (OEMs) consider imported parts and components a major problem. They found that many imported items, regardless of the source, do not meet quality standards. As a consequence, in many companies even though the purchasing department heads want to increase imports, technical staff on the shop floor often resist. With the sharp appreciation of the yen, such intraorganizational conflicts became more frequent in the second half of 1986 because purchasing managers could point to the considerable cost savings derived from imports, while the technical specialists continued to worry about quality. Generally, such debates are won by the quality-control technicians whose arguments carry more weight than those of the purhasing specialists. Many Japanese companies have established a worldwide reputation as high quality producers; not surprisingly, they are not willing to risk such a reputation just because the government wants to increase imports. Official exhortations worked in the past, but they do not have the same effect in the second half of the 1980s.

Industrial imports were also limited by manufacturing considerations, particularly the widely used *kanban* (just-in-time) inventory system. Successful application of the *kanban* depends largely on the firm's suppliers. In this system, suppliers must provide the buyers with small lots of high quality parts delivered frequently and coordinated precisely with the buying firms' manufacturing schedules. There is very little or no safety stock; thus, the quality, quantity, and timing of the deliveries are extremely critical. Dependable and readily available suppliers are a necessity.

It is, of course, possible that in the future the *kanban* system will become less important because with the strong appreciation of the yen, manufacturers that currently use the system may have to reconsider the tradeoffs among lower import prices, higher inventory carrying costs, quality, and delivery before they can make rational economic decisions concerning imports. This assumes that the questions of quality and delivery can be resolved in a satisfactory manner. However, during the first year of the Action Program such tradeoffs were not feasible.

Other traditions and long-established practices also hamper imports. Most of these are rooted in the commercial practices of the past, and thus, could not be as readily changed through government directives as, for example, product standards or import procedures. Government surveys have shown that despite the yen appreciation, the price of many foreign products had not decreased during the first half of 1986, because traditional importers of such products wanted to obtain higher profits or maintain brand image or both. While the government wanted the benefits of the yen appreciation passed on to the consumers, there was no easy way to convince importers to reduce prices since it cannot dictate price-policy to private sector companies.

The effectiveness of the Action Program during the first year was also reduced because it was not possible to raise the export-orientation of foreign, particularly American, companies. The Japanese import promoting delegations of the large, private sector corporations, for instance, came back with mixed feelings from America.[23] The representatives of Toyota and Hitachi reported that they found U.S. companies whose products they liked, but the managements of these firms were indifferent to exporting. Others were reluctant to adapt their products to the Japanese marketplace. Moreover, even companies which were export-oriented could not take advantage of the new opportunities on such short notice. Managers need time to develop business plans and to undertake the necessary financial as well as human investments required for entering the very competitive Japanese marketplace.

The Japanese government was concerned about the modest results and, in August 1986, urged the top managers of Japan's major department stores and supermarkets to increase the import of consumer goods manufactured abroad under licensing arrangements. The MITI Minister personally told managers to purchase more clothes and household merchandise produced mostly in Asian countries. Moreover, the minister asked that managers develop plans to return the windfall profits obtained through the yen appreciation to the consumers. The requests were made in August because department stores and supermarkets import about two-thirds of their foreign products during the fall and winter seasons. The heads of the retail firms promised to do their best, but such admonitions no longer carry the same weight as in the past; therefore, only time will reveal the effectiveness of the government's import promotion followup measures.

Ongoing U.S.–Japan Trade Conflicts[24]

The FY 1985 trade statistics were received abroad with the usual critical comments. Most of the response emphasized that the decline in imports was more proof of the closed nature of the Japanese marketplace.

The August 1, 1986, official Action Program report, on the other hand, was hardly noticed abroad. Most American and European newspapers mentioned the report in their news sections but failed to publish any analyses of the results. It seemed that the world had forgotten about the program which had been introduced amid a great deal of publicity and commentary only one year before.

Official reactions throughout the world, particularly in the United States, where most of the responses had been critical when the program was announced, were also muted. Members of the U.S. Congress were occupied with the tax reform bill and were also busy preparing for the fall 1986 mid-term elections. President Reagan was on vacation in California, and most key members of his trade-policy staff were also out of town.

Furthermore, shortly after the report was published, the U.S. trade figures for July 1986 were announced. The merchandise trade deficit had soared to $18 billion, a new monthly record. Administration officials and members of Congress expected that trade would be a major issue in the Congressional elections later that year; therefore, they focused on these trade statistics rather than on the Japanese government report.[25]

At that same time, the U.S. government continued to pressure Japan on what it considered to be several unresolved issues. These included the admission of foreign lawyers under the Action Program and increased access to the Japanese tobacco and car parts markets under the new round of MOSS negotiations which began in mid-1986.

The Admission of Foreign Lawyers

In May 1986, in accordance with the Action Program commitment, the Diet passed legislation admitting foreign lawyers to practice in Japan beginning in April 1, 1987. The United States had been pressuring Japan on this issue for some time; Americans viewed the admission of lawyers as a part of the campaign to open Japan's service markets. Moreover, they told the Japanese that admitting foreign lawyers was in Japan's interest because specialized legal services were needed to undertake the complex international transactions in the newly liberalized financial markets.

Not surprisingly, the Japanese lawyers disagreed, and *Nichibenren*, the Japanese Federation of Bar Associations, strongly rejected the American arguments and formed a countermeasures committee to deal with the matter. Members of the organization were concerned about the influence foreign lawyers could have on the legal profession's traditionally harmonious interaction with Japan's consensus-based society.[26] Moreover, they claimed, the standards of the legal profession are among the highest in Japan; thus, the admission of foreign lawyers could affect these standards.

The legal profession in Japan is very selective. To become a lawyer, candidates must first complete an undergraduate university education, and then apply to the nation's only law school, the Legal Training and Research Institute. Of the several thousand applicants, only a maximum of 500 are admitted annually if they pass the rigid admissions exam. In 1984, for example, of the 35,000 applicants, 500 passed and were admitted, a success rate of 1.4 percent. The curriculum is based on a two-year apprenticeship in trial practices, drafting legal documents, and other related matters. At the end of two years, candidates must sit for a routine final examination which all of them pass. The graduates may then become assistant judges, public prosecuters, or *bengoshi*.

The *bengoshi* are specialists in civil law and criminal defense, and may, therefore, represent clients in court. Others, such as patent or tax attorneys, differ from the *bengoshi* in that they represent clients only in their special fields. Most of the *bengoshi* practice in Tokyo where they are members of small firms, usually comprised of two to five lawyers.

Of course, in addition to the legitimate concern about how foreign lawyers would fit into such a differently structured legal system, the *Nichibenren* was also trying to protect the vested interests of its members. Most Japanese lawyers were afraid that their small firms would be overrun by New York-based or Washington-based law firms with hundreds of lawyers and support staff.[27]

The legislation ultimately approved by the Diet became effective on April 1, 1987. It is based on the principle of reciprocity insofar as it admits only those foreign lawyers whose native countries admit lawyers from other nations, including Japan. Approval to practice requires five years of experience, is limited to the lawyer's home country law, and prohibits the formation of partnerships and the employment of Japanese lawyers. Moreover, while the Ministry of Justice maintains general oversight, *Nichibenren* was authorized to exercise disciplinary control over foreign lawyers.

The American Chamber of Commerce in Japan and the European Business Council in Tokyo were among the first to object to the specifics of the legislation. They argued that the law was not an internationally appropriate solution as promised by the Action Program. They were joined by a group of American lawyers who petitioned the United States Trade Representative (USTR) to begin an investigation under Section 301 (Unfair Trade Practices) of the 1974 Trade Act.

American lawyers objected to most features of the legislation, but were particularly upset by the reciprocity requirement. Their concern stemmed from the fact that in the United States, legal licenses are issued by the states, and because in 1986, only New York, Michigan, Hawaii, and the District of Columbia had a policy of reciprocity, lawyers from all but these four areas are barred from Japan.[28] To placate American critics, the Japanese government promised to continue consultations on the ordinances implementing the bill, but it also made clear that "the basic framework is not going to change."

The legislation is undoubtedly restrictive, but it was the best that could be achieved under the circumstances. The *Nichibenren* had an agreement with the government dating from the early 1980s in which it agreed to solve the admission problem on its own. Moreover, the bar association is politically influential association with strong ties to the legal *zoku* in the LDP policy-formulating apparatus. The association effectively used its influence during the consensus formulation process that preceded the submission of the bill to the Diet. Thus, the government had no choice but to go along even though the legislation did not meet all the expectations at home and abroad.

The events surrounding this legislation have shown that as far as the vested interests of professional groups are concerned, the Japanese government is subject to the same kind of pressures as, for example, the American or West German state and federal governments. The political influence and restrictive practices of the American and German Medical Associations exercised under the guise of maintaining professional standards are legendary. Naturally, for the sake of the world economy, restrictive professional practices, whether in Japan or abroad, should not be accepted indefinitely. Changes, however, must be introduced gradually and multilaterally; otherwise the vested professional interest groups throughout the world will continue to fight even the most modest proposals for change.

At the same time, the strong reaction of U.S. lawyers to the Japanese legislation reflected a curious point of view. Reciprocity limitations are not unusual in the world's professional service markets. In the United States, lawyers licensed in one state wishing to practice in some other state must often pass the bar examination of that other state before being allowed to practice there, regardless of their previous experience. Most importantly, the exclusion of all American lawyers from Japan, except those from New York, Michigan, Hawaii, and the District of Columbia, could easily be remedied through the acceptance of the reciprocity principle by those states that presently reject it.

Thus, the lawyers' petition requesting an "unfair trade practices" investigation by the USTR was more of a reflection of a narrowly defined self-interest than a genuine concern over general access to Japanese service markets. American lawyers were motivated by the same self-serving considerations as the *Nichibenren* which was trying to keep them out of Japan.

Fortunately, despite the unreasonable position taken by the American lawyers, reason prevailed in Washington. On June 10, 1986, the USTR declined to initiate a Section 301 action. He did so because of the continued exchange of views and because the Japanese legislation became effective only one year later, in 1987, at which time the implementation process could be reviewed to see if any additional action was necessary.

Thus, this curious episode in U.S.-Japan trade relations came to a well-deserved ending.

Nonetheless, increased access to Japan's service markets is a legitimate goal of American trade policy, particularly if the pressure for it is accompanied by the reciprocal liberalization of the service sectors in the United States. If all goes well, the new Uruguay round of GATT negotiations may provide a multilateral framework for such actions by 1990.

Tobacco and Car Parts Imports

In the fall of 1986, the United States also expressed concern about the tobacco and car parts markets to which, the Americans argued, access was still restricted. This claim was made within the framework of the new 1986 MOSS talks, as well as in reference to the overall market access commitments made by the Japanese government in the Action Program.

The American demand for more access to the tobacco market presented a difficult problem for Japan. When the former Japan Tobacco and Salt Public Corporation monopoly was replaced by the Japan Tobacco, Inc., to increase competition, conditions in the marketplace remained restrictive because the new company retained a monopoly over domestic leaf buying, tobacco processing, and cigarette manufacturing. This was demanded by the tobacco *zoku* which claimed to protect the livelihood of the approximately 90,000 domestic tobacco leaf growers against low-cost foreign competition. Prime Minister Nakasone had no choice but to agree to the demand, because otherwise he could not have obtained a consensus for even the partial dismantling of the monopoly.

While politically unavoidable, the arrangements made little economic sense. The Japan Tobacco, Inc., pays about three times the world market price for tobacco leaves to growers, and as a result of this price support, by 1985 more than a year's supply of surplus leaf tobacco had accumulated in the warehouses. Even under the best of circumstances, such a surplus can be eliminated only in three to five years, or around 1988, at the earliest. Circumstances, however, are not the best, because the demand for cigarettes appears to be stagnating or perhaps decreasing.

Although over 310 billion cigarettes were sold in FY 1985, this represented a 0.6 percent decrease from the previous fiscal year. While the evidence is not yet entirely clear, it is possible that the Japanese are beginning to pay more attention to the health hazards associated with smoking. In a January 1987 report the Japan Tobacco Inc. announced that the estimated number of smokers declined by about 3.6 million from the 1978 peak of around 35 million to a little over 31 million in 1986. Moreover, the report emphasized, the estimated smoking population decreased by slightly over 1 million during 1985–1986 alone. Such developments, if they develop into long-term trends, could have very adverse effects on the domestic leaf growers because the share of foreign tobacco (cigarettes and pipe smoking tobacco) rose to 2.4 percent in FY 1985 and 3.3 percent by June 1986, from 1.8 percent in FY 1984.[29] Increased sales of imported cigarettes are attributed to the narrowing price gap due to an increase in domestic prices, as well as the diversification of consumer tastes.

Thus, by the fall of 1986, the Japanese government was in a difficult situation. The partial dismantling of the tobacco monopoly satisfied neither the American government nor the other foreign governments. At the same time, the influential *zoku* was not about to give up its protectionist stance to satisfy foreign, particularly American demands for a more open market. The *zoku* members believed that the Japanese government should not be concerned about the foreign demands because the former public monopoly is now a private firm and the market share of imported cigarettes is on the rise. Others, including members of the Diet, were angry at the United States because just as American medical and government authorities were trying to reduce smoking, U.S. negotiators pressured Japan to buy more tobacco. Moreover, they argue, in response to an October 1986 report by the U.S. Academy of Sciences concerning the negative effects of "passive smoking" or the involuntary inhalation of smoke by nonsmokers, the American authorities are more ready than ever to limit smoking. This reminded some of the Japanese of imperial Britain which forced the Chinese to consume opium during the nineteenth century to achieve its commercial aims.

However, from the outset, the United States argued that were it not for the restrictive practices, American producers could obtain a substantial share of the estimated $14.8 billion Japanese market. To lend weight to the criticism, the Office of the USTR independently initiated a Section 301 investigation in September 1985. The American position was further hardened when the Japanese introduced an excise tax of 11 cents per package in May 1986, thereby effectively nullifying the anticipated price benefits of the declining dollar. It is noteworthy, however, that in the fall of 1986 when the yen had already apreciated more than 40 percent against the dollar, American cigarettes continued to sell at Y 280 or $1.81 in 1986, per pack, a price which U.S. manufacturers had maintained for a long time. In other words, they were not willing to take advantage of the stronger yen and reduce the price of their cigarettes to be more competitive with the domestic brands which sold for Y 200-220 or $1.30-1.50 per pack. The

Americans took the position that they did not increase the Y 280 price when the dollar was strong or when the Japanese government imposed a higher excise tax in May 1986; thus, they should not be expected to reduce their prices now. This was a curious response from a marketing viewpoint insofar as increased market shares are usually achieved through price reductionse when other competitive factors remain unchanged.

The U.S. government's demands were straightforward. It asked the Japanese either to eliminate the high import and excise taxes or, if they wanted to retain them, to allow foreign manufacturers to produce cigarettes in Japan. To underline the seriousness of its demands, the United States set September 15, 1986, as the deadline by which the Japanese should respond or suffer retaliatory action. September 15, however, coincided with the opening day of preparatory talks for the new GATT round, and the United States did not want to add to the already tense atmosphere in Punta del Este, Uruguay, and consequently postponed announcing the measures it planned to take against Japan for three weeks.

However, shortly before the new deadline expired, the Japanese, after intense negotiations between the government and the tobacco *zoku*, accepted the American demands and "suspended" the 20 percent tariff on foreign tobacco effective April 1, 1987. Japan also agreed to introduce a formula for the automatic approval of retail prices, to shorten the minimum application period for price changes from 60 to 30 days beginning on January 1, 1987, and improve cigarette distribution based on "fair and mutually advantageous" commercial terms. Thus, the U.S. threat that America would restrict a wide range of Japanese manufactured imports unless the tobacco conflict was resolved was effective, and as a consequence the average price of U.S. cigarettes declined from $1.81 to about $1.64.

The accord was important politically to the Reagan Administration, particularly in the Southern states, where Republican candidates for the 1986 congressional elections were already under strong fire for the President's veto of the textile-quota legislation earlier that year. As soon as the agreement was reached, the President instructed the USTR to suspend the Section 301 proceedings against Japan, but emphasized that the office should monitor implementation of the Japanese measures.

While the political aspects of the disagreement were settled, the economic effects were open to question in that the agreement still left American cigarettes more expensive than the domestic brands which sold for $1.30–$1.50 per pack. Thus, the American cigarette manufacturers still had to demonstrate that they could to take advantage of a long-term market share opportunity instead of just cashing in on windfall profits.

During the fall of 1986, the United States also raised the issue of Japanese car parts imports at a subcabinet level meeting during the first stage of the new MOSS negotiations. The U.S. side insisted that Japan must provide American auto parts manufacturers with equal business opportunities to sell original equipment and repair or replacement components to Japanese car manufacturers. They supported their demand by pointing out that U.S. producers have only a relatively small share of the parts market whereas the Japanese car manufacturers have more than $24 billion in annual sales in America. They advised the Japanese that this amounts to almost half the entire trade deficit with Japan in 1985, and that in the same year, America exported only $130 million in car parts to Japan, whereas its imports of such parts amounted to more than $2 billion.

Thus, intraindustry trade in car parts between the two nations was tilted in Japan's favor. However, the reasons for this imbalance were more complex than the standard U.S. explanation that it was the result of the closed Japanese marketplace. The reasons, rather, were rooted in manufacturing differences and divergent buying practices.

One of the major manufacturing differences is the extensive use of *kanban* by Japanese car makers. In addition to all the well-known requirements of the system, *kanban* users normally do only random checks on parts obtained from Japanese suppliers who have low defect rates, whereas American suppliers themselves admit that they have quality problems with 5–10 percent of their output. This quality problem is compounded by the traditional practice of Japanese car manufacturers to work with their supply companies when designing parts specifications. Since U.S. suppliers do not participate in the development of these various specifications, they cannot always meet the car manufacturers' exact requirements.

Buying practices also differ in the two countries. While U.S. car manufacturers select parts suppliers annually, the Japanese have long-term relations with the parts producers. Most American manufacturers also use a larger number of suppliers than do their Japan rivals. According to industry insiders, during the first half of the 1980s, General Motors still used more than 3,500 suppliers whereas Toyota made do with less than 250.[30] Moreover, Japanese manufacturers often invest in the supplying companies, and provide them with a variety of supporting services to maintain a reliable and high quality supply line. Thus, most manufacturers are reluctant to replace such a system with an arrangement that they consider untested and potentially more costly.

The non-Japanese manufacturers which have successfully overcome the competitive and structural hurdles have done so by aggressively marketing high quality products and supporting them with the necessary financial resources and management commitment. Most have established permanent liaison offices in Japan as well as assembly operations either wholly owned or through joint ventures with well-established local partners.

Most American car parts manufacturers were slow to realize what was necessary to succeed in the Japanese marketplace. Nonetheless, the United States pressured the Japanese government to ensure increased imports from America. However, the Japanese manufacturers strongly resented such pressures. They argued that governments should not get involved in matters which concern private corporations. They believed that because of the essentially technical nature of the intraindustry trade imbalance, the search for a mutually acceptable solution should come from the affected industries, and should not be imposed by government bureaucrats through politically motivated measures.

MITI officials, already resentful of the constant barrage of overseas citicism of Japan's economic policies, were also taking a more aggressive stance during the car parts negotiations. They argued that the United States was asking for the impossible, for changes in traditional private business practices which are outside governmental control. The officials repeatedly pointed out that there were no government restrictions on trade in car parts, and that whatever problems may exist should be resolved by the industries without any governmental interference.

Of course, in addition to the competitive and structural reasons, car parts imports were also limited by the desire of the Japanese manufacturers to protect their markets. However, with the sharp appreciation of the yen, they may not be able to do so much longer. In the fall of 1986, for example, Nissan Motor Manufacturing Company selected an American supplier to provide the shock absorber assemblies or struts that it will use in the 1989 Sentra cars built in the United States. In addition to the better price, Nissan chose the U.S. supplier because the quality was acceptable, thus creating a price-quality relationship which they found better than any other. Similar developments can be expected in sourcing by domestic car manufacturers in Japan where American suppliers are gradually becoming more competitive. Thus, it is likely that this U.S.-Japan trade conflict may indeed be resolved by market forces without any industry, let alone government intervention.

The Unrecognized Benefits of the Action Program

The Action Program was the result of specific American demands backed by moralistic rhetoric and the threat of punitive congressional action together with the Japanese desire to somehow contain American anger through a set of measures which addressed at least some of the U.S. concerns. Not surprisingly, because the program did not address the fundamentals and focused on what was politically possible within a relatively short period of time, it had no effect on the bilateral trade balances, thus, in the end frustration cynicism prevailed. Despite the optimistic official views, the overlapping MOSS negotiations were viewed the same in both Japan and the United States.

The Action Program, however, did result in some lasting long-term benefits, which, unfortunately, were not recognized, let alone acknowledged on either side of the Pacific. During program formulation and implementation, the Japanese government, politicians, and public at large were repeatedly forced to scrutinize the image of their nation within the global context. The debates surrounding the consensus formulation process helped the Japanese to understand that their nation is no longer seen around the world as a small weakling country, but as an economic power whose actions, or inactions, affect the entire world economy. It was in this sense that even the narrowly conceived Action Program stimulated the long-overdue debate about the broader aspects of the internationalization of the Japanese economy which took a momentum of its own in the spring of 1986.

Notes

1. In 1986, out of consideration for the sensitivities of neighboring Asian countries, he refrained from visiting the shrine again. A number of his cabinet members, however, made the pilgrimage.
2. *Nemawashi* is an informal, private, and usually face-to face exchange of views in advance of reaching a decision. It involves persuasion to obtain understanding, agreement, and support.
3. Kasumigaseki is a district of Tokyo where most of the ministries and government agencies are located.
4. *Amakudari*, or descent from heaven, is the traditional one-way retirement of government officials to industry. In the past, former high-level officials frequently became top managers in the industries which they regulated while in the bureaucracy. Until the mid-1970s, this was one of the key factors in the close government-business relation that characterized the Japanese society.
5. In 1985, for example, a record 318 senior career officials transferred to jobs in the private sector.
6. Seizaburo Sato and Tetsuhisa Matsuzaki, "Policy Leadership by the Liberal Democrats," *Economic Eye* (December 1984), pp. 25–32.
7. *Ibid.*, p. 26.
8. It is interesting to note that never before have so many *zoku giin* bosses been appointed

simultaneously to ministerial posts as they were in December 1985 when Prime Minister Nakasone reshuffled his cabinet. Among them were Finance Minister Takeshita, Transport Minister Mitsuzuka, and Agriculture, Forestry and Fisheries Minister Hata, each boss of the respective *zoku*.

9. "Bureaucrats Rebellion Against Nakasone," *The Oriental Economist* (July 1985), p. 12.
10. Remarks made at a policy review meeting; Tokyo, June 18, 1985.
11. *The Action Program for Improved Market Access*, chapter I, sec. 2.2.
12. *The Action Program for Improved Market Access*, chapter II, sec.2.
13. *The Washington Post* (July 31, 1985), p. F-1.
14. *Ibid.*
15. "U.S.—Japan Joint Report on Sectoral Discussions," by Secretary of State George Shultz and Foreign Minister Shintaro Abe (Washington, D.C.: U.S. Department of State, January 10, 1986).
16. A report on the progress of the Action Program, released in September 1986 by the joint U.S.—Japan Trade Study Group (TSG), reviewed specific trade issues on a product-by-product and service-by-service basis, comparing observations and conclusions of its 1984 report with the Action Program progress. This study group consisting of Japanese and American businessmen found that although a great deal of work still needs to be done, a lot of progress has been made in opening the Japanese marketplace to foreign goods and services. See, "TSG Progress Report 1986" (Tokyo: September 1986).
17. For a summary of the report, see appendix E. This appendix also presents some information on the November 27, 1986, report which updated the Action Program results.
18. *The Wall Street Journal* (August 29, 1986), p. 20.
19. The value of imports amounted to $100.4 billion, $4.3 billion less than the expected $104.7 billion.
20. *The New York Times* (January 18, 1986), p. 36.
21. *The Japan Economic Journal* (March 29, 1986), p. 5.
22. *The Japan Economic Journal* (August 30, 1986), p.1.
23. *The Wall Street Journal* (October 23, 1985), p. 36.
24. The continuing controversy over agricultural imports is discussed in the next chapter.
25. Despite the generally poor reception of the report, there was one part of the program which was appreciated abroad. Almost all interested parties agreed that the liberalization of Japan's financial sector was moving along well, and that inspite of some complaints concerning the establishment of foreign bank branches in Tokyo, the Japanese were fulfilling their commitments on schedule. Nonetheless, in September 1986 the United States expressed its displeasure about what it considered to be the slow pace of liberalization.
26. The majority of Japanese were afraid that the admission of foreign lawyers would reduce the traditional emphasis on social harmony.
27. In 1986, Japan had just over 12,000 lawyers; in the United States, there were more than 600,000, with the largest American law firms employing between 400—800 attorneys. From *The Washington Post* (September 15, 1986), p. A10.
28. California may join these states sometime in 1987. The admission of Japanese lawyers to California is strongly demanded by the Ministry of Justice as a part of the overall settlement of the issue.
29. *The Japan Economic Journal* (September 6, 1986), p. 28.
30. G.H. Manoochehrix, "Suppliers and the Just-In-Time Concept," *Journal of Purchasing and Materials Management* (Winter 1984), p. 18.

4 THE MAEKAWA COMMISSION REPORT AND THE POTENTIAL CONSTRAINTS ON INTERNATIONALIZATION

The Maekawa Commission Report was released amid a lot of domestic and international publicity on April 7, 1986, and, expectedly, it received a great deal of attention around the world. Most people abroad believed that this was the first time that the topic of internationalization of the economy was raised in Japan. Consequently, they characterized the report as a historic event. Undoubtedly, the report was important because it was prepared by Prime Minister Nakasone's private "brain trust," therefore reflecting his views. Moreover, the report was released at a time when Japan's current and trade account surpluses had reached new heights.

However, the Maekawa Commission was not the first to investigate the idea of internationalization. Other groups, most notably MITI's Industrial Structure Council, have broached the subject before 1986. Therefore, the idea was not new, although the previous studies and reports treated it in a more general and speculative fashion. Furthermore, in most cases, internationalization played a secondary role to problems such as energy dependence and industrial restructuring. Nonetheless, the earlier publications raised the same questions and considered measures which were similar to those the Maekawa Commission eventually included in its recommendations.

Selected MITI Visions and Other Views

One of the first MITI visions which raised the question of internationalization was published in March of 1980.[1] The document, which was prepared by the Industrial Structure Council, emphasized that during the 1970s Japan had become a major economic power whose actions impact the rest of the world. Based on this recognition, the Council suggested three national goals for the 1980s and beyond: (1) increased international contributions; (2) the reduction of resource dependency; and (3) development of private-sector vitality and improvement of the quality of life ("relaxed ease").

The section on internationalization was brief and general; nonetheless, its inclusion indicated that the Council recognized the changing role of the Japanese economy in the world. It called for the maintenance of the free trade system through improved market access and an increased international division of labor. Furthermore, it emphasized that Japan must increase manufactured imports and modify institutions and practices which restrict imports and, thus, internationalization.

A similar document was prepared by the Economic Planning Agency (EPA) in 1983.[2] This study concluded that Japan was undergoing major changes marked by internationalization, the arrival of a maturing economy, and an aging society. The report emphasized that Japan no longer tried to "catch up" with the industrialized world because it was now part of it. Thus, to move into the 21st century, the nation needed a "grand design" charting a new long-term course. However, because there were no appropriate development models to adopt, the Japanese had to create their own. This model needed to be unique, but at the same time, it also had to take into account the effect of Japanese actions on the world economy. In particular, the model needed measures to help revitalize international economic growth, improve market access, and aid in the resolution of global food and environmental problems.

In August 1983, the Economic Planning Agency published another set of future views which the Nakasone government adopted as policy guidelines for the period FY 1983 through FY 1990.[3] This document identified the 1983–1990 period as a turning point for Japan and listed four policy priorities. First, there was the completion of administrative and fiscal reforms, focusing on the reduction of the size of government and the fiscal deficits; second, the revision of the existing industrial structures to provide for more economic growth; third, the integration of the private sector in the economy; and finally, the promotion of international cooperation and Japan's assumption of leadership in this area. To achieve all this, the EPA paper called for stable international relations, an economy and society full of vitality, and a secure and affluent life for the people.

The Industrial Structure Council of MITI published another vision "in search of Japan's contribution and cooperation in bringing about innovative growth of the international economic system" in early 1986.[4] The objective was to determine the desirable form of industrial structures in the new age, moving toward the year 2000. The new structures were sought with regard to three concerns: (1) the contribution of the structures to the international economy and community; (2) changes in domestic economic factors; and (3) new cultural lifestyles. The full report will be published in several parts; the February 1986 section deals with the first concern, the contribution of the new structures to the international economy and community.

The Council recognized the undesirability of the growing current and trade account surpluses for both the world economy and Japan. At the same time, it emphasized that although Japan could begin to reshape its macroeconomic policies to moderate the surpluses, by itself Japan could not significantly reduce the imbalances; only a comprehensive, multilateral effort could accomplish this. Nonetheless, the report urged the Japanese government to develop economic policies to support the growth of the world economy and to help preserve the free trade system. It also urged the country to adapt its savings and technological development patterns to the needs of the world economy and to establish global rapport with other nations. The Council further recommended that the Japanese government help stabilize exchange rates at a reasonable level, foster economic growth through the increase of domestic demand, continue with the implementation of the Action Program, and show initiative and leadership in cooperating with other nations. Thus, in contrast to the others, this MITI vision went beyond generalities and identified the shift from export-led to domestic demand-led growth as a key element of the internationalization process, and outlined the various means through which this should be done.

Another MITI report was published in April 1986 by a mixed group of Japanese and non-Japanese academicians and business executives.[5] Rather idealistically, they argued that nations must work together to build a new global economic system in which emphasis on the common good replaced self-interest.

However, in a more realistic fashion, the group also pointed out that Japan is a major economic power, and thus, its policies must respond to the new global situation. Specifically, the nation must begin to take on a leadership position; it can no longer sit idly by while other countries try to resolve international economic problems. To this end, Japan should continue to foster domestic economic growth in a way that will help the international community, and it should share its economic achievements with others. Finally, Japan should encourage free trade particularly in its region, and thereby improve the economic well-being of Asia and the other developing countries.

The group recommended several specific ways to achieve these goals. These included the promotion of free trade through increased market access, the coordination of international economic policies with other nations to stabilize exchange rates and to minimize imbalances, and the encouragement of foreign direct investment. In addition, Japan should also provide for the economic growth of the less-developed nations through the international exchange of human, scientific, and technological values and knowledge. While not specifically identifying the need to shift from export-led economic growth to domestic demand-led growth, the group's recommendations were similar to those made by other groups.

The private sector's views on Japan's future was published in March 1986.[6] Although not a detailed long-range vision of the future, this policy statement was important because it represented the opinions of the *Keidanren* (the Japan Federation of Economic Organizations), an influential private sector business group. The *Keidanren* recognized that the Japanese government had made progress toward internationalization, but believed that even greater efforts were necessary, because as a major economic power, Japan must help protect the free trade system which is vital to its long-range interest. More specifically, the federation urged the government to implement the Action Program, to play a major role in the preparation and management of the new GATT round, to help liberalize trade in services, to promote foreign direct investment and to provide for a more constructive exchange on international economic matters throughout the world.

Thus, when the Maekawa Commission began its work in the fall of 1985, it had a number of previous contributions concerning the internationalization of the economy from which to draw. This is not to minimize the Commission's insights and efforts; it achieved as much as possible in a relatively short period of time and under intense pressure from abroad. Nonetheless, the past efforts of the other groups should be credited with laying the groundwork for the Commission's recommendations.

The Maekawa Commission Report and Its Reception

Prime Minister Nakasone appointed the 17−member brain trust composed of academic, business, and government leaders and chaired by former Bank of Japan governor Haruo Maekawa, in early November 1985. The Prime Minister created this group at a time when he had two things uppermost in his mind: the increasing trade conflict between Japan and the United States, and the annual economic summit conference of the industrialized nations scheduled for Tokyo in May of 1986.

At its first meeting, Nakasone defined the group's mission as the search for policy options through which the government could pursue the "harmonization of Japan's economic relations with other countries." The assignment was difficult because by the fall of 1985, Japan already faced a stronger yen, slower growth, weakening export markets, and generally increasing foreign criticism. Because the Prime Minister wanted to use the Commission's recommendations to shift Japan's export-led economy to a domestic demand-led one in the interests of the world community, the government once again found itself in a reactive rather than proactive stance. Thus, in a sense, the Maekawa Commission began its work where the Okita committee, whose recommendations formed the basis for the Action Program, left off a year earlier.

The final Maekawa Commission report was released on April 7, 1986, just in time for the Prime Minister's visit with President Reagan in Washington, and approximately four weeks before the Tokyo summit. Expectedly, it cited the need for long-term changes to reduce exports and expand domestic demand in order to "transform the Japanese economic structure into one oriented toward international coordination."[7] Rather than establishing any blueprints for these structural changes, the report set forth six general recommendations:[8]

1. The government should strive for economic growth.
2. The government should promote basic transformations in the nation's trade and industrial structure.
3. The government must work for the realization and stabilization of the exchange rate at an appropriate level.
4. The government must further promote the liberalization and internationalization of the nation's financial markets.
5. Japan must actively contribute to the well-being of the world community through international cooperation.
6. The government should review the preferential tax treatment of savings.

Under these six broad recommendations, the report suggested specific guidelines on meeting the overall internationalization goals. It indicated that measures derived from these recommendations and the guidelines should be implemented on the basis of market principles as well as from global and long-term perspectives to strengthen the free trade system.

The report called upon the government to open Japan's market wider to imported goods, including farm products and manufactured goods. In this respect, it called for the thorough deregulation of cumbersome government rules from the premise of "freedom in principle, restrictions only as exceptions," language taken directly from the Action Program. Furthermore, the Commission suggested that coal mining and other declining industries be phased out, and that their products be replaced by imports.

As for suggestions to expand domestic demand, the Commission cited housing construction and urban redevelopment through private sector "vitality," stimulation of private consumption through tax reductions, and local government promotion of investments aimed at improving the social infrastructure. Another consideration focused on revising labor laws to reduce average working hours and to increase the minimum number of paid holidays.

One last noteworthy area of reform investigated by the Commission was Japan's international role with respect to less developed countries. The report proposed expansion of official development assistance (ODA) to these countries and an increase in the importation of their goods. The Commission also urged the government to encourage the international division of labor through positive industrial adjustment and an increase in foreign direct investment, without sacrificing small-sized and medium-sized enterprises.

Two weeks after the release of the report, the government, in an effort to follow through on the Maekawa Commission recommendations, unveiled its own guidelines containing a list of measures designed to produce an economy driven by domestic demand and to promote imports. These guidelines were formally approved May 1, 1986, at a meeting of a special task force established under the chief cabinet secretary to implement an overall program based on the Maekawa report. In addition to elaborating on the contents of the report, the guidelines called upon the government to influence the business community to be more flexible about raising wages and increasing summer vacations to allow consumers to increase leisure spending, and to ensure that the benefits of economic growth were passed along to all citizens.

The guidelines also recommend that in order to change the national economy as dramatically as proposed by the Maekawa Commission, the bureaucracy should manage the allocation of resources, particularly fiscal resources. However, the guidelines stress the necessity to maintain the nation's basic economic position by limiting any new issues of deficit-financing government bonds.

The Domestic Response

Shortly after the publication of the Maekawa report, the Japanese government also announced a set of economic measures designed to ease the deflationary effects of the sharp rise in the yen's exchange value and to expand domestic demand in the short run.[9] Thus, domestic reaction to the Maekawa Commission's recommendations was influenced by the views on the short-term economic stimuli.

Not surprisingly, public reaction was mixed. Most mass media commentators agreed with the long-term aims of the proposed changes but questioned the generality and abstract nature of the recommendations. They claimed that the absence of specific measures to implement the proposals could partly be attributed to the composition of the committee in which 8 out of the 17 members were former high level government officials. The ex-bureaucrats supposedly favored realism over idealism and managed to prevail in the writing of the final report. Some critics referred to the report as *sakubun*, a clever piece of work without any practical significance because it lacked clear operational definition. Others pointed out that the government can no longer dictate to private industry; consequently, the recommendations may be difficult to implement regardless of their degree of specificity. Moreover, they argued, the various *zoku giin*, whose interests are affected by the recommendations, would not support proposed changes such as substantially increasing agriculture imports or phasing out some of the declining industries.

Economists were concerned that the short-term economic stimuli announced in conjunction with the report were not significant enough to propel the economy forward, and that this would make the implementation of the long-term recommendations impossible. Most of them speculated that the officially predicted 1986 growth rate of 4 percent could not be achieved, particularly in light of the continued appreciation of the yen. Such views were supported by private research institutions which forecast the average growth for FY 1986 at about 3 percent or less, a notch below government expectations.

Opinions in political circles were also splintered. The Prime Minister's supporters agreed with the necessity to restructure the economy over the longrun, although most of them were concerned about the specific ways to do so. In contrast, Nakasone's political rivals seized the opportunity to reignite the debate over domestic demand stimulation which preceded the Action Program. They wanted to take Nakasone's place, and thus, they tried to raise their political visibility by highlighting policy differences with the Prime Minister. Again they called for sweeping measures to expand domestic demand, including the reissue of government bonds, the issue of construction bonds to finance public works projects, and broad tax incentives for new housing. However, before another major debate on demand stimulation could fully develop, Nakasone caused a political uproar in Japan.

Armed with the proper *Miyage* (present), that is, the Maekawa report and the package of economic stimuli, Prime Minister Nakasone met with President Reagan in Washington on April 12–14, 1986. Although the meeting was intended as a preparatory session for the Tokyo summit in May, it was devoted mostly to a discussion of the bilateral trade problems. In order to moderate strong American criticism of his economic policies, Nakasone tried to convince the Administration and Congress that Japan would shift from export-led to domestic demand-led growth in the future, substantially increase imports, and thereby, reduce the trade imbalances as recommended by the Maekawa Commission. He emphasized that the government would set up a special headquarters to work out the schedule for the implementation of the recommendations. Furthermore, he agreed to the creation of a joint Japanese-American advisory board which would monitor the entire process. Following his meetings with the President, Nakasone also met with members of Congress and declared that Japan accepted "the challenge" of implementing recommendations to fight protectionism and to improve relations with the United States.

Top level Administration officials expressed satisfaction that the Prime Minister was serious about implementing the "historic changes," and speculated that the new measures could signal a turning point in bilateral trade relations. They also suggested that Nakasone's remarks to the President and Congress implied that he accepted virtually all of the Maekawa Commission's recommendations. None of the officials, however, claimed that the Prime Minister had made a formal commitment.

Nonetheless, Nakasone's statements in Washington were interpreted by his political opponents in Tokyo as a "casually made national pledge of a mere set of proposals formulated by a privately appointed advisory committee." The critics charged that Nakasone made a *koyaku*, an internationally binding commitment, to the United States without first obtaining the necessary consensus through *nemawashi* within the LDP and the bureaucracy. From the critics' point of view, the Prime Minister violated the most basic tenet of Japanese political life, and exposed the nation and the party to potential harm. The critics claimed that changing industrial structures to increase imports is the same as sacrificing certain economic sectors which are not internationally competitive, such as agriculture. Others argued that the joint Japanese–American monitoring of the implementation process is unfair because Japan alone is to be monitored even though a number of reasons for the bilateral trade imbalances are rooted in America's domestic economic policies. Even a number of the Prime Minister's supporters believed that he acted hastily, and that by generally endorsing the Maekawa recommendations in Washington, he provided the Americans with an opportunity to exert unilateral pressure on Japan.

As soon as he returned to Tokyo, Nakasone met with his critics in a government–LDP liaison meeting comprised of 11 cabinet members and 11 key officials of the party. He explained that he did not make a *koyaku* or formal commitment to the United States, and that the mass media had made a mountain out of a molehill. Still, he was strongly criticized for "going his own way" and not consulting adequately with the LDP leadership before commenting on matters of national importance. The chairman of the Policy Affairs Research Council even refused to accept the Maekawa report as a basis for policy deliberations because the advisory panel that prepared the report "lacked authority," and therefore, in legal terms, the document represented little more than the private views of it members. While Nakasone's explanations were eventually accepted, the LDP party leadership's dissatisfaction with his method of placing private advisory groups ahead of the party policy formulation apparatus continued. Thus, by late spring of 1986, the Prime Minister was walking a narrow path between the demands of the United States and the demands of his LDP critics.

Not surprisingly, Nakasone's explanations to the LDP leadership were not well received in the United States. The mass media and a number of politicians on Capitol Hill viewed his statements as soft-pedaling the commitments to implement the Maekawa recommendations, and thus, to reduce Japan's current and trade account surpluses. Some in the media made critical references to the Prime Minister as a politician who "keeps reading from two different scripts" and who cannot be relied upon.[10] More importantly, in a speech to a group of businessmen in Washington, USTR Yeutter stated that when Nakasone returned to Tokyo, his government started to back away from the Maekawa recommendations. Yeutter emphasized that this was a dangerous game that could lead to very harmful consequences for Japan. Already under pressure at home, the Japanese government's response to such high level criticism from abroad was immediate and tough; a spokesman labeled the remarks "irresponsible," and stated that the USTR and other American government officials did not appreciate the Japanese efforts. While the matter was eventually settled, the USTR's remarks provided Nakasone's critics and opponents with a weighty political argument. They could point to the remarks as proof of their predictions that the Americans would use the Prime Minister's Washington statements to immediately increase pressure on Japan.

Nakasone's political opponents used the Washington incident to attack the Prime Minister continuously. Moreover, in early June the Chairman of the LDP Executive Council and the Chairman of the LDP's Policy Affairs Research Council unveiled a set of economic proposals which were critical of the government's fiscal austerity policies. They argued that as a result of the yen's sharp appreciation, Japan was in a critical situation, and that only a comprehensive set of pump priming measures could save the economy from stagnation. Such proposals were in line with the policy adopted at an earlier LDP leadership meeting concerning the provision of a more than $20 billion supplementary budget during the second half of 1986. Although Nakasone endorsed the supplementary budget in order to win support for his double-election plans in July, he referred to the proposals as "personal opinions" prevalent in the party.

Expectedly, the LDP's overwhelming electoral victory in July 1986 reduced the volume of criticism and substantially enhanced Nakasone's position. While the Maekawa Commission's report was not an election issue, and Nakasone was criticized during the campaign for the rapid appreciation of the yen, the voters seemed to endorse his plans for the future. Following the election, the Prime Minister declared his intention to move ahead and shift Japan's economy to domestic demand-led growth. He told the mass media that the government would "faithfully" follow the recommendations of the Maekawa Commission.

To emphasize his commitment, Nakasone again stressed the necessity of structural adjustments at a meeting of the Economic Council in September 1986. The Council, another one of Nakasone's blue-ribbon private advisory panels, established a special committee headed by Haruo Maekawa, to promote economic restructuring and to increase imports. As a first step, the Committee set a specific numerical target for the reduction of Japan's current account surplus which amounted to an all-time high of 3.7 percent of GNP in 1985, and was expected to be more than 4 percent in 1986. The Committee announced that this proportion should be reduced to about 1.5 to 2 percent over the next five to seven years, and it considered the target as a reasonably well-defined goal for the internationalization process. While the Council is a highly respected body that usually prepares the five-year social and economic outlook for the government its recommendations are not binding. Moreover, in the past some of its recommendations were made irrelevant by the rapid change of economic circumstances. Nonetheless, it is significant that it has tried to set a specific goal for the internationalization process, and that it also formed two additional subcommittees to study the problems of stimulating domestic demand and of the potential rise in unemployment.

Thus, despite strong opposition within the party and criticism from other circles, Prime Minister Nakasone not only engineered an electoral victory but eventually also managed to have the basic propositions of the Maekawa Commission accepted by the LDP leadership as the centerpiece of future economic policies. While the details still had to be worked out through the customary consensus-seeking procedure, the overall direction of the Japanese economy was set. The extension of his LDP presidency and, thus, Prime Ministership for another year beyond October 1986, and the inclusion of his strongest LDP opponents in the newly formed government, provided Nakasone with the political flexibility he needed to begin the consensus-seeking process in earnest.[11]

Reactions Abroad

The international response to the Maekawa report was muted. European media and government circles, for example, expressed scepticism and took a wait-and-see attitude. They argued that the Japanese had issued too many reports and market access packages in the past, none of which had substantially altered the massive current and trade account surpluses. A number of commentators criticized the absence of specific details and concluded that the report was just another window-dressing exercise to promote Nakasone's April visit to Washington and his stewardship of the May Tokyo summit.

In the United States, the White House expressed optimism and hailed the report as a turning point in Japanese history. Administration officials calculated that in praising the recommendations, they could enhance the probability of their implementation. Furthermore, they also wanted to strengthen Nakasone's domestic position because he was known to be in favor of harmonious international economic relations. Thus, when USTR Yeutter's critical remarks caused indignation in Tokyo, top Administration officials quickly distanced the White House and said that Yeutter spoke only for himself.

The Administration's view of the Maekawa report reflected a shift in policy from emphasizing procedural market access to encouraging domestic growth as a means of reducing the bilateral trade imbalances. American policy formulaters were clearly concerned about the delayed impact of the dollar devaluation, the persistent budget deficits, and the continuing decline of American's international competitiveness. They were searching for more comprehensive and effective measures than the market access packages of the past. Thus, the Maekawa Commission's recommendations were in accord with the United States' new approach to international economic problems in general and to bilateral trade conflicts with Japan in particular.

Congressional views were less enthusiastic. While even the most vehement critics of Japan conceded that the recommendations were important and that if implemented, they could go a long way toward easing U.S.–Japan trade relations, many members of Congress expressed scepticism about the readiness of the Japanese to follow through. Some senators cited past experiences with market access plans, and as usual, did not recognize the power of the *zoku* and placed the blame on Kasumigaseki by arguing that the Japanese bureaucracy would not accept most of the recommendations. Others stated that only time would reveal how serious the Japanese are about internationalizing the economy, and cautioned that if the recommendations were not implemented at an early date, protectionist pressures in the United States would reach new heights in the fall 1986 midterm elections, and possibly beyond, since the Democrats could gain control of Congress, as they did.

The U.S. media response was mixed. Some newspapers compared the recommendations with changes that took place in Japan during the Meiji Restoration in the nineteenth century. A few argued that the plan called for a switch from the mercantilist policies of the past to policies which may redress the global imbalances Japan created over the past 30 years. Others, however, criticized the report for a lack of specifics and noted that the recommendations were more philosophical than pragmatic in nature. Moreover, they also claimed, the Prime Minister did not have the support of the bureaucracy for the proposed changes. All of this, the U.S. critics claimed, would make it very difficult, if not impossible, for the Prime Minister to call double elections and remain in office beyond October 1986, let alone obtain censensus for the recommendations. As it turned out, such views, as usual, underestimated Nakasone's political skills.

Not surprisingly, the harsh views were moderated after the July 1986 electoral victory. Critical members of Congress and the media conceded that the Prime Minister apparently had sufficient support among the voters and in the party to realize his plans. Some even considered the election results a direct vote of confidence in the Maekawa Commission's recommendations.

The Domestic Discussion of Internationalization

The beginning of a new year in Japan is traditionally a time for introspection by individuals, families, and society as a whole. At such times, people think about the past year's events and speculate about the future. The media usually play a major role in this self-examination; newspapers with circulations of several million copies and the major television stations present articles, commentaries, and special programs on where Japan stands and what the next few years may bring.

At the beginning of 1986, the major theme of the national self-reflection was the necessity to live in harmony with the rest of the world. The question of coexistence with other nations is, of course, not new in Japan. It had been discussed many times, in a number of settings, with varying intensity and results since the Meiji restoration. However, never before had the discussion been as intense and focused as at this time. The media, government officials, politicians, intellectuals, business leaders, and others referred to the internationalization of society in general and the economy in particular as one of the great new tasks. It is not an exaggeration to say that by the early months of 1986, there was a consensus on the desirability of internationalization, and anyone opposed to the process was regarded by most people as acting against the national interest. However, this consensus was at a philosophical level and did not include an appreciation of the practical measures which would have to be taken, or more importantly, on how such measures could affect the daily lives of people. Apart from the speculative newspapers and magazine articles, no other interpretations of the potential effects of the internationalization process were available.

Of course, the restructuring of an entire society and its economy is an immensely complicated undertaking, and it is, thus, well-nigh impossible to identify the measures and changes that are needed to reach what is, in essence, a vaguely defined and continually moving target. Not surprisingly, this caused confusion among the public, and even today many Japanese fear that the changes could be destructive. They are concerned that the emphasis on increasing domestic demand, or spending, could turn into self-indulgence and undermine the Japanese tradition of self-sacrifice and hard work which made the economic achievements possible. Others, influenced by the intense foreign pressures for increased market access, believe that internationalization means simple procedural adjustments as exemplified by the numerous market access packages of the past, including the 1985 Action Program.

Some critics noted that internationalization as promoted by the Nakasone government is too partial to the United States and does not involve sufficient consideration of other nations.[12] The adoption of a lot of "Americana" during the postwar years, the argument goes, has created the illusion that internationalization is the same as accepting American influence and recognizing English as the *lingua franca*. These critical observers sought a broader interpretation of internationalization because although other nations do not complain as noisily as the United States, the economic gap between them and Japan is rapidly increasing. Hence, Japan must pay attention to their expectations as much as it does to those of the United States and, to a lesser degree, Asia.

The Japanese preoccupation with the United States and Asia was confirmed by the results of the Public Polls on Japan's Foreign Relations, released by the Office of the Prime Minister in June 1985. The findings showed that North America and Asia are the highest scoring among the geographic areas in which the Japanese showed the most interest. Over the period May 1980 to June 1985, interest in North America and Asia ranged from between 30 to 40 percent, reaching a virtual equality of 35 percent in June 1985. The remainder of the world accounted for only 30 percent of interest.

Potential Sociocultural Constraints

All nations have images of themselves and of how others perceive them. Usually, such images are a mix of reality and myths, and are perpetuated by the educational system, the mass media, writers, social scientists, and politicians, among others, for a variety of reasons. In the case of Japan, there are a variety of *nihonjinron* or Japan theories which supposedly explain the nature of society and its implications for fields of human endeavor from economic behavior through politics to the arts. While such views are usually oversimplifications of very complex issues, they are still seen by most people in Japan and abroad as helpful explanations of how society functions and how it interacts with the outside world. Thus, although many propositions of current *nihonjinron* may be questionable, they are widely accepted and seem to contain enough truth to shed some light on the potential sociocultural restraints on internationalization.[13]

Although the Maekawa Report deals only with the economic aspects of internationalization, its basic recommendation, the shift from an export-led growth to a domestic demand-led growth, cannot be accomplished without some modification of the sociocultural aspects of *nihonjinron*. Naturally, this cannot mean the eradication of the Japanese self-image, however disagreeable this image may have become to some nations which have difficulties accepting Japan's growing self-assertiveness. The modifications, however, must be made to the degree that the Japanese can accept them without damaging their sense of identity, and which at the same time, is enough to halt the world's growing perception that Japan wants to be treated as an equal but continues to insist on considering itself unique.

Such abstract interpretations of what internationalization ought to mean cannot be readily translated into pragmatic policy proposals. Consequently, it is not surprising that the Japanese are still searching for the practical measures through which internationalization can become a reality without the loss of a strong self-identity based on a centuries-old heritage. The debate continues, and in light of clashing generational values, external pressures, the appreciation of the yen and its deflationary impact on the economy as well as the continued emphasis on fiscal austerity, the search for possible answers is not getting any easier with the passage of time. Whereas abroad this may be construed as hesitation, reluctance, or even diversionary tactics to maintain the status quo, uncertainty and uneven progress are an unavoidable consequence of the immense scope of the internationalization task.

Self-Perception — 'The Ugly Japanese?'

Most contributors to the conventional "Japan theories" have long noted that Japan is a group-oriented society that values reciprocity and social harmony above all else. Whereas the Western societies, particularly the United States, focus on individual rights and legalistic procedures, the Japanese rely on a complex network of unspoken mutual obligations and pragmatic ad hoc adjustments. Moreover, while the Japanese were receptive to Western influence, particularly after the Meiji restoration, they themselves always decided what to accept and how to modify it. For example, the Japanese rejected two of the most conspicuous elements of Western culture, the Christian religion and the Roman alphabet. Instead, they adapted Buddhism to their values without forfeiting Shinto and assimilated Chinese characters into written Japanese. It is this pragmatic and flexible manner of absorbing foreign influences that helped the Japanese to maintain their self-perception as a unique nation. At first such an attitude was viewed with curiosity by the rest of the world, but it was gradually resented when combined with economic success. The attitude of uniqueness became particularly distressing to the industrialized nations because they believed that the Japanese were using this notion to justify a variety of trade practices that conflicted with the customary standards of international economic behavior.

Not surprisingly, many Japanese are, therefore, uneasy about internationalization. They see it as an externally imposed demand that may damage their identity. This is particularly worrisome because many Japanese believe that it was their uniqueness that made the economic success possible in the first place. In their view, foreign demands for change may endanger the economy's international competitiveness created through hard work. Such opinions are unintentionally reinforced by the Japanese government's reactive rather than proactive foreign policy in general and international economic policy in particular. The government promotes internationalization more as a necessary survival response to external forces than as a transition from an industrializing nation to a mature economy with corresponding improvements in the quality of life.

Because of the uncertainties throughout the national self-examination process and subsequent discussions, many thoughtful Japanese raised questions about the willingness of the nation to internationalize.[14] A major catalyst for such doubts was an article by the late Theodore White.[15] The American author argued that 40 years after it lost the Pacific War, Japan is defeating the United States in trade, and that the "real winner of the war" will be decided in 10 years. He argued that the United States must never again be merciful and generous toward Japan because such policies allowed the Japanese to protect their markets while launching an assault on the U.S. economy, thereby dismantling American industries.

Although most Japanese understood that White's views did not represent the majority opinion in the United States, his harsh words raised concerns about how various long-standing domestic practicees may be perceived abroad. Newspaper editorials, for example, referred to the multiple fingerprinting of the Korean minority living in Japan and of other non-Japanese residents on working visas as a "relic of postwar Japan" that stands in the way of internationalization.[16] Others pointed to the rejection of Vietnamese refuges and the Labor Ministry's frequent denial of visas to foreigners as well as the limited number of foreign students in Japan's universities as a reflection of an insular attitude that may be difficult to overcome.[17] There were references to the low number of international conferences held in Japan relative to other nations and to the Japanese "cultural free ride" mentality which, from the outside, shows the nation as a combination of a "third-rate culture" with "first-rate economy."[18] Some described the plight of new arrivals in Tokyo who find it very difficult to overcome the discrimination of Japanese landlords against foreigners.[19] Others criticized the practice of some corporations that still reject Japanese graduates of foreign universities because they do not want employees shaped by a *gaikoku daigaku* (foreign university), but young men and women with characteristics that can be honed only in Japanese universities.[20]

A recent EPA survey found that the attitudes in which such practices and behavior are rooted are still widespread and strong.[21] The survey asked 3,000 male and female respondents between the ages of 15–74 their views about the influx of people, products, and information from abroad. The overall finding indicated that whereas the Japanese are receptive to foreign products and information, they are uncomfortable with the idea of more people moving to Japan from abroad and, thus, decreasing the homogeneity of their society. Many Japanese still share a closed mentality toward foreigners living in their country either for work or study, the EPA noted in its report.

More specifically, the survey found that 73.3 percent welcome foreign technology, 79.2 percent foreign news, 78.6 percent foreign tourists, and more than 50 percent are in favor of increasing food imports and bringing more students from abroad. However, only 28.3 percent had no objection to more foreign workers, and a mere 26.7 percent supported the idea of international marriages. Moreover, increased foreign direct investment in Japan and an increase in the number of Japanese children educated abroad was acceptable to only 40 percent. A large percentage of respondents, 73.8 percent, rejected overseas assignments for themselves and their families, and 50.1 percent had negative views on renting living space to students from abroad.

A number of eminent Japanese express deep concern about these *shimaguni konjo* (insular attitudes). Some are particularly worried that these attitudes might turn into prolonged arrogance toward other nations, especially America, which are less internationally competitive today. A high level government official and member of the Maekawa Commission pointed out that ". . . a growing number of politicians, businessmen, mass media people and other opinion leaders here are becoming undeservedly smug and prone to cavalier utterances."[22] Such people argue that only the Japanese can manufacture first-class products, and if the Europeans and Americans worked harder, they would not fall behind in economic competition. Moreover, they accept the idea that "Made in U.S.A" is a label of lesser quality as an article of faith, regardless of the nature of the products in question. They believe that Americans do not pay enough attention to detail, since, for example, their clothing falls apart, cars sound tinny, and appliances waste energy.

Conversely, concerned Japanese point out, the executives of large

Japanese corporations which are very successful in the American markets are firm believers in the principles of free competition, and believe that there is nothing wrong with sending large quantities of products to the United States as long as American consumers want them. They are particularly proud of the fact that they never received any government support, and argue that their success is due to superior productivity, constant technological improvements, and the provision of high quality products. American industries which cannot meet such competition should not complain because they have created their own problems. While there is truth in these arguments, if repeated too often and too loudly, they create the impression of arrogance and lack of concern for the economic well-being of other people, and thus, generate an image of "the ugly Japanese."

The strength of the *shimaguni konjo* mentality based on the "uniquely homogeneous" nature of Japanese society is well illustrated by the events surrounding Prime Minister Nakasone's remarks about American minorities and educational levels in September 1986. In a speech to young LDP political workers in the Shizukoka foothills of Mount Fuji, Nakasone explained that the minorities, particularly blacks and Hispanics, have negatively affected the American intellectual and educational levels.

While his remarks created an uproar in the United States, some of Japan's national newspapers did not even mention the speech until after the U.S. reaction. Others put it into inside-page columns which usually chronicle various minor political developments. Only Nakasone's political opponents in the Japan Socialist Party and other critics immediately recognized the potential international implications of the remarks. Most other Japanese believed that he was talking common sense, saying that ethnic diversity creates confusion and discord, and that societies function best when they are homogenous. Those who faulted him did so mostly for voicing his opinion, not for having it. The uproar in America was eventually moderated through an explanation and a formal apology by the Prime Minister addressed not only to the United States but also to the Japanese people for embarrassing them. Moreover, a number of U.S. newspaper articles informed the American public about the background and context of Nakasone's remarks, and thereby helped settle the matter.[23] This was important because most Americans did not know that the Japanese lived in isolation from the rest of the world for 250 years, and that even today, less than 2 percent of the population represent minorities, and that during the nineteenth century, the Japanese were the subject of racial slurs by Western "scientists" who declared them to be an inferior race.

However, while the self-perception of being unique is not only widespread and may manifest itself in a sense of superiority, it should be noted that many Japanese of all ages admire certain American and European technical, artistic and fashion skills and tastes. In particular, the younger generation appears to be less insular in its outlook and, thus, more receptive to influences from abroad. They travel more than their parents, and they are more at ease when interacting with people from other cultures. Despite the employment practices of some businesses, more of the young Japanese are studying abroad, if only for a year or two, to obtain the experience, insight, and linguistic ability required to become internationally oriented.

It is, however, unavoidable that as the younger generation gradually takes over the reins of political and economic leadership and as they occupy opinion-making positions throughout society, Japan as a nation will become more self-assertive. Not burdened by World War II guilt feelings, buttressed by a powerful economy and rooted in a rich cultural heritage, the younger generation cannot be expected to continue playing the "little brother of America" role. Thus, what in some circles throughout the world is seen as the emergence of the ugly Japanese is in reality an expression of regained self-confidence. Of course, such self-confidence can easily turn into arrogance and a sense of superiority. However, there are internationally minded Japanese who understand the dangers lurking behind such attitudes, and who can be relied on to speak up if such attitudes appear to be more than just sporadic outbreaks by people with extreme views.

The Communication Gap

Throughout their history, the Japanese have never been good at communicating with the rest of the world. This is partially due to the insular mentality, that is, the strong sense of uniqueness just discussed, lack of exposure to the international community, and their inability to master Western languages well because of the substantial grammatical differences between Japanese and Western languages. Other reasons include the reticence to strike up casual conversations with foreigners who are not well known to them or accepted as friends.

What is true for society at large is also true at the official level. The Japanese government's reactive rather than proactive stance has been mentioned several times, in different contexts, as a restraint on Japan's foreign relations. The extensive use of lobbyists abroad, particularly in Washington, is another case in point. Given the nature of the American political system, foreign governments or businesses must have knowledgeable representatives in Washington other than their diplomats because the city is not only the seat of political power but also a rich source of information provided by the federal agencies and private think-tanks. Regardless, the Japanese probably employ far more lobbyists than necessary to obtain the benefits of direct unofficial representation. Whereas the impression outside of Washington is that heavy representation is effective in influencing U.S. policy toward Japan, the reality is more somber. The Japan lobby is a large but rather diversified conglomerate of economic and political interests which do not act in unison and, thus, are usually not that influential.

An example of this ineffective use of lobbyists which involved communications problems was the visit of LDP Vice President Susumi Nikaido to Washington on October 8–10, 1985, to moderate the protectionist mood in Washington, and to pave the way for Prime Minister Nakasone's meeting with President Reagan at the United Nations. To arrange the visit, the LDP reportedly paid 100 million yen to a Washington lobbying firm.[24] Although the delegation represented the LDP and not the government, the visit of high-level Japanese politicians could have been arranged through the embassy or by other intermediaries at much lower cost. In the end, the delegation failed to convince U.S. lawmakers to moderate their stance on trade relations, met with Vice President Bush for 20 minutes, and as a result of a disagreement between the Japanese embassy and the American lobbying firm, saw President Reagan only for a five-minute "photo-opportunity." Veteran Washington political observers were stunned by the ease with which the Japanese paid $400,000 to obtain such limited results. Most Japanese with an appreciation of the Washington political system believed that the incident reflected the lack of international savvy on the part of the responsible LDP officials.

The Japanese often think of themselves as a nation misunderstood by the rest of the world. While such contentions are sometimes self-serving, in many instances, they are true. One of the major reasons for this is the often shallow foreign press coverage of Japan. This is partially due to the inability of most foreign correspondents to speak Japanese and their editors' demands for sensational headlines rather than solid, informative news. Moreover, in the case of the U.S. press, newspapers regularly report more about European than Japanese political, economic, and social affairs because most Americans have European heritages.

There are, however, other reasons for the often superficial coverage. The more than 500 foreign journalists permanently assigned to Japan have difficulties obtaining insightful information because of the traditional Japanese press club system. Although the Foreign Press Center was established as a commercial venture in 1976 to help foreign reporters by providing various services, the press system continues to tightly control the flow of reliable information from the source to the media. The clubs are omnipresent; they cover the cabinet, the Diet, and every one of the 37 government ministries and agencies. Special clubs cover the Tokyo Stock Exchange and even religious affairs in Kyoto. Only the staff of the newspaper companies of the Japanese Newspaper Publishers and Editors Association can be full members. Foreign correspondents and even Japanese journalists who are not members cannot take advantage of the benefits the clubs provide through the government ministries, agencies, or other institutions that sponsor them. The benefits include, among others, furnished offices, administrative help, free domestic and international telephone calls, and guaranteed access to a continuous flow of information.

Foreign journalists may be admitted as special members upon application. At press conferences, however, they must ask questions in Japanese; thus, for practical purposes, most foreign reporters do not join the clubs. Consequently, they find it difficult, if not impossible, to obtain information directly from primary sources.

The traditional reticence of most Japanese to communicate openly with foreigners also makes reporting about the country difficult. This is particularly true if the journalists are more aggressive and probing than the standard Japanese reporter. Therefore, direct insights into Japanese political, economic, and social life may be distorted or simply unavailable through primary sources, forcing reporters to rely on secondary sources provided by others which may be quite accurate, but still lack the journalistic intimacy so important to good reporting.

At a time when Japan is undergoing a series of difficult economic adjustments, the policy formulation power is shifting from the bureaucracy to the politicians, the Maekawa Commission recommendations are gradually implemented, and the external pressures to reduce the current account surpluses continue unabated, the rarity of nonsensational, insightful reporting casts a shadow on the internationalization process. Friend and foe alike throughout the world are finding it difficult, if not impossible, to consistently keep up with the scope and complexity of events happening in Japan. The result is what many Japanese lament as the lagging foreign perceptions behind Japanese realities, a condition which has long affected the country's international relations.

Education

Because of their highly competitive and demanding educational system, the Japanese are among the most literate people in the world. In international academic competitions, Japanese students are consistently among the top performers, particularly in mathematics and the sciences. Compared to the United States, Japanese students must learn as much math by the ninth grade as American students need to graduate from high school. Moreover, while only 75 percent of high school students graduate in the United States, more than 90 percent graduate from high school in Japan. At the higher educational level, with a university population one-fifth that of America, Japan produces about 75,000 graduate engineers annually as compared to 72,000 in the United States. However, in spite of such impressive results, the Japanese basic and higher education systems are under increasing scrutiny today. There is a debate about the future of the systems, and the outcome of these discussions may have implications for the internationalization process.

Educational reform ranks high on Prime Minister Nakasone's list of policy objectives. In 1984—85 he stimulated a public debate on education, and as a consequence, the Special Education Council has put forward various plans to revamp the educational system.[25] However, the Prime Minister was not pleased with the recommendations because they did not address what he considered to be the basic problems inherent in the post-World War II system developed during the occupation. Nakasone argues that the current 6—3 system (six years in primary school followed by three years in junior high school) is a "borrowed system that has no roots in Japanese society." He believes that the current educational system produces a generation which is devoid of discipline, respect for its elders, and love of the nation. The Prime Minister and the private advisory group he appointed to study the matter are convinced that a strong dose of moral education and more emphasis on responsibility to society are the answers. This, of course, is a reference to the nation's traditional values of loyalty, discipline, and hard work which the Prime Minister would like to see reinforced.

Debate over educational reform has a long history in Japan. Immediately after the establishment of an educational structure modeled after the West in 1872, there was an intense discussion of how such an alien model should be adapted to Japanese conditions. After World War II the system was again changed under the orders of the Allied Occupation Authorities, and thus, a discussion evolved over how the American model should be modified to fit the Japanese context characterized by a rapidly growing school-age population. When economic growth accelerated, another discussion began over how the educational system could be made more responsive to the needs of the economy.

The major issues of the current debate, however, are different from those of the past. The rapid growth of the educational system is slowing; the population of five-year-olds peaks in 1989 and then begins to decline. Moreover, industry no longer demands continuous reform because there is a balance between the needs of the economy and the quality of individuals available for employment.

Today's education debate centers on the attitudes of the new generation of students. More Japanese students exhibit an "anti-school" attitude than ever before. Disillusionment, dislike of school, and violence have become so widespread that they have aroused concern throughout the nation. Most education experts consider the high level of *gakureki shakai* (educational credentialism), which generated one of the world's toughest entrance examination systems, the major culprit for such resentful attitudes. Unless exceptionally bright, most youngsters must attend the *juku* (special cram school) to pass through the "examination hell," and be able to attend a prestigious high school or university. Moreover, the Headquarters for Youth and Children of the Management Coordination Agency reported in 1986 that young Japanese between the ages of six and the early twenties are not anxious to take on the responsibilities of adulthood, and want to maintain their present status as long as possible. The Agency found that almost all the young men and women are satisfied with their present way of life; in the case of senior high school and university students, over 80 percent were content, and in the case of young workers, over 70 percent. The majority of them are optimistic about the future and believe they can fulfill their personal expectations about life in general and their careers in particular within about 10 years. However, only 5 to 10 percent of the total expect to serve society or to have a career through which they can contribute to the improvement of society. The report concludes that today's youth is very different from the young people of the past in that they exhibit a strong desire to embark on an individualistic way of life rather than to follow a "grand dream based on a noble spirit."[26] Not surprisingly, the older generation, with some discomfort, refers to the young as *shinjinrui* (the new human breed).

Thus, according to many Japanese, a far-reaching education reform is in order, although it is too early to predict what changes will take place once a consensus is developed concerning these reforms. In the meanwhile, it is noteworthy that the interim report released by the Advisory Curriculum Council of the Ministry of Education in October 1986 called for nurturing of the young generation's consciousness and sense of duty as Japanese in the world community, as well as the teaching of the cultural traditions of the nation.

Competition for admission to Japan's universities is intense. Passing the university entrance examination is the major educational concern of most high school seniors. Competition is intensified by the stratified nature of the higher educational system which was the result of the rapid increase in such institutions during the postwar years. At the end of World War II, there were 48 universities and colleges; by 1985, that number had increased to 446. Most of the new institutions are private, and many of them are not well endowed; thus, they must rely on tuition as the major source of income. Although all universities are officially equal and employers no longer offer pay differentials according to a university's ranking, most Japanese continue to evaluate institutions in terms of unofficial rankings. Moreover, the present structure and practices of even the most prestigious Japanese higher education institutions are not entirely in accord with international customs. Although these institutions provide a quality education, through their traditions, they continue to promote the image of Japan as a close-knit, homogenous, and thus unique society which is difficult for foreigners to penetrate.

An illustration of this is that as of May 1, 1985, there were only 15,009 foreign students in Japan, most of them from Taiwan (29.4 percent), the Republic of Korea (20.9 percent), and the People's Republic of China (18.2 percent).[27] While increasing, these numbers are still small in comparison to the number of foreign students in the United States (over 350,000 in 1986) and the major Western European countries, each of which had more than three or four times the number of foreign students in Japan. One of the major reasons for this relatively low number is the time and effort involved in learning the language well enough to benefit from instruction. To deal with this problem, most institutions are beginning to provide intensive language training and are establishing other ways to ease the difficult academic and social adjustment period for foreign students.

However, all of these arrangements can be effective only if the Japanese institutions also allow foreign faculty to become active participants in the universities. At present, the hierarchical structures of Japan colleges and universities make it difficult for foreign faculty, even if they speak Japanese, to become integrated into the decision-making system. Many institutions use the traditional *senpai-kohai* (senior-junior) system which is based on the employment of their own graduates as faculty, and thus leads to a certain amount of inbreeding and isolation. Students who want to become faculty members are guided by individual professors for whom they develop an intense personal loyalty for the rest of their career. In the resulting close-knit institutional environment in which conformity is highly valued, it is still difficult for foreign faculty members who are outside the *senpai-*

kohai system to become tenured, and thus to fully participate in the academic and administrative decision-making process.

To promote the process of change, Prime Minister Nakasone in 1986 announced a policy of increasing the number of faculty members and students from abroad, and rescinded a law that barred foreigners from obtaining tenure at national universities. According to his plan, by the year 2000, a total of 100,000 foreign students, many from neighboring Asian countries, will study in public and private colleges, universities, and research institutions. The objective for this influx of foreign students is to have a large number of young people learn *nihongo* (Japanese language, history, and culture). Another motive is the desire to have more Japanese faculty and students interact with people from abroad in a domestic setting.

These objectives, however, are not without their problems. During the first half of 1986 alone, 6,800 foreign students entered Japan under the new system of relaxed sponsorship requirements introduced by the Ministry of Justice. There is now increasing evidence that quite a few of these young men and women, particularly from the Southeast Asian countries, end up working illegally in bars and factories. Of course, Japanese law prohibits foreign residents with student visas from working, but with the yen appreciation, less expensive unskilled foreign labor has become very attractive to Japanese companies that want to remain competitive. Student visas are particularly attractive to foreigners who are lured to Japan by the appreciated yen and who want to work illegally because in most cases they are valid for six months and can be relatively easily extended if the educational institution verifies that the visa holder has a class attendance rate of 70 percent or better.

According to Ministry of Justice sources, during the first half of 1986 about 25,000 foreign nationals with official work permits have entered Japan, which is a substantial increase over 1985. If those holding student visas and working illegally are added, this number would go up substantially, claim ministry officials. Thus, not surprisingly, by the fall of 1986 the ministry started an investigation of its student visa system with the objective of reducing its misuse. In view of the Prime Minister's policy to arrange for 100,000 foreign students to study in Japan by the year 2000 and the continued strength of the yen, this is going to be difficult at best.

A special plan of the Ministry of Justice announced in the spring of 1987 may, however, be helpful in this respect. According to official sources, a number of private corporations together with the Ministry of Justice want to found a new organization with the tentative title of "The Immigration League." The organization's major objective would be the dissemination of information concerning the proper immigration procedures and the creation of a comprehensive network to deal with the domestic firms wanting foreign workers as well as with the workers themselves. In this fashion, the organizers hope, illegal immigration could be better controlled and, consequently, the problem of foreign workers could be separated from that of increasing the number of foreign students.

A noteworthy effort to promote the internationalization of the higher educational system is the attempt of the United States—Japan Committee for Promoting Trade Expansion (CPTE) to have prestigious American universities open branch campuses throughout Japan. The committee, organized by American and Japanese legislators to give U.S. business easier access to Japanese markets, considers the establishment of such branches its first major project. Under the plan, Japanese communities would provide public land free or at reduced rates together with the necessary facilities, and Japanese business groups would endow chairs and provide internships.

By late 1986, more than 20 Japanese cities and towns have indicated a willingness to invite American universities to establish local campuses in facilities financed through Japanese funds. Likewise, 62 American institutions, including some of the venerable Ivy League universities, expressed interest in the program, and sent delegations to Japan to scout the opportunities. Such projects promote interest and experience in international relations for students from both the United States and Japan.

Many hurdles must be overcome to realize these plans, however. There is the question of quality control, of high costs due to the appreciated yen, and the difficulty of obtaining a large number of scholarships for potential students. The current slowdown in the Japanese economy has also created some reluctance among businesses to make long-term funding commitments to educational institutions. Nonetheless, the program is imaginative, and even if only a small number of U.S. universities succeed in establishing these campuses, their presence would substantially contribute to the internationalization of the Japanese higher educational system.

Economic Policy Contraints

In addition to the sociocultural traditions and practices that could interfere with internationalization, there are also several potential economic policy constraints. These policies are designated to protect economic sectors which are not internationally competitive, such as agriculture and several declining industries. Other policies as, for example, the administrative and fiscal reforms, are necessary to reduce the size of government and to moderate the fiscal burden accumulated over many years.

Agriculture

When considering Japan's role in the world economy, the outside world usually sees only the immensely successful large *kaisha*. Toyota, Hitachi, and Sony, among others, dominate the world's perception of an economy which, however, also has some "soft" spots. Behind the phalanx of the industrial giants, there is for example, a small-scale, low-productivity but politically influential agricultural sector which is protected by interacting socioeconomic and political forces.

Agriculture is an economic activity with special characteristics. GATT recognizes this and provides a unique status for agriculture which is greatly affected by a variety of socioeconomic and even climatic conditions. Based on this, Japan's farm policy is governed by the Basic Agriculture Law, enacted 25 years ago to help agriculture improve its international competitiveness. This is still the objective, although the policies formulated under the law have undoubtedly placed more emphasis on the protection of farmers, and generally neglected the improvement of competitiveness as well as the Japanese consumers.

At present, Japan restricts the imports of a total of 28 agricultural and fisheries products, 22 of which are so-called "residual items" whose imports should be liberalized, but for a variety of reasons are not. According to the Japanese government, the remaining six products, including rice and wheat, are "state trade items" approved by GATT, whose import, therefore, may be limited. Although protectionist, by international comparison Japan's farm policy is not different from that of the United States, which has 13 quotas approved by a GATT waiver of 1955, or the European Community that has 60 import surcharge restrictions as well as other import curtailing measures of dubious legality in GATT terms. Thus, although the nature and effects of the national protectionist policies may be argued, evidence shows that the governments of all industrialized nations find it socially and politically necessary to protect their agricultural sectors.[28] Japan is no exception.

Japan's agricultural policies are subject to continual criticism because of the worldwide problem of overcapacity created by high support prices, particularly in the United States and the European Community. The U.S. government, for example, in July 1986 asked the GATT to investigate the legality of Japanese import quotas on 12 agricultural products. The Americans charged that the Japanese policy "violates GATT rules which explicitly prohibit import quotas." The 12 items include local specialties, and thus a quick removal of the quotas could deal a heavy blow to the regional economies that produce them. Nonetheless, after an initial review in

October 1986, GATT agreed to investigate the American charges. At the same time, the U.S. side expressed a willingness to continue bilateral talks, thus keeping the possibility of a special settlement alive.

American interest in Japan's agricultural policies is intense because U.S. agricultural exports are not doing well. In 1984–1985, for example, American agricultural sales to Japan declined from $6.7 to $5.4 billion, although Japan remained America's most important agricultural export market. The decline was due mostly to the overvalued dollar and intense competition from other producer nations.

While the U.S. farm lobby is understandably very concerned about sales to Japan, the impact of agricultural exports on the bilateral trade imbalances is minimal. In 1986, for instance, a study of the congressional research service of the Library of Congress concluded that the elimination of all Japanese agricultural import restraints could increase American sales by approximately $1 billion, but this would decrease the overall bilateral trade deficit by only 2 percent.[29]

Nevertheless, in 1986 the U.S. rice industry filed a petition with the Office of the USTR to seek retaliation against Japan's import restrictions, the centerpiece of Japan's agricultural policy, on the grounds that it constitutes "unfair trade" under Section 301 of the 1974 U.S. Trade Act. The industry was represented by the Rice Millers' Association (RMA), consisting of 27 members and including farmer-owned cooperatives and independently owned rice milling companies located in Arkansas, California, and other Southern states. Others, such as 23 associate rice exporter members, have also joined the action.

The Association argued that the protectionist measures force Japanese consumers to pay $25 billion more annually for rice, and that this equals approximately half of the U.S. trade deficit with Japan in 1985. Thus, they claimed, the elimination of the restrictions would increase the purchasing power of the Japanese consumers and moderate the bilateral trade imbalance, both major goals of the Nakasone government's internationalization policy.[30]

The Reagan Administration, however, recognized the political sensitivity in Japan of the American rice growers' demand. In late October 1986, the Office of the USTR rejected the petition to retaliate against the Japanese if bilateral negotiations failed to increase U.S. rice imports. USTR Yeutter explained that he would ask the Japanese government to bring its rice policy to the table at the new round of multilateral trade talks (GATT) scheduled to begin in early 1987. According to Yeutter, an agreement reached in the preliminary trade talks at Punta del Este in September 1986 included two key provisions which could be applied to the

Japanese rice policy. The first provision declares the liberalization of agricultural trade a major goal of the multilateral discussions, and the second would require GATT member countries to roll back policy measures which restrict or distort trade.

Japan's protectionist agricultural policy has deep roots. The country has a high population density, small farms, and fertile but expensive land. The average two-acre or three-acre farms cannot compete with the large-scale farms and agrobusiness operations which are more dominant in other parts of the world. Moreover, the nation with its narrow territory, large population, and vulnerable sea-routes depends on foreign supply sources for approximately 50 percent of its food measured in calories and around 33 percent measured in value, proportions which are higher than in other industrialized nations. The 1973 unilateral American export-ban on soybeans is frequently cited as an example of what can happen if the nation relied too heavily on supplies from abroad.

Japanese agriculture would undoubtedly be more efficient and thus more internationally competitive if it were reorganized into larger units so that modern production methods and equipment could be applied. However, this would mean the end of the rural socioeconomic structures which have existed for centuries and which form the basis of the rural communities throughout the country. This is not a realistic option for a government dominated by the LDP which has its major political support in such areas.

Expectedly, major changes in current agricultural policy are strongly opposed by the agricultural *zoku* of the LDP. A case in point was the the government's inability to reduce 1986 rice prices by the originally planned 3.8 percent. Japan spends more than $8 billion annually to maintain the price support system, and Prime Minister Nakasone wanted to reduce this amount in line with his administrative and fiscal reform plans. However, the LDP rice *zoku* resisted, and consequently, Nakasone had no choice but to maintain the 1985 price level as demanded by the *zoku* and its ally the Zen-Chu, or Central Union of Agricultural Cooperatives, which comprises about 4,300 cooperatives representing 4.4 million farms and approximately 12 percent of all households. The organization also controls all aspects of Japanese agriculture including the distribution of credit, fertilizers, and feed-stuffs, thus keeping producers cost high. The political influence of Zen-Chu is illustrated by its claim that of the 359 LDP candidates for both the lower and upper house of the Diet who responded to an inquiry conducted by the organization prior to the 1986 elections, 337 supported its demand to keep rice prices in 1986 at the 1985 level or even higher.

The well-supported system is managed by the Ministry of Agriculture, Fisheries and Forestries, and it not only keeps out imports and creates a surplus but also monopolizes rice marketing. It provides growers with high prices for their crops and consumers with rice costing three to five times the world market prices.[31] Such policy, however, also has a positive side; it plays a major role in Japan's much envied income equality between farmers and urban workers. Thus, not surprisingly, Prime Minister Nakasone told the Diet in the fall of 1986 that Japan would reject the American rice growers' demands for the liberalization of imports, although he indicated that the government must expedite agricultural reforms in the future.

Japan's agricultural policy which protects the small farmers, yet results in high domestic food prices, has, by and large, been accepted by the Japanese, most of whom have family roots in the rural areas. Most people still believe that national security in terms of stable food supplies justifies current policies, particularly since it became known that during the last few years the nation's self-sufficiency in grain has fallen to about 33 percent, the lowest ratio for any industrialized nation. This has created a psychological fear of shortages in an emergency. Naturally, the Zen-Chu and its allies fan such fears to secure the support they need to maintain the price support system even at its high cost to the consumer. Table 4−1 shows to what extent consumers subsidize agricultural producers through the higher domestic prices.

Past attitudes notwithstanding, in late 1986 there were signs of growing dissatisfaction. Consumer representatives began arguing that importing less costly rice, for example, would not only reduce Japan's trade surpluses

TABLE 4−1. Comparison of domestic Japanese agricultural prices to import prices: 1985−1986*

Products	Import source			
	France	Britain	W. Germany	USA
Rice	—	—	—	8.3
Wheat	3.7	3.7	4.1	7.8
Sugar	1.8	1.5	2.3	2.9
Beef	1.2	1.3	1.7	2.6
Milk, Cream	1.4	1.5	1.5	1.9
Pork	—	1.2	1.4	2.4

* Figures shown represent the number of times that the domestic price exceeds the import price.

Source: *The Japan Economic Journal*, October 18, 1986, p. 3.

but would also stimulate domestic demand by allowing consumers to spend more money on other products. Moreover, the Japan Federation of Employers' Association published a proposal to overhaul agricultural policies. Leading industrialists of the Keidanren have also argued for some time that the protectionist farm policy must be dismantled and replaced with a competitive market system regardless of the political and socio-economic concerns. They maintain that Japan's future depends on the industrial sector; thus, the protection of agriculture is too heavy a price to pay because it creates resentment against industrial products abroad. In contrast, the farm lobby argues that it is both unreasonable and selfish to use farm products as a pawn in the attempt to earn conflict-free industrial trade relations with other nations. At one point, the debate was so intense that a farmer's organization in Hokkaido called for a boycott of Sony and a major supermarket chain. During the boycott, farm leaders pointed out that the agricultural quotas came into international limelight only as a result of the backlash provoked by the aggressive exporting of manufac-tured goods by the major kaisha and trading houses. They buttressed their arguments by pointing out that in contrast to the industrial sector, which amassed a huge trade surplus all over the world, the 1985 agricultural import deficit in the range of $24 billion reduced this surplus, thereby moderating the outside world's criticism of Japan.

Prime Minister Nakasone and a number of other politicians are fully aware of the high economic costs of the current agricultural policies and recognize the need for changes. Japan's support of the multilateral review of global agricultural policies through the Uruguay round beginning in 1987 is an indication of the Prime Minister's willingness to take both the international and domestic heat that the upcoming negotiations will un-doubtedly generate. Of course, agreed revisions will have to be implemen-ted multilaterally over an extended period of time so that the necessary socioeconomic adjustments can be made in a politically acceptable manner. In the case of Japan, the agricultural *zoku* must be convinced that any change in policy will be made in the long-term interest of the farmers.

Declining Industries

In addition to agriculture, the Japanese economy has other weak areas. These consist of industries which have experienced structural problems, mainly due to the major increase in the cost of energy and raw materials obtained from abroad, and lower demand for their products in Japan and throughout the world. Most are producers of basic materials as, for example, petrochemicals, fertilizer, paper, and aluminum, but others such as shipbuilding and steel are also included. In accord with changes in the world economy, they must be restructured to survive in the long run.

Government assistance to depressed industries is not new in Japan. It began with the recession cartels which, during the 1970s, allowed companies in an industry plagued by a temporary decrease in demand to reduce output systematically rather than to engage in destructive price competition. However, in time, MITI found that such short-term measures were no longer adequate because a number of industries became subject to long-term excess capacity problems.

As a result, MITI proposed the Temporary Measures Law for the Stabilization of Specific Depressed Industries which the Diet passed in May 1978, and which was in force until 1983. The law was designed to improve the competitiveness of depressed industries through systematic cutbacks of excess capacity. Industries identified as structurally depressed received antitrust exemption to do this according to a plan developed by MITI which was based on supply and demand projections, and included proposed cutbacks concerning surplus plant and equipment. By 1983, six industries producing 14 different products were authorized under the law to make the necessary adjustments.[32] In May 1983, the Diet renewed the law because the 1979 oil price crisis and economic recession of 1980−82 interfered with the restructuring schedule. Renamed the Temporary Measures Law for the Structural Adjustment of Specific Industries, it put more emphasis on revitalization than the previous version.

According to current policy, an industry is designated as structurally depressed if the majority of its firms are losing money and at least two-thirds of them agree to participate in restructuring. Once this requirement is satisfied, MITI, together with its Industrial Structure Council, develops a detailed plan the firms must follow. If necessary, MITI can ask the industry to form a cartel to realize its capacity reduction goals. Today there are 22 industries designated as structurally depressed; 7 were selected under the first law, the other 15 were added under the 1983 measure. Most of them produce basic materials, although the newly added industries include cement and sugar refining. Firms in these industries can receive loan guarantees to ease the problems of scrapping plant and equipment, and can also obtain low-cost funds through the Japan Development Bank to introduce new technologies and products to increase production and marketing efficiency. Modernization and reduction of capacity are also promoted through tax laws, but no direct operating subsidies are provided.

One of the industries presently facing severe problems is coal mining, which has lost its competitive edge against foreign coal producers because of large price differentials due to the combined effects of the global coal glut, lower oil prices, and the rapid appreciation of the yen. In September 1985, MITI established the Coal Mining Council, which, after lengthy deliberations, came to the conclusion that a scaling down of the industry is unavoidable. This finding is in accord with the recommendations made by the Maekawa Commission, which proposed that industries with declining international competitiveness be permitted to scale down to promote the international division of labor. The Commission specifically called for a "sizeable reduction in the domestic output of coal" and argued that coal imports be increased.

In FY 1985, the Japanese used slightly less than 110 million metric tons of coal of which 94 million tons, or 85 percent, were imported from Australia, Canada, South Africa, the United States, the Soviet Union, and the People's Republic of China, all lower cost producers than the Japanese mines. Thus, it was with this high import penetration ratio in the background that MITI presented its plan to restructure the industry in the fall of 1986. It called for the reduction of production from 16.4 million metric tons in FY 1985 to 10 million tons by FY 1991, including the ending of local production of coking coal used mainly by the steel industry, and the closing down of 8 of the country's 11 mines.

However, the proposed restructuring of the industry is not likely to result in higher coal imports from the United States which concerns some members of Congress who demanded that Japan make its coal imports from America commensurate with its 25 percent steel market share in the United States MITI officials explained that American coal, while less expensive than Japanese coal, is more expensive than other imports. On a cost-insurance-freight (CIF) basis, for example, the average 1985 import price per ton of U.S. coking and steaming coal was $67.30 and $55.50, whereas the sam Australian coal sold for $43,80 and $53.50, respectively. Under these circumstances, MITI officials argued, privately owned steel companies cannot be expected to buy American coal just to satisfy the demands of the U.S. legislators and coal industry.

The painful social consequences of the restructuring plan were well illustrated by the closing down of a colliery of the Mitsubishi Coal Mining Company in November 1986. The colliery, the oldest in the country, was losing an estimated $2.6 million each month with its cumulative deficit reaching $225 million by 1986. While the economic reasons for the shutdown were compelling, it resulted in the dismissal of 900 workers in a region where jobs are scarce.

Another example of the painful employment effects of structural adjustments in declining industries is the decision made by Nippon Steel Corporation in February 1987 to shut down five blast furnaces and to eliminate 19,000 jobs over the next four years. While management tries to reduce the human suffering associated with job eliminations through attrition and transfers, the regions in which the shut down plants are located will have lost the jobs forever.

The government's policy of supporting structurally depressed and declining industries is controversial both at home and abroad. In Japan the Fair Trade Commission, charged with the enforcement of the antitrust laws, has often tried to prevent MITI from realizing its restructuring plans. The FTC argues that MITI's efforts are in vain, because due to market forces, the capacity reductions would have occurred anyway, and that the government-orchestrated cutbacks allow inefficient producers to survive. Other domestic critics question the long-range relevance of a program that calls for capacity reductions in industries which have lost their international competitiveness and thus should be phased out. Doubts are also expressed about the ability of the government to help industries plagued by declining demand or high labor costs, magnified by the recent appreciation of the yen.

Criticism from abroad, particularly the United States, is more vocal. One high level administration official described the Japanese government's involvement in the restructuring processes as "critical," "thorough," and "definitive." The American and European governments agree that the restructuring policies are inherently import restrictive, and thus, add to the bilateral trade imbalances. This is based on the claim that the various joint activities permitted under the law, particularly officially sanctioned cartels and administrative guidance by the various ministries, enable the domestic high-cost producers to keep low-cost imports out of the country.

However, most of such criticism is leveled without supporting evidence.[33] During the MOSS negotiations in 1985−1986, the Americans provided evidence for some of their claims concerning import restrictions in the containerboard, soda ash, and aluminum industries; in most other cases, the evidence, however, was weak or lacking altogether. Moreover, the Japanese argue, the restructuring law itself does not contain any clause that restricts imports, and the low import penetration in most depressed industries is not in itself proof of restrictions. MITI and the other ministries also deny that their administrative guidance results in protectionism.

The validity of some domestic and foreign criticism not withstanding, Japan's record in dealing with structurally depressed industries relative to the rest of the industrialized world is impressive. While a large number of designated industries are still struggling years after they began the restructuring process, the country has been spared the traumatic socioeconomic dislocations which depressed industries created in other industrialized nations such as the United Kingdom. The Japanese realize that structural changes are necessary but painful, and through adjustment polices, they try to minimize the human suffering normally associated with the shutdown of businesses or industries.

The rapid appreciation of the yen in 1985–1986 has made matters worse for the structurally depressed industries. Japan's merchant seamen, for example, are facing massive layoffs as the nation's shipping industry considers employing crews from nearby developing countries who are willing to work for as little as one-sixth of Japanese wages. The Japan Shipowners Association, composed of 188 companies, claims that its recent study of industry trends shows 40 percent of seamen will be redundant within the next four to five years.

Meanwhile, because shipbuilding capacity is to be reduced by an additional 20 percent in FY 1987, an estimated 18,000 workers, or about 30 percent of the total shipyard workforce, will be redundant. Most of these workers will not be absorbed through internal reassignments, which firms typically try to do. Since shipbuilding currently provides most of the jobs in cities and towns where the industry accounts for more than 50 percent of the value of manufactured products shipped, this is a harrowing prospect for thousands of families.

Thus, from a social viewpoint the criticism of Japan's supportive policies toward structurally depressed industries is not justified. Undoubtedly, certain industries such as coal mining may have to be phased out regardless of the consequences involved. However, the government's attempts to provide other problem industries with the means to restructure is socially and politically necessary. Additionally, there are national security implications in some of the basic materials industries which are far too serious to be left entirely to market forces.

Administrative and Fiscal Reform

The problem of large government and rapidly increasing expenditures together with deficit financing is shared by all industrialized nations. Since Japan is no exception, Prime Minister Nakasone made reduction in the size of government and the reestablishment of sound fiscal conditions, or fiscal and administrative reform, a centerpiece of his domestic policy program.

Administrative and fiscal reform has a long, although not entirely successful, history in Japan. In the early 1960s, Prime Minister Ikeda created the first Special Administrative Research Council headed by a well-known businessman, but resistance from the bureaucracy and special interest groups prevented any reforms. Prime Minister Suzuki, at the recommendation of Nakasone, formed the Second Special Administrative Research Council to explore ways to introduce reforms in 1981. When Nakasone took over as Prime Minister, he formed the Administrative Reform Promotion Council in July 1983 to monitor the implementation of the reform measures recommended in the Research Council's five previous reports.

Nakasone's concern about administrative and fiscal reform is rooted in the mid-1970s when as a consequence of the recession triggered by the oil crisis in 1973, the government started its deficit financing binge. Although the Public Finance Law prohibits budget deficits, the government got by this through a loophole in the law which allows deficits generated by appropriations for investments such as public works, as long as the Diet approves. Bonds issued for this purpose are known as "construction bonds," and they usually account for about 50 percent of the deficit while the other half is comprised of deficit bonds which are sold to cover current expenditures. Beginning in the 1970s, both types of bonds were issued in increasing quantities to stimulate growth. Moreover, during subsequent years, social security outlays also increased rapidly because the government wanted to raise the standards of a system which was no longer adequate for an industrialized nation.

Deficits increased dramatically when in 1978, at the urging of the United States, Prime Minister Fukuda resorted to large-scale deficit spending on public works to expand domestic demand in accordance with the "locomotive thesis" which proposed that the Federal Republic of Germany and Japan stimulate their economies to pull the world out of the recession. This action together with increased fiscal spending in subsequent years unhinged the nation's fiscal structure. By FY 1986, total accumulated debt amounted to more than $900 billion, the annual deficit to $70 billion; interest alone represented 20.9 percent of the budget, and total government debt as a percentage of GNP reached new heights. By international comparison, Japan was ahead of the United States and all other major industrialized countries except Italy. Table 4−2 illustrates this point.

In light of these developments, throughout the years Prime Minister Nakasone stood firm on his commitment to administrative and fiscal reform. He pledged to eliminate reliance on deficit financing bonds by FY 1990; however, by late 1986, this had become a very difficult task. According to MOF officials, the original target was to cut bond issues by more than $7 billion each year beginning in 1984, but the actual reductions were around $3.7 billion in FY 1984, $4 billion in FY 1985, and $3.2 billion in FY 1986. In order to moderate the high deficits, the Prime Minister also

TABLE 4–2. Total government debt to GNP ratio in selected countries: 1985

Country	Total government debt to GNP ratio
USA[a]	48.8
Japan[b,c]	52.1
U.K.	49.1[e]
Italy[f]	76.3
France	18.5[f]
F.R. of Germany	21.4

[a] U.S. dollar figures are calculated according to the annual average exchange rates of the IMF, International Financial Statistics.

[b] Fiscal year.

[c] U.S. $1.00 = Y 238.54.

[d] End of 1985.

[e] End of March 1985.

[f] 1984.

Source: *Japan 1986: An International Comparison* (Tokyo: Keizai Koho Center, 1986), p. 83.

attacked three of the major financial drains, the so-called three Ks: *Kokutetsu* (Japan National Railroads), *kome* (rice), and *kenpo* (the medical insurance system). Privatization of the railroads (discussed in the next chapter) became a reality in April 1987, and this was a major success because for some time, the railroads generated an annual deficit of nearly $10 billion. The high cost of the medical insurance system had also been reduced through an increase in payments by the patients for medical services. However, as discussed previously, Nakasone failed to overcome resistance from the *zoku* to reduce the subsidy payments on rice.

An unexpected tax revenue shortfall of more than $6.5 billion for FY 1986 made the situation even worse. It was the first time in four years that tax revenues had decreased by more than $6.5 billion of what was estimated in the budget for the year. As a consequence, the amount of deficit financing bonds issued for FY 1986 exceeded that for the previous year for the first time in three years. The unexpectedly low tax revenues were the result of a drop in corporate tax receipts due to the declining earnings generated by the sharply appreciated yen.

Prime Minister Nakasone's cautious and austere fiscal policies did not go unchallenged. While he was supported by the Ministry of Finance, the Keidanren, and others, his policies were criticized within the LDP and by a number of private sector economists who forecast a much lower growth rate for FY 1986 and up to 1990 than the 4 percent predicted by the government. One of the private sector economists argued that fiscal austerity is a mistake because healthy public finances could be achieved by the restoration of equilibrium in the economy through an increase in government expenditures, or pump priming.[34] Through simulation he showed that in addition to accommodative monetary policy, reduced personal, and lower corporate income taxes, the government should spend about $13 billion annually on public works between 1986 and 1990 to achieve a growth rate of about 4.4 percent which would restore fiscal health. While he did not make any specific proposals concerning the funding of the tax cuts and the spending increases, he concluded that the fiscal austerity policy is incompatible with the measures which are required to reflate domestic demand, reduce the external imbalances by 1990, and set the economy on its way toward internationalization in accordance with the recommendations of the Maekawa Commission.

The Nakasone government, however, did not change its austere fiscal policies. In December 1986 it announced the FY 1987 budget which envisioned the spending of $335.09 billion, up only 0.02 percent from FY 1986, the smallest increase since FY 1955. Of the total, $201.8 billion was allocated for general expenditures, with the remainder going to debt-servicing and local government funding.

The off-budget fund for loan programs and infrastructure projects, also known as the "second budget," however, was increased by 14.1 percent to $156.58 billion. The source of these funds include deposits in the postal savings bank, pension payments, and proceeds from bond issues. At the same time, public works spending by the central government was decreased by 2.3 percent from FY 1986; this decline, however, was more than offset by the new construction projects planned by local governments. As a consequence, overall public works spending should rise by 5 percent to almost $90 billion. Government officials expect that such spending will provide some stimulation to the economy in the upcoming years.

Government borrowing was expected to amount to $65 billion in FY 1987, down $2.8 billion from the previous fiscal year but still higher than the cuts required to meet the goal of a balanced budget by FY 1990.

While the FY 1987 budget was in keeping with the government's fiscal austerity policy, private economists in Tokyo expressed continued concern about the future of the economy. Most believed that the continual emphasis on fiscal austerity would make the achievement of the expected average 4 percent growth rate during the 1986–1990 period virtually impossible.

Notes

1. Industrial Structure Council, *The Vision of MITI Policies in the 1980s* (Tokyo: Ministry of International Trade and Industry, March 1980).
2. Long Term Outlook Committee, Economic Council, Economic Planning Agency, *Japan in the Year 2000* (Tokyo: The Japan Times Ltd., 1983).
3. *Outlook and Guidelines for the Economy and Society in the 1980s* (Tokyo: Economic Planning Agency, August 1983).
4. Industrial Structure Council, Coordination Committee, Planning Subcommittee, *An Outlook for Japan's Industrial Society Towards the 21st Century* (Interim Report Focusing on International Perspective), (Tokyo: Ministry of International Trade and Industry, February 1986).
5. *Japan In the Global Community: Its Role and Contributions on the Eve of the Twenty-First Century,* Report of Roundtable Discussions on "Japan in the Global Community" (Tokyo: Ministry of International Trade and Industry, April 1986).
6. *How Can Japan Contribute to a Healthy World Economy* (Tokyo: Keizai Koho Center, March 1986).
7. *The Report of the Advisory Group on Economic Structural Adjustment for International Harmony* (April 7, 1986), p. 2.
8. *Ibid.,* p. 4.
9. Among others, the $23 billion measures included public works, the promotion of housing construction by individuals, the lowering of electricity and gas rates to pass on the exchange rate gains of the appreciated yen to consumers, and more relief to small-sized and medium-sized enterprises hurt by the stronger yen.
10. See for example, *Business Week* (May 5, 1986), p. 44.
11. For example, Kiichi Miyazawa, one of the Prime Minister's major opponents in the debate over domestic demand stimulation, became Minister of Finance, a position which made it more difficult for him to argue against fiscal austerity because the ministry is one of the major proponents of such policy.
12. *Asahi Evening News* (September 16, 1986), p. 7.
13. Two sociologists have recently challenged most of the current *nihonjinron.* See Ross Mouer and Yoshio Sugimoto, *Images of Japanese Society* (London: KPI Limited, 1986).
14. See, for example, Susumu Ohara, "An Island Unto Itself: The Roots of Japan's International Isolation," *Speaking of Japan* (May 1986), pp. 18–21; also "Thoughts on August 15," *Asahi Shimbun* (August 16, 1986), p. 9.
15. Theodore White, "The Danger of Japan," *The New York Times Magazine* (July 28, 1985), pp. 18–22+.
16. *The Japan Times* (August 28, 1986), p. 14; *Asahi Shimbun* (August 2, 1986), p. 11.
17. *The Japan Economic Journal* (January 18, 1986), p. 6.
18. *Asahi Evening News* (September 13, 1986), p.7., and Asahi *Shimbun* (May 20, 1986), p. 11, respectively.
19. *The Japan Economic Journal* (December 13, 1986), p. 6.
20. *Asahi Evening News* (May 22, 1986), p. 3.
21. *The Japan Economic Journal* (October 11, 1986), p. 11, and (November 1, 1986), p. 3.
22. Takashi Hosomi, "The Ugly Japanese," *Tokyo Business Today* (March 1986), p. 8; see also, Masahiko Ishizuka, "New Self-Assertion, But Whither," *The Japan Economic Journal* (October 11, 1986), p 6; Yoshio Okawara, "Constructive Approaches Are What We Need," *Tokyo Business Today* (November 1986), p. 10; and "The Dangers of

138   THE INTERNATIONALIZATION OF THE JAPANESE ECONOMY

Neonationalism," *Tokyo Business Today* (November 1986), pp. 22– 26.

23. See for example, Nathaniel B. Thayer, "Nakasone Is Not a Racist," *The Washington Post* (September 30, 1986), p. A15; and "Japan Under Nakasone: Image of National Pride?" *The New York Times* (September 26, 1986), P. A13, as well as Carl T. Rowan, "The Real Issue Nakasone Raised," *The Washington Post* (October 7, 1986), p. A17.
24. At the time of the visit, this was equal to approximately $400,000.
25. For a list of these recommendations, see *The Japan Times* (April 24, 1986), p. 1.
26. *Asahi Evening News* (December 20, 1986), p. 7.
27. Ministry of Education (Tokyo, March 1986).
28. An interesting case in point was the Canadian government's decision to impose a 67 percent tariff on American corn on November 7, 1986. The Canadians argued that U.S. agricultural subsidies have driven corn prices so low that Canadian farmers were forced to sell their crop for less than it cost to grow in order to remain competitive. This was the first such duty ever imposed on the United States by any nation, and only the fifth time that the Canadians used such a measure in managing their trade relations.
29. Donna U. Vogt, "Japanese Import Barriers to U.S. Agricultural Exports," Report No. 85–153 ENR (Washington D.C: Congressional Research Service, Library of Congress, 1986).
30. The Association also claimed that the liberalization of the Japanese rice market would double U.S. exports from the present 18 percent world-export share to 36 percent.
31. The policy was introduced in 1942 to stabilize prices and supplies of rice, and was continued after 1945 for essentially the same reasons.
32. The industries included, among others, nonferrous metals, shipbuilding, steel textiles, and chemicals.
33. U.S.-Japan Trade Study Group, *Progress Report: 1986, op. cit.*, p. 39.
34. Susumu Kato, "Three Scenarios for Economic Policy," *Economic Eye* (September 1986), pp. 19–22.

5 TRENDS AND CHANGES IN THE DOMESTIC ECONOMY

While the Japanese government made the decision to internationalize the domestic economy through the gradual implementation of the Maekawa Commission's recommendations as well as other policy options, a number of economic trends and changes were already underway. Some of these were unleashed on a short notice by the sharp appreciation of the yen during 1985–1986. Others were introduced earlier by the government, and others still were subtly initiated by fundamental socioeconomic forces which were shaped by the Japanese political, social, and cultural environment, but which by and large are common to highly developed nations.

The extent and rate at which the economic trends and changes promote the internationalization process is difficult to determine. They are, however, instrumental to the process and are an integral part of what some astute observers of global economic developments have referred to as the emergence of the "triad power," or the convergence of the economies and markets of the United States, Western Europe, and Japan.[1]

The Economic Trends

At the beginning of 1986, Japan faced a much stronger yen and slowing exports; nevertheless, the government estimated an annual economic growth rate of 4 percent in real terms. This optimistic rate was predicated on a substantial increase in domestic demand; official forecasters were certain that prices would remain stable and real income would increase as commodity and other import prices declined as a result of the higher value of the yen. The optimism seemed justified by the surprising fourth quarter results of 1985 when the economy grew at a healthy, inflation-adjusted rate of 1.7 percent, or at an annual pace of 7.2 percent; the 1.7 percent rate was accelerated from the July-September quarter, when the economy had expanded a more modest 0.7 percent. Domestic demand accounted for 1.5 percentage points of the 1.7 percent growth during the July-September 1985 period, with external demand accounting for remaining 0.2 percent share.

The last quarter figures for 1985 were a surprise to most economists, who had been expecting sluggish growth as a result of a slowdown in exports and the sudden appreciation of the yen following the Group-of-Five (G-5) agreement in September 1985. Even government economists conceded that the statistics did not accurately portray the state of the economy. A case in point was the large increase in inventories which in the last quarter of 1985 rose by 31 percent from the previous quarter, when they dropped 21 percent. Although most of the blame for this was placed on the yen's appreciation, which severely hurt export-oriented industries, the increase happened before the full effects of the yen's sharp rise were felt.

As the yen moved from Y 170 to Y 160, deflationary effects of the appreciation became more visible, and the calls for stimulation of the domestic economy were becoming louder both at home and abroad. Since the government was committed to fiscal austerity, increased public spending could not be used to stimulate domestic demand. Thus, the attention turned to monetary policy. Eventually, the Bank of Japan decided to reduce the official discount rate on October 31, 1986, for the fourth time that year; th first three reductions had taken place in January, March, and August, and between these cuts, the discount rate fell to 3.0 percent per annum.

The central bank's action was notable because it gave the impression that monetary policy, which had remained steady for so long, was beginning to show signs of flexibility. The discount rate drops were orchestrated through close multilateral consultations with the United States, the Federal Republic of Germany, as well as other nations, as agreed the previous year in New York. This move was also a signal to the rest of the world that Japan was serious about stimulating domestic demand.

While the reductions in the discount rate eased the burden on small businesses, many small exporters were badly affected by the yen appreciation; in 1986 alone, more than 430 businesses were forced to close their doors. Corporate profits also plummeted causing companies to slash their labor forces wherever possible, and thus unemployment rose slightly to 2.9 percent in the first quarter of 1986, when the economy showed its worst performance in 11 years. Moreover, according to a Bank of Japan survey, manufacturing profits for 1986 were expected to drop 22 percent from 1985 levels. The private sector forecasters revised the optimistic 4 percent economic growth rate downward to 1.8 percent, less than half of what it had been the previous year.

While most of Japan's large corporations were cushioned by large profits from 1984 and the first half of 1985, and were thus able to weather the rough economic climate, it became clear by mid-1986 that flexible monetary policy alone would not be sufficient to reverse the ominous trends. Thus, in an attempt to revitalize the economy, on September 19, 1986, the government announced a $23 billion set of Comprehensive Economic Measures aimed primarily at public works projects.

The reflationary package had been championed by MITI, which insisted that a sizeable increase in public spending was necessary to boost domestic demand and thereby, to reduce trade conflicts with Japan's major trading partners. This action has long been resisted by the Ministry of Finance, which spent the past five years trying to bring public spending under control. MOF officials wanted fiscal measures which were consistent with the goals of the fiscal austerity policy, such as the reallocation of funds to finance construction, regulatory changes to encourage private investment, measures to pass on the benefits of the yen's appreciation to consumers, and increased aid to small businesses hurt by the strong yen. Even so, MOF officials did not believe that expanding domestic demand could significantly reduce the trade surplus.[2]

When the Comprehensive Economic Measures were announced in September 1986, it was not clear how the government planned to raise the $23 billion to revitalize the economy; by October 31, the government announced a supplementary budget, cutting back the original FY 1986 budget by $1.6 billion and also adding a $3.75 billion construction bond issue to help finance public works. The expected shortfall in revenue due to lower individual and corporate earnings, customs, and other revenues was covered by reserves from FY 1985 and savings from other expenditures. The total amount to be spent, including additional capital expenditures by the private sector, added up to the largest package of this type in Japanese financial history. Nevertheless, many questioned whether this was too little, too late.

Not only MOF officials but also private sector economists were skeptical about the measures' ability to make a dent in Japan's current account surpluses within the foreseeable future. According to a macroeconomic model developed by Nihon Keizai Shimbun, Inc., the package could reduce the nation's current account surplus by only a maximum of $500 million in FY 1986, that is, by March 31, 1987.

In September 1986, the yen was approximately 55 percent higher than it had been in September 1985, and thus, Japan's export volume was slowly declining. On October 31, 1986, the United States and Japan announced a quietly negotiated joint agreement to stabilize the yen-dollar exchange rate. The move was seen as an attempt to help curb the stagnation of Japan's economy and also to help narrow the U.S. trade deficit. The statement, made jointly by U.S. Secretary of the Treasury Baker and Finance Minister Miyazawa, promised closer cooperation on maintaining foreign exchange stability, including joint intervention in currency markets when necessary, to allow for better policy planning and less risk exposure in the domestic markets of both nations. The agreement also pointed to tax reforms in the United States and Japan to provide incentives for growth in both economies.

In time, the high yen gradually began to generate some domestic support as economic indicators showed modest growth in demand, lower retail prices for imported goods, higher growth in the service industries, and improving profits due to lower fuel and raw materials costs at the end of the year. Plant and equipment investment for nonmanufacturing industries was expected to jump by 14.1 percent, and growth in the nonexport sector was projected to increase by 3.4 percent in FY 1986, as compared to 2.7 percent in FY 1985, with further growth of 3.9 percent in the remainder of calendar 1987, thus, gradually shifting from export-led toward domestic demand-led growth.

The tertiary sector and especially the service industries are playing an increasingly larger role in this process.[3] In 1985, the tertiary sector accounted for 61 percent of the nation's GDP and employed slightly more than half of the labor force. According to a MITI survey, by the end of FY 1985, the tertiary sector had expanded 20 percent since 1980.

While industries such as land transportation, telecommunications, and tourism have expanded in excess of 30 percent, deregulation in the domestic markets has had a dramatic effect on the growth of financial and insurance sectors, which have experienced a 53.6 and 76.2 percent growth, respectively, in the same five-year period. Growth in business services has been consistently high within the service industries, due chiefly to the rising importance of services as a component of business activities and growth in the importance of information in company operations, particularly information obtained from outside sources. Conversely, consumer services showed relatively slow growth over this period. Government officials, however, hope that as domestic structural changes take hold and reach consumers in the form of reduced working hours, increased leisure time, and higher disposable income, the volume of services purchased by households will also gradually increase.

Changing Consumer Markets

The Japanese marketplace in the second half of the 1980s is a vastly different place from that of only 10 years earlier in the mid-1970s. The most impressive feature of this change was the steady increase in private consumption. In spite of slower economic growth during the early 1970s, private consumption grew from $106.2 billion in 1970 to $602.8 billion in 1980, the highest growth rate among industrialized countries for this 10-year period. Table 5-1 shows an international comparison of private consumption growth rates as a percentage of GNP between 1970 and 1980.

However, during the first half of the 1980s, a change occurred. According to a 1986 report of the Economic Planning Agency (EPA), despite favorable effects of the stronger yen and lower crude oil prices on consumer living costs, the Japanese propensity to consume declined in FY 1985, hitting 77.1 percent, down from 78.6 percent in FY 1984, and reaching the lowest level since 1982.[4] The EPA attributed the decline to growing consumer uncertainty about the future caused by the deflationary effects of the appreciating yen.

Emerging Market Segments

Japanese consumption patterns are undergoing gradual changes. As the government encourages domestic demand and promotes imports, as the appreciating yen makes imports more attractively priced and increased foreign travel makes them more acceptable, the Japanese are developing varied tastes, and thus the consumer market is developing into several distinct segments. This is quite different from the recent past when mass production, mass marketing, and mass consumption prevailed.

When considering the emerging segments, however, it is important to remember that even though there is a divergence in tastes, the Japanese continue to be among the most demanding consumers in the world in terms

TABLE 5-1. International comparison of changes in private consumption: 1970-1980

	Japan		USA		UK		FR Germany	
	1970	*1980*	*1970*	*1980*	*1970*	*1980*	*1970*	*1980*
Nominal GNP (billion $)	311.2	1,003.5	992.7	2,626.1	124.0	523.6	185.5	820.8
Private final consumption expenditure (billion $)	162.9	584.9	621.4	1,672.8	76.3	315.2	100.4	452.3
Private consumption expenditure as percentage nominal GNP (%)	52.3	58.3	62.6	63.7	61.5	60.2	54.1	55.1
Per capita income ($)	2,427	6,920	3,945	9,318	1,719	6,919	2,399	10,275

Source: *Comparative International Statistics* (Tokyo: Bank of Tokyo, 1983), p. 9.

of product quality, durability, reliability, and design. At the same time, consumer demands for quality are accompanied by expectations of reasonable prices, particularly as growth in disposable household income has slowed over the years. Evidence has shown that Japanese consumers exhibit a propensity to spend money on either high-priced items of superior quality or on inexpensive products, but do not support a middle market.

Although in the past nearly 90 percent of Japanese classified themselves as "middle class," and the differential between the highest and lowest income brackets was smaller than in most other industrialized countries, income segmentation is now an important factor in determining consumption patterns. The ownership of nonessential consumer durables and nondurables tends to rise significantly with income level. For example, the proportion of households owning "essential goods," such as hot water heaters and vacuum cleaners, is fairly constant in all but the lowest income group. Goods like televisions and stereos enjoy a high market penetration in all income brackets, but the highest income group owns twice as many televisions and stereos as other households. Other retail figures indicate that the higher the income level, the more propensity there is for change in lifestyle, especially in terms of adopting modern patterns.

The dynamics of geographic segmentation are changing rapidly. In the past, those wishing to market products to Japanese consumers needed to pay strict attention to where the consumers were located, because not only did tastes vary significantly from region to region but different regions had different infrastructures, such as different electricity cycles, which created problems for "nationwide" product launches. Recently, however, this variety has become less pronounced as the Japanese experience more things as a nation rather than as a region. For example, consumers throughout Japan are watching the same television shows and reading the same newspapers, so that news, fashion, and lifestyle trends spread quickly throughout the country. Thus, in this respect, the consumers have become more homogeneous.

While segmentation on a geographic basis is still important, the segments tend to break out in urban/nonurban segments rather than specific regions. Due to large retailing chains, fashionable clothing and household products are available even in small cities. Prices for these items show little variation because of nationwide dissemination of information and relatively constant consumer expenditures for such products. Variations do occur, however, when comparing expenditures on items such as food, housing, education, and entertainment. Expenditures on food are higher in cities because of increased consumption of high quality and gourmet foods as well as processed foods, and more frequent dining out in restaurants.

Housing, eduction, and entertainment costs are also higher in cities because they are in higher demand in urban than in rural areas.

Within the changing geographic consumer segmentation trends exist the
more rapidly changing demographic segments of Japan's marketplace,
particularly with respect to age groups. People live longer in Japan now
than they did 20 years ago, and as more people live long, healthy lives past
the mandatory retirement age of 55 or 60, demand for special products and
services is growing. Moreover, different lifestlyles are also emerging which
should be recognized as separated market segments within the demographic segments, such as salaried male workers, women, students, and
subsets of these groups.

Salaried male workers fall into two basic subsegments based on age. The
first identifiable group consists of the young professional male under the
age of 30. This period in a Japanese man's life, when he is first out of school
and joining the workforce, is relatively burden-free. They work hard and
play hard, so this group is important to the emerging leisure industry.
Approximately 55 percent of young working men own cars, as compared to
19 percent of women in the same age group; they also own more televisions, stereos, and sporting equipment. Free time as distinguished from
work time is becoming more important to this segment, and these men are
willing to spend a relatively large portion of their income on leisure
activities; in 1984, men in this age group spent approximately $500 per
month and saved the rest. Of this sum, about 10 percent was spent on
consumer durables, and 25 percent on education and entertainment. The
emerging trend, however, is that as they become more involved with their
work, their priorities change and they become more conservative, focusing
on cost of living and business concerns rather than a flashy lifestyle.

The second subsegment of salaried males emerges as the Japanese men
grow older and their salaries increase; at this point their buying patterns
also change. Unless they are saving to buy a new home, men in their
thirties and forties tend to spend more money on their business appearance, on such items as suits, shoes, and watches. Once they are well
established in their companies, their styles and appearance becomes very
important and usually much more conservative than that of their younger
counterparts because they are then representatives of those companies.
They also continue to buy sporting goods and hobby items such as stereo
equipment and personal computers; however, as consumers in this subsegment, they are replacing the systems they bought as "young salaried
workers" with much more expensive, sophisticated equipment. Within the
family decision-making process, the male head of household has little
influence over purchases other than big ticket items such as the family car.

All other financial decisions and purchases are either decided jointly with their wives or are made by the wives alone.

Women in Japan are increasingly taking on a multiplicity of roles in the marketplace. Traditionally, married women control their households and manage the family money. Generally the only contact a man has with his paycheck is to turn it over to his wife, who in turn gives him an allowance out of which he purchases his suits and shoes. Other daily purchases such as socks, underwear, and toiletries are made by the wife. She also takes the lead in making purchases in the home, although both husband and wife have influence on large purchases such as furniture and appliances. Since housewives are responsible for such a large portion of these types of purchases, they have been the major force behind many consumer movements in Japan that have accomplished goals such as better labeling and stricter environmental controls.

In light of the decline in real disposable household income over the past few years, more women both single and married have entered the workforce. In 1985, 35.9 percent of the workforce were women, and approximately 20 percent of those were part-time. In order to balance the full time job of running a household and raising children while also helping with the family income, many wives work part-time out of their home. Part-time work satisfies the needs of both the demand and the supply side of the marketplace, because for women, it does not interfere with their household responsibilities and they can work freely during the hours they choose; for companies, part-time workers' wages are relatively low and their level of employment can be easily adjusted. A major change in such two-worker households has been a move away from traditional eating patterns to more convenience foods and more dining out.

Women in their early twenties form another important market segment in Japan. This age group roughly corresponds to the market segment of young salaried male workers, although their buying patterns are very different. The greatest percentage of working women are found in this group, and they work largely in the service sector. Although they are paid less than men of the same age, unmarried women in this segment usually live at home, have fewer expenses, and therefore have higher disposable incomes. Most women recognize this period as a transtion until they get married, so they save some money for their wedding and their own home. By and large, they own more furniture than men, but spend less on electronic gadgets. Even after these expenditures and savings, this group spends much more money on clothing, accessories, and cosmetics than any other group, and are still able to have enough money to travel domestically and abroad.

Special Buying Times

While it is important to recognize the buyer behavior of these various consumer segments, there also exists another dimension to spending patterns which accounts for volume sales in Japan, namely the compensation system and the major ceremonial events. While these are not new trends or changes, they are important characteristics of the Japanese marketplace which differentiates it from all the major consumer goods markets throughout the world.

The nature of the compensation system affects consumer spending because for the most part, compensation is predictable since it is determined well in advance, and major expenditures can be planned years ahead of time. Generally, employees are paid on a monthly basis, and when they retire, they recieve either a pension from their company or a large lump-sum payment.

The other major method of compensation is the bonus system which is a bi-annual payment received in addition to the monthly salary. The bonus, usually worth between one and three times a monthly paycheck, is paid in December and midsummer, which coincides with the two major gift-giving seasons in Japan, *Oseibo* and *Ochugen*. *Oseibo* which literally means "year end" is Japan's largest gift-giving season. Although it coincides with Christmas, it is distinctly different in spirit and extremely important to both personal and business relationships. *Oseibo* is a way of showing that a person is grateful for someone's time, respect, or patronage, a kind of settling of accounts. On a personal level, gifts are exchanged from children to their parents, students to their mentors (even if they are no longer students), and, to a lesser extent, between friends. On a business level, companies give presents to any organization or its representatives with whom they do a significant amount of business. Companies can spend upward of $1,500−2,000 apiece for *oseibo*, which nowadays is usually in the form of high-priced gourmet delicacies, and sometimes contract stores to organize the execution of their gift-giving. *Ochugen*, the midsummer gift-giving time, is less official and more optional than *oseibo*. Bonus seasons are peak periods for marketing consumer goods, because typically, half of the bonus is saved and the other half is used for large purchases or loan repayments. While this would seem the perfect opportunity for boosting import sales, many imported goods are overlooked because they lack the festive packaging expected by the Japanese.

The major ceremonial events in Japan entail massive expenditures on clothes, presents, and entertainment. Entering a new school at any level requires new clothes and school equipment; traditional children's festivals require expensive ceremonial kimonos and gift exchanges. Likewise, school graduations are big gift-giving occasions, as are "coming of age" celebrations.

Perhaps one of the largest cash outlays, next to buying a house is a wedding. Marriage is assumed to be an essential step, and the occasion is duly celebrated. It is an expensive affair, requiring large sums of cash for the ceremony itself, the honeymoon, and new furnishings, and thus the ancillary markets for this occasion are quite large. The average cost of a wedding in Japan is about $15,000–20,000. a substantial part of which comes from the newlyweds' savings, the rest is paid by the parents.

Consumer Credit

The Japanese are primarily cash-and-carry customers which some economists believe has had a dampening effect on consumer spending. An estimated 80 percent of transactions involve cash because the consumer credit system remains limited. The biggest barrier to the development of a consumer credit system similar to that of the United States is the law which limits credit cards allowing payments over time. Charge cards that require full payment of the monthly balance have been in use since the mid-1970s; however, they have met with little acceptance because they are only moderately better than cash. Purchases made by credit cards recorded about $12 billion in 1983, which accounted for slightly less than 2 percent of total personal consumption spending in that year, and it is estimated that by 1990, credit card sales will make up only a modest 2.9 percent of total personal consumption spending.[5] Most of the potential users of consumer credit are among the younger generation who enjoy the convenience as well as status image of carrying credit cards. For the most part, however, consumer credit remains mired in tight regulations and excessively high interest rates which has forced financial firms to investigate new types of consumer debt instruments.

One possible solution has been the development of debit cards. American companies started offering debit cards in 1984, but the highly developed state of consumer credit in the United States makes deducting purchases directly from the bank account less desirable than paying for purchases over time. Since the debit cards do essentially the same thing as the credit cards currently used in Japan, the debit card potentially has a lot of appeal since it eliminates the extra step of paying the bill.

Reaching Consumers

As the marketplace is more and more marked by product differentiation, traditional means for reaching the consumer are changing from both a promotional and distribution perspective. The consumer is becoming more knowledgable and discerning, so traditional mass marketing techniques no longer trigger the same buying response as in the past. As a result, mass retailing is in trouble and advertising expenditures are stagnating. The notion of niche marketing, or highly segmented population targeting, is becoming increasingly important to domestic and foreign suppliers as consumers struggle to sort out their choices and perferences.

Promotion of products in Japan takes many forms, especially as the government wants to step up domestic demand in both the consumer and industrial markets. Presently promotion mixes consist of direct sales efforts, point-of-purchase promotions, media advertising, direct mail, and product exhibitions and fairs, among others. When discussing advertising of any nature in Japan, a fundamental difference must be noted. Ads and commercials are not designed to extol the virtues of a product but merely to evoke a mood. Typically they do not even identify the product until the last line or the final second.

Although commercial and ads fail to communicate a "real" sales message, it leaves the viewer with a certain sensation. This type of advertising dominates in Japan because too much direct verbal communication is considered awkward. The purpose of "mood" advertising is to entertain and thus instill a good feeling toward the company and its products, or to create public reaction and thereby interest that will lead to increased public awareness of the product.

The relationship established between a company, its product, and its consumers through effective "mood" advertising is considered imperative to the buying decision in Japan. For most foreign companies, even those with international brand name recognition, advertising in Japan is a difficult procedure of establishing this required relationship with the customer while getting the message across that they offer a quality product, without alienating their customer by a direct approach. In many instances this requires more time, money, energy, and patience than most foreign companies consider reasonable. In some cases, this frustration has been alleviated by positioning products as luxury imports and pricing them as such. Insofar as the Japanese tend to associate price with quality, the relationship is established; however, this type of strategy severely limits any hope of growing sales volumes. Another strategy has been to link advertising with a Japanese company in the same industry, and rely on the "relationships" pre-established by the Japanese company. This has been successful only to the degree that the import does not cannibalize sales of the domestic product, at which point the domestic company usually withdraws support.

Japan is the second largest advertising market in the world behind the United States, yet the flat growth and sluggish consumption rates have created stagnancy in the advetising field. In 1985, the combined ad revenues of the basic four mass medium (newspapers, magazines, radio, and television) rose only 2 percent, down from the 1984 gain of 4.6 percent. The year-to-year growth rate slowed in each medium.

The decrease in advertising expenditures is directly related to a decrease in sales due to consumer saturation. Many experts are wondering just how much more the consumer can buy, especially since Japan is not a "throwaway" or replacement society by nature. Advertisers recognize the necessity for keeping their products in front of the public, even if they are not buying, and therefore they are seeking alternative means to media advertising.

One method is direct marketing, or catalog sales. Since Japan does not allow for bulk postage rates on advertising items, direct mail is not as inexpensive as it is in the United States, but it is still less expensive than media advertising. Due to traditional personal sales relationships between consumers and retailers, direct marketing has been slow to gain acceptance. Recent social trends, however, have allowed direct marketing to take root. The most significant of these has been the increasing number of women in the workforce. With more disposable income but less time to spend it, these women are receptive to the conveniences of direct marketing. As a result, direct marketing sales are growing about 10 percent per annum, as compared to 1 percent annual growth in overall retail sales.[6] Increased computerization has also facilitated targeting the proper markets for direct mail campaigns through updated mailing lists and efficient invoicing.

Catalog marketing is extending to foreign goods as well. Overseas catalogs representing merchants of Gucci to camping equipment are available to Japanese consumers at mail-order centers opened in Tokyo by the Manufactured Imports Promotion Organization. Some consumers see mail ordering direct from foreign manufacturers as a way of capitalizing on the yen appreciation savings, previously enjoyed mostly by the distribution intermediaries. Others see it as their contribution to narrowing the trade surplus, although purchases under $1,200 are not officially recorded for the trade statistics.

Trends in the Quality of Life

The Maekawa Commission recommendations have a potentially major impact on the quality of life in Japan over the longrun. From the viewpoint of the Japanese, this aspect of the internationalization of the economy is as important, if not more so, as the reduction in the current-account and trade-account surpluses. Most people abroad do not appreciate this because they do not realize that behind the great success of the large kaisha in the international marketplace is an economy which has weak spots and which has not yet fully distributed its accumulated wealth.

In 1985, Japan's nominal per capita GNP was $11,190 compared to the $16,702 of the United States at the prevailing exchange rate of Y 235 to the dollar. However, as a consequence of the rapid appreciation of the yen, by mid-1986 Japan had caught up to the United States at Y 157.5 to the dollar.[7] Of course, such simple measures cannot be used to compare standards of living because they ignore a number of additional pertinent considerations such as the domestic purchasing power of the respective currencies. Nonetheless, they provide some interesting insights into the standard of living trends of the two nations.

The Japanese have done well over the years, and despite declining interest rates, the nation's personal savings jumped a record amount in FY 1985, topping the $2 trillion mark for the first time, according to the Bank of Japan. In comparison to FY 1984, the balance of personal savings, that is, the funds placed by individuals in banks, post offices, securities houses, and insurance companies, was up by 9.3 percent. By mid-1986, the Bank of Tokyo reported that household savings were up by 6.3 percent from the year before, the ninth consecutive yearly increase despite a 4.3 percent average decline in take-home pay.[8] According to the bank, retirement, education, and the high price of homes were the major reasons given by a sample of savings account holders for their continued high savings propensity, which makes the Japanese one of the most frugal people in the world.

At the same time, due to a steady increase in tax and social security payments, the growth of disposable income in real terms has continued to decline for the last 10 years. Whereas until 1976, when it began the steady decline, average disposable income made up over 90 percent of total monthly income; this share was down to 84 percent during the early 1980s and thereafter. In particular, the share of housing loan repayments has continued to grow which together with the increased tax and social security payments were the major reasons for the decline and the sluggish consumer demand in the recent past.

Apprehension about the potential effects of the sharply appreciating yen on the economy has also resulted in more modest wage gains during the traditional *shunto* or wage drive in 1986. This was in line with the modest average salary increase of 0.68 percent over the 1976–1986 period.[9] According to the Ministry of Labor, in the spring of 1986 employees at major private corporations obtained an average monthly wage increase of 4.55 percent.[10] In comparison to the 5.03 percent increase in 1985 this represented a 0.48 percent decline, and is the third lowest increase since such data were first reported in 1956. Such modest wage increases combined with the reported trends in disposable household income during the last decade, represent a disquieting trend in an economy where private personal consumption accounts for about 60 percent of gross domestic product (GDP), which is quite high by international standards. Not surprisingly, the Nakasone government's interest in the course of wage settlements appeared unusually strong in 1986. While not trying to directly influence the negotiations, the government's desire to increase domestic demand made it an unlikely bedfellow with the labor unions, which were also concerned about the forthcoming wage increases.

The outlook for 1987 was even worse. Faced with a difficult economic environment, labor leaders informally predicted that the 1987 pay increases would probably be held to 3 percent at best. This level would not only be below the 1986 increase of 4.55 percent, but even less than the record low of 4.4 percent increase in 1983. The president of the influential Japan Federation of Employers' Associations pointed out in a speech to a federation meeting in early 1987 that the average increase should not exceed the difference between the real economic growth rate and the rate of growth in the number of employed workers.

Together with the limited wage increases, for about a year following the sharp appreciation of the yen beginning in September 1985, the Japanese consumers were also denied the benefits of the exchange rate adjustments. The domestic price effects of the approximately 56 percent appreciation of the yen against the dollar did not emerge before the late fall of 1986. According to MITI officials, in late October 1986, prices fell for about 8,300 imported products in department stores and supermarkets, thus finally contributing to the improvements of the quality of life for the average Japanese citizen.

MITI officials found that of the 8,300 items with reduced prices, 40 percent were foodstuffs, 35 percent clothing and related items, 12 percent everyday household goods, and 13 percent sporting and other consumer products. Approximately 80 percent of the price reductions fell into the 10–30 percent range. While these results surpassed the findings of an earlier report issued by MITI in June 1986, when only 1,650 items registered a price decline of a lesser degree, the price movements did not reflect the appreciation of the yen. This conclusion was confirmed by a report submitted by the Round Table on Wages, Prices and Employment to the Minister of Labor in October 1986. The report also found that for Japanese purchasing power to be equal to that in the United States in the fall of 1986, import prices should have come down a great deal more. Thus, members of the Round Table argued, it is necessary to develop measures through which price cuts of food imports, electricity, and gas could be enforced.

Concerns about the quality of life also extended to taxation. By the early 1980s, over 80 percent of the population were dissatisfied with the system.[11] The majority of people believed that it lacked equity and that the rates were too high. However, over 50 percent wanted to retain the tax-exempt *maruyu* or small savings which the Maekawa Commission wanted to eliminate. Moreover, an unexpectedly large proportion of the people also wanted an indirect rather than direct tax as part of a reform, because they believed that the rich could more easily avoid the latter. In comparison to previous surveys on taxation, the 1986 results also showed that more and more people were frustrated about what they perceived as the inequities of the system and the ever-growing tax burden. The frustration was especially high among salaried workers with annual incomes of $36,000—$48,000 and those in the $60,000 or higher bracket. Most of the salaried workers were concerned about the different methods of reporting income by those who are self-employed, and they believed that tax evasion by such people is very frequent.

However, in spite of some of the disquieting trends of recent years and the concerns over import prices and tax reform, measured by conventional standards, the Japanese have done very well over the last 20 years. They have improved their quality of life relative to the past and relative to other nations. According to an assessment by the Economic Planning Agency, the quality of life in Japan is quite satisfactory, and in some respects, better than in a few of the other industrialized nations.[12] These findings were obtained through the EPA's New Social Indicators for 1984, which are designed to probe beyond the purely financial measures of the standard of living and to gauge the quality of life in a broader fashion. The indicators are made up of 148 indexed items in eight different categories which reflect the entire scope of quality of life considerations ranging from health through economic security to community, social, and cultural activities.

More specifically, the EPA found that life has substantially improved from the viewpoint of economic security, environment, health, and working conditions, but has deteriorated as far as the family is concerned. In comparison with America, the United Kingdom, the Federal Republic of Germany, France, and Sweden, Japan obtained higher scores in several areas, including the environment, general security, health, and even family life.

In comparison to the 1980 levels (rated as 100), the quality of life improved, for example, in health (101.9 in 1984), education and cultural activities (101.6), working life (101.4), the environment and general society (101.0). The improvements in health were achieved, among others through longer average life expectancy and declining infant mortality. The environment and general security was rated higher because of the expansion of sewage systems and a decrease in the number of felonies.

The major deterioration (98.2) in family life was reported to be due chiefly to an increase in divorces resulting in households headed by women with small children and a rapid increase in the number of the aged living alone. In 1985, for example, 30.3 percent of all suicide, 26.6 percent of fatal traffic accidents, and slightly over 16 percent of all victims of various financial swindless were 60 years or older.[13] These problems are likely to multiply in the future; the Health and Welfare Ministry reported in 1986 that the "graying" of Japan's population is progressing more rapidly than earlier predicted. According to the ministry, by the year 2007, people aged 65 or over will exceed the number of children age 14 or under, and in 2020, people over 65 will account for approximately 25 percent of the total population. In comparison, the proportion of older Japanese (65 and over) was 10.2 percent in 1986. Internationally, this compared with Sweden, where 17.1 percent of the popultion was over 65, and the Federal Republic of Germany and the United Kingdom with around 14 to 15 percent of the citizens in that age category in the same year. According to demographers, Japan will surpass Sweden as the "oldest" society in the world at the beginning of the twenty-first century, thereby raising a whole new set of social concerns which are likely to affect the quality of life in the future.[14]

Moreover, in its 1986 White Paper on the national life, the EPA also concluded that in spite of its positive international comparison of Japan's quality of life, most Japanese arc dissatisfied with the inadequate social infrastructure, expensive housing, high food prices, available free time to pursue leisure activities, and the hard school life of their children. These findings were reinforced in a survey conducted by the Prime Minister's Office in 1986 which found that of the respondents polled, 31.7 percent want the government to take action on taxes, 30.7 percent on social insurance and welfare, 28.4 percent on high prices, and 20.3 percent on youth and education.[15]

Such concerns were also reflected in the daily press.[16] Newspaper editorials were representative of the concerns expressed in the EPA White Paper. Some pointed out that there are "ominous signs of a materialistically affluent but spiritually deficient" national life. Others argued that in spite of the positive official reports, the quality of life is not holding up as well as it should, and that such a development is not a proper reflection of the great wealth which the nation has accumulated over the past 30 years.

In light of these findings, the EPA recommended in its White Paper that to catch up with the quality of life in the United States and Western Europe, Japan must invest more in social infrastructures and housing, improve the productivity of its agricultural sector, and attain larger wage increases and shorter working hours. The EPA called on the nation to seek "a new and unprecedented national goal to attain an affluent lifestyle through international harmony," objectives which are in accord with the Maekawa Commission's recommendations.

Deregulation of the Financial Markets

Of all the domestic policy options to internationalize the economy, the deregulation of the financial markets was already well advanced by early 1986 when the Maekawa Cmmission's recommendations were released. The Ministry of Finance (MOF) carefully began orchestrating the gradual deregulation process during the 1970s because it wanted to avoid major upheavals in the financial markets and loss of control over monetary policy.

In the early 1980s, as trade conflicts grew, so did American criticism of the financial markets. U.S. pressure for reform was based on the belief that Japanese financial regulations had driven down the value of the yen by making it an unattractive currency. U.S. officials argued that freer capital markets would increase international use of the yen, thereby raising its value and also moderating some trade problems. Moreover, American financial firms wanted greater access to Japanese capital markets, and complained that Japanese regulations hindered them from playing a larger role in competing for institutional and private investments, particularly the lucrative pension funds.

The result of this pressure was the November 10, 1983, Yen-Dollar Accord covering specific measures to liberalize Japan's financial markets. The agreement was hammered out by the Japan-U.S. Yen-Dollar Committee, and jointly approved by the U.S. Secretary of the Treasury and the Minister of Finance. The Yen-Dollar Accord set out measures for changing the treatment of Japanese financial markets in the following areas: (1)

liberalization of capital flows; (2) internationalization of the yen; (3) expanded foreign participation; and (4) the deregulation of domestic capital markets.

A working group of the Yen-Dollar Committee was established to monitor the progress of these measures and to pursure additional steps, which were ultimately reflected in the Action Program's section on financial market liberalization. In this respect, the Action Program served as a reaffirmation of the commitment undertaken by the Yen-Dollar Accord.

Liberalization of capital flows primarily focused on easing restrictions on financial transactions. Deposit interest rates, money market instruments, and certain lending activities were deregulated. Guidelines for interest rates on large deposits were relaxed, and then were completely removed in the spring of 1987.[17] Banks can now issue short-term certificates of deposit (CDs) and money market certificates (MMCs) more easily, and remaining restrictions on issuances of this type are also expected to be eased.[18] Interest rates on residents' foreign currency deposits were completely liberalized.

In the money market, the ban on sales of foreign commercial paper and CDs was abolished in April 1984. This step, originally planned for 1982, had been delayed to avoid depressing the yen through large capital outflows; however, now CD repurchase agreements, bankers' acceptances, and treasury bills are traded freely, though still on a limited scale, and foreign currency swaps and Euroyen borrowings are rapidly increasing. Banks are now permitted to deal in government bonds, and security brokers have begun to deal in CD and bankers' acceptances markets, thus expanding the scope of the traditional roles of these financial institutions.

In the capital market, guidelines for issuing unsecured bonds have been relaxed, and rating agencies have been established. The futures market for government bonds began operating at the end of 1985, and banks were permitted to participate in the currency futures markets by the end of 1986.

The internationalization of the yen focused on deregulation of external transactions and efforts to increase the yen's use in order to increase its foreign exchange value. Although the overall share of yen in global foreign exchange reserves doubled from 2 percent in 1976 to 5.2 percent in 1984, it is small relative to the U.S. dollar's 65.1 percent share and the West German mark's 12 percent share. Given the size of Japan's economy, the percent of its trade denominated in yen is also small, only 3 percent; West Germany denominates approximately 40 percent of its foreign purchases in German marks. Due to the recent establishment of the bankers' acceptance market and the lifting of certain lending restrictions in Japan, Japanese importers are no longer forced to obtain trade credits abroad, although due to complex rules governing this market, they still find it easier to do so.

The Euroyen market has undergone a great deal of change since 1984. Domestic and foreign banks now issue and trade short-term negotiable CDs outside Japan, although issuance of this instrument had lagged because the maximum allowed maturity of six months is too short. Another important development was the relaxation of rules governing Samurai bonds (yen-denominated bonds issued in Japan by nonresidents) and Shogun bonds (foreign currency denominated bonds issued in Japan by nonresidents) which led to a sharp increase in the use of these instruments in 1985.

In addition to these internal mechanisms for stimulating yen use, restrictions of foreign participation in financial transactions were eased. Nine foreign banks gained approval to engage in trust banking and participate in the government bond underwriting syndicate. Also, 36 foreign securities firms have approval to operate in Japan, and in an unprecedented move in October 1985, six foreign firms were allotted seats on the Tokyo Stock Exchange (TSE). Lastly, 30 major foreign firms, among them Proctor & Gamble and Chrysler Corporation, were listed on the TSE as of September 1, 1986; this number increased by the end of 1986. Thus, Japan's financial markets have expanded and are nearing integration with financial markets abroad.

Many of these changes have been made possible because of the changing roles of traditional financial institutions. As the liberalization and internationalization of the yen continues, there is growing preference of borrowers, lenders, and investors to go into the capital markets rather than engaging in conventional bank financing. "Securitization" has not noticeably advanced in Japanese markets because domestic commercial paper cannot be traded, and banks do not engage in the sale of loan portfolios, but to a certain extent, the separation between commercial and investment banking is blurring. The government has allowed the securities subsidiaries of foreign banks to open branches in Japan, which has permitted some foreign banks like American Express Bank, Ltd., to convert their Japanese banking presence into a securities business. The MOF seems intent on creating a financial center like New York or London by granting foreign banks entry into the lucrative investment business, although to date, the same permission has not been granted to domestic banks.

Interntionalization of the financial markets continues. On December 1, 1986, the Tokyo offshore banking facility began operations to provide nonresidents with financial services free of federal taxation and other Japanese regulations. The government hoped to spur 24–hour trading, promote the growth of Tokyo as an international financial center, and increase use of the yen as an international currency. Bankers, however, were less enthusiastic about the importance of the offshore facility because of a number of regulations they believed limited its usefulness. In an attempt to insulate domestic financial markets from the influence of the offshore facility and to preserve the efficacy of monetary and tax policies, the MOF banned net inflows from offshore accounts to domestic accounts, imposed a variety of local taxes on the transactions, and prohibited offshore accounts from issuing domestic CDs or holding foreign securities. Bankers maintain that for as long as the restrictions remain, the facility will be little more than an offshore depository.

Foreign Direct Investment in Japan

Foreign direct investment represents an inflow of capital; thus, it is not one of the policy options recommended by the Maekawa Commission to reduce the current account surpluses. Nonetheless, it needs to be reviewed because by enhancing the international division of labor, such investments aid the integration of Japan into the global-economy.

Foreign direct investment began in Japan shortly after World War II, although to protect the nation's precarious balance of payments position and the exchange value of the yen, the government exerted strong control over it for many years. Moreover, already during the early days, the Japanese viewed such investments primarily as a source of technical and managerial know-how rather than as a source of capital; thus they were very selective in issuing investment permits. Beginning in the 1960s, policies became even more restrictive because Japan wanted to protect its "infant industries" until they became internationally competitive.

Between 1967 and 1980, policies were gradually eased. Investment laws were reshaped from "basically restrictive" to "basically free." The 1980 revision of the "Foreign Exchange and Foreign Trade Control Law" completed this process in that it made all foreign direct investments "free in principle," although the Ministry of Finance retained a certain amount of control.[19] Nonetheless, this measure brought Japan into compliance with the OECD foreign direct investment guidelines observed throughout the industrialized world.

From the beginning, the number of direct investment projects initiated annually showed a fluctuating but generally upward trend. In FY 1976, for example, a total of only 196 such projects were started whereas a little less than 10 years later in FY 1985, the total reached over 800. By the end of

TABLE 5–2.   Foreign direct investment in Japan by country: end of 1985

	No. of firms	Amount (U.S. $ million)
USA	2,329	3,495
UK	409	360
Switzerland	266	335
Germany, FR	315	238
Netherlands	129	164
France	252	133
Canada	76	124
Panama	—	36
Belgium	—	7
Other	—	1,761
Total	6,286	6,653

Source: *Japan 1986: An International Comparison* (Tokyo: Keizai Koho Center, 1986), p. 58.

the calendar year 1985, the accumulated number of such projects was over 6,000, with the United States accounting for most of the investments (37 percent). Table 5–2 shows the accumulated totals by country as of the end of calendar year 1985.

As for the method of investment, until a few years ago, most of them involved the establishment of start-up operations or the buy-out of joint venture partners. Acquisitions were rare because traditionally Japanese companies are viewed as "communal organizations," that is a collection of people and not of assets that could be readily sold. Other reasons included the high debt-equity ratio which made it difficult for the stockholders, owning only a small percentage of the company, to gain control. More-over, in many companies, nonshareholders or holders of only a few shares in the organization still could maintain strong control through well established personal relation.

While acquisitions attempts have become more frequent during the last few years, hostile takeovers are still frowned upon. The Japanese word *nottori* means both hostile takeover and hijacking. Not surprisingly, the first, heavily publicized major hostile takeover attempt was made by an Anglo-American partnership and not a Japanese company, Trafalgar-Glen International Finance Services Co., in 1985. Trafalgar-Glen wanted to acquire Minebea Co., Japan's leading miniature ball-bearing manufacturer. The Anglo-American company tried to exercise warrants and convertible bonds in its possession which amounted to 30 percent of Minebea's stock, and eventually made a $1.4 billion tender offer for Minebea's outstanding stock.

The takeover attempt was rejected by the institutional holders of the Japanese company's stock. In addition, the MOF delayed its approval for several months, and in 1986 a Japanese court dismissed Trafalgar-Glen's subsequent suit to stop Minebea's defensive moves as a restraint on competition. While there can be no doubt that with the increased internationalization of the Tokyo capital markets and the desire of foreign companies to quickly establish themselves in Japan that hostile takeovers will be attempted again, it is unlikely that the Japanese will change their views on such acquisitions. Japanese takeovers are mostly friendly transactions using the services of a trusted *nakodo* or go-between because neither side wants to experience major disruptions, particularly from the employees' viewpoint. Also, the lessons of the hostile takeover insider deals which rocked Wall Street in 1986−1987 will not be lost on the Ministry of Finance, domestic financial institutions, and corporate managers.

With respect to the industrial sectors, in the past, most foreign direct investment went into distribution, particularly wholesaling. This reflected the strategy of foreign companies to set up a strong sales organization to establish themselves in the Japanese marketplace. Next came the service sector, with financial and information technology business services leading the way. Manufacturing, in third place over the years, was represented chiefly by high-technology companies, particularly in the field of electronics, although investments were also made in the more traditional nonelectronic machinery, transportation, communication, and fabricated metal products industries.

By the second half of the 1980s this pattern, however, was beginning to change. More foreign companies decided that the only way to stay in the highly competitive Japanese marketplace was to establish a manufacturing and maybe even a research and development base. They concluded that investments in distribution facilities alone would not be sufficient in the future because not only does a production and research base enhance competitive abilities but it also makes the acquisition of the increasingly significant Japanese research findings much easier.

A case in point is the Eastman Kodak Corporation of Rochester, New York. Although the first Kodak products were sold in Japan almost 100 years ago, for many years the company's direct representation was limited to a small office staffed by a few Americans. Independent Japanese firms distributed the Kodak products, and handled all marketing decisions, including promotion and pricing. It was not before 1984 that the company increased its expatriate staff to more than 20 and acquired some distribution channels of its own. Moreover, it entered a joint venture with another distributor, and took a 10 percent minority position in Chinon Industries, a Japanese camera manufacturer.

In 1988 Kodak plans to open its own $65 million research and development center in Yokohama. According to industry sources, Kodak intends to invest more in Japan than in any other nation except the United States, although the Japanese market accounted for only 5 percent of its $11.5 billion worldwide sales in 1986. Kodak is making this investment because it not only intends to market its products in Japan but also hopes to learn from Japanese firms about electronics and other high-technology areas in which these firms are world leaders. Kodak wants to follow technology developments directly from inception to implementation, instead of finding out about Japanese technological advancements after they are embodied in products and marketed throughout the world.

To underline its new commitment to the Japanese marketplace, Kodak also changed its marketing strategy in 1986. For the first time, it began selling its film in boxes labeled in Japanese, and supported its marketing effort through extensive promotional campaigns. Moreover, to meet the expectations of Japanese amateur photographers, who are the most demanding in the world, Kodak introduced a new, highly sensitive color film. Thus, after taking the Japanese market for granted for nearly 100 years, Kodak made the kind of commitment that is necessary for long-term success in the Japanese marketplace.

The recent changes in the investment climate also have a great deal to do with this new approach by foreign investors. The deregulation of the capital markets not only brought in many financial institutions from abroad but it also helped provide the necessary support services for foreign direct investors. Furthermore, the privatization of Nippon Telegraph and Telephone (NTT) and the deregulation of the telecommunications market created entirely new opportunities. In the pharmaceutical industry eased regulations made it not only possible but necessary for the major American and European manufacturer to establish both a production and a research and development base in Japan.

In line with its policy of internationalizing the economy, the government now actively encourages and aids foreign direct investors. For example, MITI, once the guardian of the domestic industries, is now providing site and other related investment information through its Industrial Policy Bureau. Foreign business representatives have been treated so well by the staff of this bureau that in 1986 a number of them made special courtesy

calls following their final investment decisions to express their appreciation. This new MITI attitude, however, is not generally applauded. While
some foreign investors only remain sceptical about MITI's new policies,
Japanese critics have started to refer disparagingly to the ministry as
"foreign," particularly "American lackeys." Whatever the case may be,
the fact remains that in contrast to the past, MITI now actively promotes
not only imports but also foreign investments.

Another government agency trying to increase foreign direct investment
in Japan is JETRO, which in the past was in charge of Japan's exports
throughout the world. Today JETRO, through its worldwide network,
offers investment information and other supporting services to foreign
firms interested in Japan. Other agencies such as the Japan Development
Bank have also started programs aiding foreign investors.

However, while the overall environment for foreign investment has
improved markedly over recent years, some problems remain. As a result
of the sharp appreciation of the yen, foreign direct investments have
become more expensive. Particularly, the cost of maintaining expatriate
executives in Japan's major cities is exorbitant. Also, because the majority
of able Japanese are already employed by domestic firms, many of which
still provide lifetime employment, it is not easy to find experienced
employees for a new venture. Moreover, very often those who are available for employment do not want to work for a foreign company that may
not succeed and leave Japan on short notice. Thus, it is understandable
that foreign investors still believe that the quickest, most effective, and
least frustrating way to invest in Japan is through the acquisition of an
existing company or a joint-venture rather than the establishment of a
start-up operation.

However, even during the second half of the 1980s this is not always
easy to do, particularly when it comes to large, well-established companies.
A noteworthy exception to this is the joint-venture between Toshiba
Corporation and Motorola, Inc., announced in November 1986. The two
semiconductor manufacturers decided to establish a manufacturing facility
in Japan and to exchange a broad range of microprocessor and memory
chip technologies. According to industry sources, the joint-venture is
designed to help overcome basic deficiencies in both firms. Motorola is
strong in the manufacture of microprocessors, but has virtually given up
the memory chip market. In contrast, Toshiba is very efficient in the
production of memory chips but failed in its attempt to develop competitive microprocessors.

Acquisition opportunities tend to be more available in troubled industries such as chemicals, pharmaceuticals, metals, foods, and even consu-

mer electronics. Here a relatively large number of small-sized to medium-sized (less than 300 employees) companies are receptive to friendly take-overs, or, at least, to substantial foreign equity investments. As more of such companies face financial difficulties due to the appreciation of the yen and the resulting loss of export profits, it is likely that even more of them will be open to acquisitions by foreign investors in the near future.

Notes

1. Kenichi Ohmae, *Triad Power: The Coming Shape of Global Competition* (New York: Free Press, 1985); also Michael E. Porter, ed., *Competition in Global Industries* (Boston: Harvard Business School Press, 1986).
2. MOF officials estimated that each Y 1 trillion ($6.5 billion) increase in domestic demand would generate less than Y 77 billion ($500 million) in additional imports.
3. The tertiary sector includes the service industries, government, and utilities.
4. *The Japan Economic Journal* (November 1, 1986), p. 3. The report is the EPA's annual *White Paper on National Life for FY 1986*.
5. *The Japan Economic Journal* (April 12, 1986), p. 22.
6. "Can Japan Go Direct?" *Tokyo Business Today* (October 1986), p. 28.
7. *The Japan Economic Journal* (June 7, 1986), p. 2.
8. *The Japan Economic Journal* (October 18, 1986), p. 28.
9. Reported by the Research Institute for Labor Administration; *The Japan Times* (March 7, 1986), p. 2.
10. Although wage negotiations take place on a company-by-company basis, average figures and projections play a major role in the eventual settlements reached.
11. *The Japan Times* (July 28, 1986), p. 2; see also, *The Japan Economic Journal* (November 15, 1986), p. 28.
12. *The Japan Economic Journal* (March 22, 1986), p. 20.
13. *Asahi Evening News* (July 23, 1986), p. 5.
14. *Economic Survey of Japan (1984–1985)* (Tokyo: Economic Planning Agency, 1985), p. 177.
15. *White Paper on National Life: FY 1986* (Tokyo: Economic Planning Agency, 1986), and *Survey on National Attitudes on Living Standards* (Tokyo: Office of the Prime Minister, 1986).
16. See, for example, "Living Standards: A Self-Admiring Portrait," *The Japan Times* (March 18, 1986), p. 14.
17. As of September 1, 1986, interest rates on time deposits exceeding Y 300 million ($1.9 million) were removed. Interest rates on the deposits of Y 1 billion ($5 million) or more were first freed in October 1985, and the ceiling was lowered to Y 500 million ($3.1 million) in April 1986. *The Japan Economic Journal* (September 13, 1986), p. 3.
18. *Ibid.* Measures implemented on September 1, 1986, expanded issuance of CDs and MMCs to 2.5 times of the bank's shareholder's equity from 2.0 times.
19. The government can restrict foreign investments in areas where foreign ownership over 25 percent could harm national security, public order, or welfare, or adversely affect the national economy.

6 THE DOMESTIC POLICY OPTIONS

By 1986, the Japanese government was committed to the gradual implementation of the Maekawa Commission recommendations to internationalize the economy. Prime Minister Nakasone, banking on his influence generated by the overwhelming July 1986 electoral victory, forged ahead with his plans. Moreover, the underlying trends and changes in the economy were setting the stage for the implementation of the recommendations. At the same time, the govenment had no illusions about the difficulties that lay ahead. Its outlook was clouded by social and cultural traditions, economic policies based on narrow interests, its own fiscal austerity and the unclear impact of the yen's rapid appreciation on the economy as a whole, at least in the short run.

The domestic policy options chosen to internationalize the economy in the second half of the 1980s include personal and corporate income tax reform, increased infrastructure and housing investments, the continuing promotion of private sector vitality through privatization, deregulation and increased basic research, as well as the reduction of working hours to increase leisure time.

The Tax Reform

Dissatisfaction with the tax system is not new in Japan. Over the years people referred to it as the *ku-ro-yon* (nine-six-four) system, meaning that salaried employees paid 90 percent of their tax obligations, businesses 60 percent, and farmers only 40 percent. By the fall of 1985, the concern among ordinary citizens and even corporate managers was so high that the government had to act; thus, Prime Minister Nakasone appointed a Tax System Advisory Council comprised of government officials and business executives. The advisory body was instructed to review the tax system in light of the fiscal austerity policy and the internationalization of the economy. More specifically, the Council was told to consider the equity of taxation, the fairness of tax rates, economic growth, and the economic opportunities for individuals and businesses in its deliberations. Concurrent to the Council's deliberations, the LDP's Tax System Research Commission also began its discussions, and in early 1986, both bodies made interim recommendations. These included personal and corporate income tax cuts, particularly for middle-aged salaried workers, and an emphasis of the need for simplification of the 15−bracket progressive structure.

The underlying economic scenario for the proposed tax reforms was developed by the Ministry of Finance in October 1986. According to MOF's estimates, the overhaul of the system incorporating total tax cuts of about $28 billion would boost GNP in real terms by about 0.1 percent and capital spending also by 0.1 percent during the first year of the reform. Moreover, people in almost all brackets would benefit, despite the elimination of the tax exemption on the *maruyu* or small, tax-free savings interest and the introduction of a new indirect tax.

All of this was based on the assumptions that personal income and residential taxes would be cut by $17 billion, corporate income taxes by approximately $11 billion, and that a new indirect tax together with a tax on the interest of *maruyu* savings, would generate about $28 billion, thus making the reform revenue-neutral. MOF also estimated that while overall consumer spending would be unaffected in the short run, the eventual expansion of domestic demand could reduce the current account surplus by about $500 million a year.

The proposed changes in the personal income tax system were designed to shift the burden so that salaried employees would pay slightly higher taxes during the first few years of their career and after they turn 60 years old. However, they would pay substantially less during their forties and fifties, when the progressive tax structure was most punishing under the old system. To maintain the "revenue neutrality" of the reform, the Council proposed eight different versions of a new indirect tax without, however, identifying which was most appropriate.

In its report the Council also recommended lowering the effective corporate income tax rate from 52.92 percent to 49.99 percent. It emphasized that the corporate tax rate should be reduced gradually together with the personal income tax rates, and it supported its recommendation with the argument that the 52.92 percent effective tax rate was higher than in the United States, the United Kingdom, and France, and lower only than West Germany which had a 56.52 percent effective rate.[1]

The reduction of corporate income taxes was supported by MITI's advisory group, the Research Council on Corporate Vitality and Taxation, which argued that Japan's effective corporate tax burden was the "heaviest among all Western economies" and that this began to seriously affect the nation's international competitiveness. The group called for a substantial reduction in corporate taxes, more policy-based corporate tax breaks, and changes in the statutory depreciation schedules. In addition, it also proposed special tax cuts to facilitate research and development, acquisition of resources and energy, improvements of social infrastructure, and the promotion of medium and small businesses. These arguments and recommendations were also supported by the Keidanren which in the spring of 1986 released its own tax reform plans.

On the basis of MOF's assumptions and these considerations, the Tax System Advisory Council submitted its final recommendations to Prime Minister Nakasone in late October 1986. The recommendations included a reduction of personal income and residential taxes through a change of the tax brackets so that a basic tax rate of 15 percent would apply to the incomes of most of the Japanese wage earners. However, taxes would be progressively increased by 10 percent for each higher income bracket, with the maximum rate set at 50 percent. The minimum rate would be set at 10 percent for the lowest earners, and the *maruyu* system would be abolished.

The centerpiece of the proposed corporate income tax reform was a reduction of such taxes through a change of the effective tax rate from 52.92 percent to 49.99 percent as put forth by the Council. As expected, Prime Minister Nakasone sent the entire tax recommendations package to the LDP's Tax System Research Commission to develop the final version of the plan so that it could be submitted for Diet approval in early 1987.

By the first week in December the Commission reviewed the proposals and issued its final recommendations. It supported a total tax cut of $27.7 billion a year comprised of a reduction in personal income taxes by $11.8 billion, personal residential taxes by $4.7 billion, and total corporate income taxes by $11.2 billion. More specifically, the Commission reduced the number of income brackets from 15 to 6, cut the maximum rate from 70 percent to 50 percent, set the minimum rate at 10 percent and the basic rate at 15 percent. It also agreed to reduce the effective corporate income tax rate from 52.92 percent to 49.99 percent.

At the same time, however, the Commission also recommended the introduction of a maximum 5 percent value-added-tax and the imposition of a 20 percent tax on interest earned on *maruyu* savings. These measures were expected to raise $18 billion and $10 billion, respectively, thus generating a total of $28 billion in new revenue.[2] Moreover, the Commission recommended the exemption of firms earning less than $625,000 annually and of certain basics such as medical care and food from the VAT. Elderly people, the handicapped, and single-parent families were also allowed to retain the tax-exempt status of their *maruyu* savings.

The Commission decided to carry out the personal income tax cuts beginning in FY 1987 over a period of two years and the planned corporate income tax reduction over a period of three years. The tax exempt status of the *maruyu* would be repealed in October 1987, and the new VAT would be introduced in January 1988. However, the income tax cuts would be phased in gradually so that tax reductions would equal the modest expansion of some lesser levies such as the property ownership transfer and license tax. In this fashion the tax reductions and increases beginning in FY 1987 would be balanced throughout the year, insuring the revenue neutrality of the reform. According to critics, had the tax cuts been fully implemented in the beginning of 1987, the Japanese would have enjoyed and approximate $18.5 billion tax reduction in real terms during the first year. Nonetheless, some Japanese economists predicted that there could be a short spur in spending before the introduction of the VAT, giving the economy a much-needed boost.

Thus, by early 1987 the first major tax reform in 36 years was in sight. This was a considerable achievement, because although the LDP discussed tax reform several times before, previous governments could not carry it off. Even this time it took lengthy and often heated negotiations to reach consensus. Resistance was particularly strong from the postal-savings *zoku* which opposed abolishing the tax exempt status of the *maruyu*. It took the three top LDP leaders, Secretary General Takeshita, Executive Board Chairman Abe, and Policy Affairs Research Council Chairman Ito, to develop a plan which the postal savings *zoku* and its bureaucratic ally the Ministry of Posts and Telecommunications (MPT) was willing to accept. The compromise plan consisted of expanding post office financial services and easing restrictions on MPT's management of funds collected through postal savings. The key role of the LDP Tax Systems Research Commission and of the top LDP leadership in reaching the necessary consensus on the reform is another illustration of how policy formulation power has shifted from the bureaucrats to the politicians.

Expectedly, critics immediately objected to the plan. Prime Minister Nakasone's opponents claimed that the reform breaks a pledge made by the Prime Minister prior to the July 1986 elections when he declared that no large-scale indirect tax would be introduced which the Japanese people and the LDP could not support. Others objected to the regressive nature of the VAT which puts the same burden on the rich as on people with more modest means. Particularly strong concern was expressed about the ease with which the VAT could be raised in the future, because taxpayers would not feel the change directly. Critics pointed to the Federal Republic of Germany where the initial 10 percent VAT rate was raised to 14 percent, and to the United Kingdom which increased its original rate from 10 to 15 percent. The European experience is relevant, they argue, because in 1986 Japan's tax and social security contributions accounted for only 36.1 percent in comparison to major Western European nations where the same ratio stood at well over 50 percent. Thus, the critics claim that as soon as the government finds it necessary to raise additional revenues, it can point to the relatively low tax-social security burden in Japan and increase the VAT.

In response, supporters of the reform pointed out that the maximum 5 percent VAT is not large scale and that the LDP has agreed to its introduction. Moreover, the exemption of small firms and of certain basic goods from the VAT minimizes the regressive features. Most importantly, they emphasized, any proposition to increase the VAT in the future would have to go through the same lengthy and complicated consensus seeking process as the tax reform had to.

Infrastructure Investments

As reported by the Economic Planning Agency, by the end of March 1986 (FY 1985), Japan had an estimated $2 trillion in social infrastructure assets stated in 1980 prices.[3] Moreover, the EPA pointed out, in FY 1982 (the only year for which breakdowns are available), of the $1.4 trillion total in that year approximately 31.7 percent represented sewage systems, parks, schools, and other environmental facilities. About 44.6 percent represented transportation and communication facilities such as roads and railways,

9.8 percent national land, and about 11.7 percent agriculture, fishery, and forestry infrastructures.

The FY 1985 social infrastructure of $2 trillion is high by international comparison. However, a more detailed breakdown reveals that the diffusion level of social infrastructure in Japan is lower than in most industrialized countries. For example, the diffusion of sewages was 72 percent in the United State and 97 percent in the United Kingdom in the late 1970s, but only 33 percent in Japan in 1983. In 1983, only slightly over 53 percent of Japan's roads were paved as opposed to West Germany's (99 percent), the United Kingdom's (96.4 percent), and France's (95 percent). Furthermore, during the early 1980s, Tokyo had the lowest per capita park space, 2.1 square meters, among the world's major capital cities, while Washington, D.C., had 45.7, Bonn 37.4, London 30.4, Paris 12.2, and Stockholm and impressive 80.3 square meters.

The major reason for the discrepancy between the reported value of social infrastructure and its diffusion rate is due to the high cost of construction in Japan relative to other industrialized nations. These higher costs do not include land prices; consequently, the decisive factor may be the topography, which is characterized by mountainous regions. Moreover, most of the social infrastructure in Japan was built after the 1960s whereas in Western Europe or the United States, the infrastructures were built over longer periods of time and were, therefore, less costly.

Japan's urban infrastructure in particular leaves much to be desired. This is borne out by a May 1986 report on Japan's urban policies published by the Organization for Economic Cooperation and Development (OECD) at the request of the Japanese government.[4] The report emphasized that while Japan was once a rural nation, by the early 1980s around 77 percent of its population lived in cities, thus making it the most urbanized of all 24 OECD member countries. Therefore, the government should now give priority to urban policies, in particular to the improvement of urban social infrastructures, not only to increase domestic demand but most importantly, to improve the quality of life for its citizens. As for funding, the OECD suggested that this could be obtained through the use of private savings for the national budget's infrastructure investment and loan programs.

In addition, the report also chided the Japanese authorities for their apparent lack of interest in making Japanese cities more pleasant for their inhabitants. At the same time, it counseled caution concerning the plans for the deregulation of the various current controls to stimulate private sector activities in urban redevelopment. In view of the OECD urban experts, Japan's current regulations still leave enough room for improvements without a possibly overhastened deregulation which could disregard traditional concerns and, thus, cause problems in the long run.

Public efforts to improve the social infrastructure are already under way.[5] By mid-1986, the Ministry of Construction proposed 51 projects, the Ministry of Transport 18, and MITI 98; once possible duplications are eliminated, probably more than 100 projects will remain on the list. Moreover, if joint projects between the private sector and local governments as well as independent local initiatives are also included, the total may rise to 150. All of these projects will be financed with public funds complemented by substantial private sector investments which are expected to have a multiplier effect throughout the economy.

The single largest building project, the Kansai Cultural and Scientific Research City, is a Ministry of Construction project in the Kinki area, the western Japan counterpart of Tsukuba Academic City in Ibaraki Prefecture near Tokyo. The new planned city will include not only public research institutes but also universities, private research institutes, recreational facilities, housing and parks in a bid to create a pilot model city for the twenty-first century and an international center of research and culture. It will be built in an area that reaches into three prefectures — Nara, Osaka, and Kyoto — covers approximately 25 million hectares, and will house a population of about 120,000 people when completed. Total investment is expected to reach about $30 billion of which $22 billion is expected to be provided by the private sector. The construction is already under way.

Another major construction project in the same area is the new Kansai International Airport. The $8 billion project is due to be completed in 1993, and will service about 18 million passengers and 660,000 metric tons of cargo annually. In addition, the Osaka Prefectural Government tentatively calculated that the new airport will require additional services such as food and communications, thereby creating new demands of perhaps $32 billion over the next few years. The airport is unique in that it will be built on an artificial island of about 1,260 acres, the construction of which is already under way. Kansai will be Japan's first 24—hour airport, and it will be connected to the mainland by a 2.4 mile-long bridge. The Kansai International Airport Co. was established to oversee construction; the company is capitalized at $500 million of which over 60 percent is borne by the Japanese government, and the rest by local authorities and the private sector. This is the first time that local authorities and private firms have participated in building an airport; until 1986, such projects were undertaken only by the government.

The major infrastructure project under construction in the Tokyo area is the Trans-Tokyo Bay Highway, to be completed by 1996. The highway will run across the central part of Tokyo Bay and will be linked with the Tokyo Bay Shore Highway and other roads to form a major beltway system. The four-lane expressway (two additional lanes will be built sometime in the future) will cross one of the most crowded sea areas of the bay; consequently, it will consist partially of roads, tunnels, and one bridge connecting two man-made islands. Total costs are estimated to reach $10 billion, but total spending, including all the necessary additional investments, is predicted to reach $16 billion. The multiplier effect of the project is also expected to be substantial as the Ministry of Transportation, for example, is already planning to build hotels, a yacht harbor, and housing facilities on the two artificial islands.

In addition to such major national undertakings, local governments also intend to develop regional projects envisioning the creation of industrial and urban areas around high-technology and information-oriented corporations and the expansion of urban facilities in general. In Tokyo, for example, plans are evolving to build a large "Central Park" in the heart of the city, and to install underground electric cables which would replace the traditional poles. Such a project would probably require $30 billion or more because it would mean the installation of some 560 kilometers of cable over a period of 10 years. However, given the tightness of local government budgets, the realization of such plans may be impossible without substantial private-sector investments.

While the stimulating effects of such mammoth infrastructure projects on domestic demand is generally acknowledged, there is concern about the extent to which such undertakings can increase imports. A case in point is the building of the Kansai International Airport which gradually developed into another U.S.–Japan trade conflict. Washington was lobbying vigorously to obtain a share of the $8 billion project through an open bidding system. While the airport was the immediate focus of this effort, the broader goal of the United States was to get a foothold so that American companies could bid for the estimated total of $60 billion public infrastructure projects as they become available in the future.

However, under Japanese construction laws, foreign firms need permission from either the Ministry of Construction, the governor of the prefecture, or the local authorities concerned to engage in construction activities. Moreover, the traditional Japanese "designated" bidding system is quite different from the open bidding system that American and other foreign companies are used to. Under the designated bidding system, the organization in charge of a project selects about a dozen or so firms from the list of registered contractors on the basis of their established capabilities. These so-called "designated companies" then submit bids, and the lowest bidder is awarded the contract. Officials justify this restriction on eligibility as a means to prevent below-standard or unscrupulous firms from getting involved with projects and conceivably causing major problems.

The United States was concerned because by February 4, 1986, a few weeks before the original bidding deadline, the Kansai International Airport Company, which was in charge of construction, had already reached an agreement with six Japanese consulting firms to develop a master plan for the airport terminal. Furthermore, by early 1986, planning for the construction of the artificial island was also well advanced; this included the geological survey of the site and the development of the project ship, which had been awarded to domestic private and public organizations 10 years earlier. In a response to the outcry from abroad, both the Ministry of Transportation and the Ministry of Construction pointed out that while they cannot reconsider the contracts already awarded, foreign companies will be able to compete for contracts in the various other stages of the project, such as the construction of air terminal facilities and buildings and the provision of navigational assistance. Officials also pointed out that while there were more than 30 American companies among the large number of firms from abroad which had registered for the project, none of them expressed official interest in the first stage. Only firms from the Republic of Korea expressed a desire to participate in this stage.

Nonetheless, by the spring of 1986, the U.S. government and the American construction industry were highly critical of the Japanese handling of the project. The U.S. side claimed that as early as 1985, they asked the Ministry of Transportation to use an open bidding system for the project. While the ministry was noncommittal, the U.S. argued, the 1985 Action Program promised that the Japanese government would liberalize the bidding procedures on public projects. Moreover, the Americans pointed out, while U.S. companies are virtually excluded from the Kansai project, Japanese construction companies have obtained contracts in excess of $1.7 billion in the United States in 1985 alone. The Japanese argument, that the Kansai construction is being handled by a "quasi-governmental" corporation (Tokusku Kaisha) and is thus a private project, was refuted by the U.S. side, which insisted that the government owned two-thirds of the Kansai International Airport Company, and that more than 100 of the company's 150 employees came from the public sector.

The handling of the Kansai project and the imbalance in bilateral construction-trade angered Congress, and in June 1986, Japan was harshly criticized during the hearings on trade in construction services. Senate Republicans even asked the USTR to investigate whether Japan is violating international agreements by refusing to allow foreign companies to bid on the first stage of the Kansai project and by not allowing open bidding in general. In the end, through extended bilateral negotiations, the Americans obtained a commitment that U.S. companies and other construction companies would be able to bid on the future stages of the project, albeit, under the traditional Japanese designated bidding system.

The president of the Kansai International Airport Company made it clear that the system is rooted in the traditions of the Japanese construction industry, and that he would not accept demands to replace it. He pointed out that changes would create great confusion, inefficiency, and bankruptcy in the industry. His arguments were of course supported by the more than 6,700 domestic companies that had expressed interest in the airport project. The Japanese, however, agreed to designate foreign companies for phases two and three of the project if they can offer appropriate technology and demonstrate their ability to carry out the contract. Moreover, they agreed to hold a seminar on the Japanese designated bidding process in September 1986 to familiarize foreign companies with the special characteristics of the system. Prime Minister Nakasone personally instructed his transportation and construction ministries to assure that the traditional system be applied in a "reasonable manner" so that foreign companies are not discriminated against. It is noteworthy that the majority of American companies represented at the seminar were manufacturers of construction and electronic machinery; less than ten were construction companies. Of these, by the end of November, only two companies expressed the wish to participate in the first-stage construction project. At the same time, it must also be pointed out that the Japanese construction companies that received the first-stage contracts are reluctant to consider the possibility of subcontracting work to qualified foreign companies because they "see no benefits in such arangements."

At the conclusion of this special seminar, the U.S. side decided to drop its demand for a switch from the designated to the open bidding system as long as the Japanese guarantee "fair access" to the upcoming projects for all foreign firms. This contrasted with previous U.S. Administration demands that the Japanese eliminate the traditional arrangements. However, while the official U.S. attitude was conciliatory, representatives of the American construction industry expressed great dissatisfaction with the outcome of the seminar, and promised to lobby the new Congress, controlled by a Democratic majority in both the House and the Senate, for retaliatory action.

By the middle of December, the industry's dissatisfaction apparently has had some effect. In a reversal of its position following the special seminar, the U.S. Administration declared that despite the intervention by President Reagan and Prime Minister Nakasone, only "extremely limited" progress has been made in efforts to enable U.S. companies to compete for contracts of the Kansai airport project. The Administration raised the possibility of formal actions, although it did not specify what those would be. Some Washington observers believed that the new stance was an attempt to preempt harsh actions by the protectionist-minded new Congress controlled by the Democrats.

American construction companies were apparently upset because they confused the designated bidding system with what is known as the *Dango* system in Japan. This alleged bidding practice is based on prior mutual consultation under the leadership of the top construction firms which established vertical control over the other companies in the industry. Decisions concerning who can bid on projects and the final selection of the winners are all made through the *Dango*, which functions as an industry cartel.

The Fair Trade Commission investigated the *Dango* system during the early 1980s. It concluded that the system limits competition and issued an order prohibiting it. Of course, this does not mean that some firms in the industry are no longer practicing it. However, projects of the magnitude of the Kansai airport are not managed through the *Dango* system and, consequently, non-Japanese companies should have a reasonable chance to obtain contracts during the second and third stages as long as they are qualified.

As a result of consistent pressure and lengthy discussions, some American companies have in fact obtained modest contracts by early 1987. The Caterpillar Corporation was awarded a $86.7 million contract to supply construction equipment. Others, for example, the Bechtel Corporation, obtained smaller supply and consulting commitments. This brought U.S. participation to $87.4 million, undoubtedly a paltry sum in relation to the $8 billion that will be spent on the project. Nonetheless, the awards represented a breakthrough and could very well lead to additional supply, consulting and even construction contracts in the later stages of the project.

Increased Housing Investments

According to the 1986 OECD report on Japanese urban policies, the nation enjoys an excess supply of housing units in relation to the number of households, but if other factors are also taken into account, the total housing situation is much less satisfactory.[6] There are large numbers of vacant housing units comprised mainly of substandard, small wooden constructions in metropolitan areas. Moreover, when compared with other OECD nations, Japan has far fewer (320) housing units per 1,000 inhabitants than the others (around 400), and the floor area available per person (26 sq.m.) is also smaller than in most OECD countries (35–40 sq.m). Size is a particular problem in the large metropolitan areas such as Tokyo, where, according to Japan's Construction Ministry, over 30 percent of the people live in homes with less than 39 sq.m. of space. This is the result of too many people moving to metropolitan areas to seek employment and of the dramatic increase in land prices. Table 6–1 shows an international comparison of housing provisions during the first half of the 1980s.

As the data show, in comparison to a select group of OECD countries, Japan with the largest average number of persons per household (3.3) has the second fewest (323) number of houses per 1,000 inhabitants. This, combined with the small scale of the units, illustrates why housing investments are especially important for the improvement of the quality of life. Haruo Maekawa, chairman of the Maekawa Commission, stated, "The most urgent tasks at present are housing policy and urban renewal .... From the viewpoint of improving the quality of the people's living, we are more inferior to other nations in housing than in any other areas."[7]

While such views are frequently heard in Japan, it is interesting to note that according to a late 1985 survey by the Prime Minister's Office, 71.2

TABLE 6–1.   International comparison of housing provisions

	Number of houses per 1,000 persons	Average number of persons per household
Japan	323 (1983)	3.3 (1983)
Denmark	427 (1982)	2.5 (1981)
France	444 (1983)	2.8 (1982)
Germany	438 (1984)	2.4 (1981)
Netherlands	367 (1984)	2.8 (1985)
New Zealand	322 (1983)	3.1 (1981)
Sweden	441 (1980)	2.3 (1980)
United Kingdom	391 (1983)	2.7 (1981)
United States	398 (1981)	2.7 (1980)

Source: *Urban Policies in Japan* (Paris: Organization for Economic Cooperation and Development, 1986), p. 77.

percent of the Japanese people are "more or less" satisfied with current housing conditions, and only 28 percent indicated that they were dissatisfied. Moreover, officials point out, the percentage of satisfied respondents has increased with each successive survey on the topic. However, some observers suggested that such results were possible only because most of the respondents compared the present housing situation to the immediate post-World War II years, and not to the American or Western European standards which should be applied to the Japan of the 1980s. This is in line with official views expressed in the Construction Ministry's latest housing plan, which envisions the matching of Japan's housing conditions with those of the United States and Western Europe by the twenty-first century.

Japan's specific housing goals are usually announced in five-year construction plans prepared by the Construction Ministry on the basis of the Housing Construction Program Act of 1966. The plans spell out the number of units to be built, and set the guidelines concerning minimum, average, and residential environmental standards. During the 1981−85 period, the plan called for the construction of 7.7 million units, which was a decline from the 8.6 and 9.6 million units of the two previous planning periods. Typically around 40−45 percent of the units are publicly financed, and the achievement rate is about 85−90 percent. The total amount spent on housing is around 6 percent of GDP, which is the highest among all OECD countries.

The most recent five-year housing plan for the FY 1986−FY 1990 period calls for the construction of 6.7 million units, 1 million units fewer than the previous FY 1981−85 plan. The total investment is projected to be more than $500 billion at 1980 prices.[8] Of these, 2.25 million units will be financed through loans from the governmental Housing Loan Corporation, 280,000 will be built and owned by the public sector, and 130,000 units will be constructed by the Urban Development Public Corporation. About 3.3 million units will be built through public funds, which will be about 200,000 units fewer than during the previous five-year housing plan.

The Construction Ministry noted in its plan that because slightly more than 10 percent of Japanese households are made up of married couples with two children who are living in units which are smaller than the minimum size set by government standards, the newly constructed homes will have more floor space; the total space will also be expanded to accommodate aged family members. Furthermore, the ratio of owned to rented houses will change from 7:3 in the past to 6:4, indicating that more people will be renting houses instead of owning them. The reason for this is the increase in land prices, particularly in major metropolitan areas where most people want to live.

To promote new housing development, the government also intends to reduce the various regulatory requirements which in the past have seriously hampered private-sector investment. In 1983, Prime Minister Nakasone specifically instructed the Construction Ministry to develop ways to change zoning laws under which local governments promote and at the same time control urbanization to prevent disorderly development. Not surprisingly, such laws made it difficult to increase the supply of housing; consequently, the cabinet issued a directive to the Construction Ministry in 1985 (see appendix F) to advise local authorities to be more flexible about zoning changes from "urbanization control areas" to "urbanization promotion areas." As a result, by 1985 a number of prefectures, among them Hokkaido, Kyoto, and Kanagawa, reassessed their zoning policies and freed some 39,000 hectares for housing developments. Moreover, around 1,100 cities, towns, and villages have also established new development guidelines which will ease the regulation of new constructions. While progress was made, zoning requirements still pose a problem throughout most of the country and are likely to continue to hamper private-sector housing investments in the future.

In addition to zoning rules, new housing investments are also affected by the high cost of housing relative to disposable household income. According to the 1986 OECD report, based on recent construction costs and income data, the rate of increase in both is about the same in Japan as in other OECD nations. However, the housing cost-income ratio is much less favorable in Japan due to the scarcity of land and the resulting high land prices. Between July 1985 and 1986, for example, land prices throughout Japan rose by an average of 2.7 percent, with residential and commercial areas showing a 2.2 and 5.2 percent increase, respectively.[9] Not surprisingly, land prices went up most in metropolitan areas; within one year in Tokyo, for instance, commercial land prices increased by 34.4 percent and residential land prices by 18.8 percent. In the fashionable Tokyo areas such as Ota and Setagaya wards, residential land prices jumped by more than 90 percent. According to the National Land Agency, such explosions of land prices can be attributed to the influx of businessmen from abroad due to the internationalization of the Japanese economy in general and of the financial sector in particular, the growing demand for office buildings in metropolitan areas, especially Tokyo, and the growing number of luxury homes purchased in the outer suburbs by individuals who are selling their centrally located real estate holdings. Moreover, the agency claimed, increasing land speculation among investors has also contributed to the surging real estate prices. The easy-money policy of the Bank of Japan in combination with the continually high savings rates and the reduced demand for credit from the business sector, has made this possible. Some economists expressed concern that speculation may siphon funds away from the small cities and towns as well as the industrial areas where new investments are needed. They are calling for a public policy that would encourage and reward investments going into such areas.

Privatization

Both the government's administrative reform plans and the Maekawa Commission's recommendations emphasize the need to reduce the size of the public sector. Traditionally, the government owned and operated a large number of corporations. These played a major role in the economic development of the nation, particularly during the post-World War II years when rapid growth provided a financial cushion to protect even the most inefficient public corporations as long as they offered a socially necessary service.

Nippon Telegraph and Telephone (NTT), the Japanese National Railways (JNR), Japan Air Lines (JAL), and the Japan Tobacco and Salt Public Corporation (JTS) were among the largest of the public corporations. Demand for their services was rapidly growing during the 1950s and 1960s; therefore, most of them did reasonably well. However, increasing energy costs, economic slowdowns, and declining demand during the 1970s turned a number of them into money losers, contributing to the growing fiscal deficits which the government could not afford. Moreover, the emergence of new technologies such as telecommunications required more flexible and dynamic organizations than the unwieldy giants that were mired in bureaucratic red tape. At its peak, for example, the Ministry of Transportation, in charge of JNR and JAL before privatization, was known as the "Ministry of Rules and Permissions."

In 1983, the special Commission on Administrative Reform concluded that NTT, JTS, and JNR should be privatized, although the government would continue to own their stock, for a while at least. Prime Minister Nakasone, who initiated the current administrative reform drive before he took office, was personally committed to privatization as a means of bringing government deficits under control. He also viewed privatization as a way to revitalize the private sector and, in the case of NTT and JTS, to reduce bilateral trade conflicts with the United States. The Prime Minister's expectations were supported by a 1986 Bank of Japan study which concluded that privatization together with private sector investments would generate enough domestic demand to boost GNP by 1.1 percent over the next year or two. The study emphasized that the privatization of NTT alone would generate $20 billion worth of domestic demand through new investments over the next five years. Moreover, investments by financial institutions in computerized and other related services as a result of liberalization of the financial markets would also generate $15 billion worth of demand over the same period. Significantly, the study reported, part of this demand would have to be satisfied through imports, particularly from the United States whose telecommunication and information systems industries are very competitive internationally.

The first major public corporation to be privatized was NTT which changed its status as of April 1, 1985. The Diet passed the necessary legislation in December 1984 after long negotiations between Prime Minister Nakasone (supported by MITI), the telecommunications *zoku* and the Ministry of Posts and Telecommunications (MPT). At first, the *zoku* and MPT proposed a bill that would have enabled the ministry to retain much of its regulatory power and thus moderate competition in the industry. Competition, however, was important, because during the late 1970s and early 1980s, the procurement practices of NTT, which obtained almost everything from its "family" of about 1,000 domestic firms, was one of the centerpieces of the U.S.-Japan trade conflict that dragged on for some time and left bitter feelings on both sides.

The Prime Minister and his supporters eventually overcame the telecommunication *zoku's* resistance, and NTT became the largest public corporation to be turned into a private company since 1934, when the state-owned Yawata Steel Company went private and was reorganized into Nippon Steel Corporation. Today, with some 320,000 employees, NTT is Japan's largest private company, organized around dozens of wholly owned subsidiaries and joint venture partnerships. Expected to be innovative and competitive, the new subsidiaries have enough authority and are small enough to fulfill their role.

Although the legislation was passed and the organizational arrangements were made by 1985, the new private NTT still faced a number of problems. It had a difficult time with the foreign companies that wanted a share of the newly competitive telecommunications market. The problems centered on the ministerial ordinances which implemented the privatization legislation because historically, such ordinances were always drafted behind closed doors by the relevant ministries together with industry advisory councils. This tradition was in sharp contrast to the American practice of holding open hearings to shape the operational details of comprehensive legislative actions. The resulting U.S.-Japan tensions were heightened by the spring 1985 "Japan-bashing" exercise in Congress and the generally anti-Japanese mood that prevailed throughout most of Washington. However, after some additional discussions, the matter was settled, and foreign business representatives, including Americans, were invited to participate in the advisory councils.

At the end of its first year as a private company, NTT showed impressive results.[10] The company's pre-tax profits for FY 1985 were 56 percent higher than projected. While no year-to-date performance comparisons were possible because NTT used different accounting methods as a public corporation, informal estimates indicated that the FY 1985 pre-tax profits increased by 50 percent from the previous year. This placed NTT in third place behind Toyota Motor Corporation and Tokyo Electric Power as Japan's top performers. This was naturally welcomed by the government which began selling NTT shares to 1.65 million investors chosen through a national lottery in the fall of 1986. When the shares were first traded on the floor of the Tokyo Stock Exchange (TSE) in February 1987, exchange officials had to put together a special set of rules to prevent demand for stocks from getting out of hand. The government's goal was to sell 12.5 percent of the total stock every year for four years so as to bring the government's share down to 50 percent, with 30 percent ownership as the long-range target.

Japan's newly deregulated telecommunication market is very competitive. Immediately after NTT's privatization, more than five companies obtained a license in the Sector I communications business (basic common carriers), and more than 200 entered Sector II businesses in which firms have access to the basic facilities and without licensing requirements can provide a variety of services. While foreign firms cannot enter Sector I, they are free to do business in Sector II; a number of American companies are already very active in this market.

One of the most successful foreign companies is Northern Telecom of Canada. The company expects its annual sales in Japan to double in two years, and its management ascribes its good prospects to adaptability. The Canadian company developed its relations with NTT over a period of five years before obtaining its first major order, and does not expect to earn a profit before 1990. Moreover, it became a member of the trade and standards associations of the industry and keeps in touch with all relevant public and private sector organizations.

However, while the telecommunications market was quickly becoming competitive, NTT's procurement from abroad, particularly from the United States, during FY 1985 was much less encouraging. The total value of equipment and materials imported by the newly privatized corporation amounted to about $200 million in FY 1985, up 5 percent from the previous year; purchases from the United States represented $180 million or 90 percent of the total. The FY 1985 data, however, were discouraging because the rate of increase was lower than during previous years, particularly in the early 1980s.

Moreover, in October 1986, the U.S. Department of Commerce reported that during the first half of the year, U.S. telecommunications and electronics sales were lower than during the same period in 1985. This was disturbing to the United States because telecommunications and electronics were areas in which the Reagan administration expected large sales increase as a result of the MOSS negotiations. At the same time, while American officials expressed disappointment, they did not blame the results on the closed nature of the Japanese markets. They acknowledged that the markets were open but pointed out that the purchasing attitudes of the Japanese were changing slower than expected. In contrast, the Japanese argued that the deflationary effects of the rapidly appreciating yen and the resulting economic uncertainty were the major reasons for the disappointing import results. This did not mollify the Democratic members of Congress who were preparing for the November 1986 elections, and thus blamed the Reagan Administration for not realizing that Japan will not give up "its traditional way of doing business." Others claimed that the results will "...add fuel to those protectionist fires."

However, such harsh words may have been somewhat misplaced. Apart from the deflationary effects of the appreciated yen on the domestic marketplace, there were other reasons for the poor sales of the U.S. telecommunications companies.[11] While American Telephone and Telegraph (AT&T) is not representative of the entire industry, its performance in Japan to date has not escaped the attention of potential buyers of American telecommunications equipment. In 1983, AT&T was one of the first U.S. corporations to sell a major piece of telecommunications equipment to NTT. However, the equipment failed, and in early 1986 AT&T also unexpectedly withdrew from a computer service venture because of technical problems. It unfortunately also violated some basic business practices in a country where implied commitments are taken seriously. Moreover, AT&T had difficulties modifying the internal software of its station-use switching systems for Japanese end-users. To overcome all of these handicaps, AT&T signed an agreement with Fujitsu in December 1986 under which the Japanese company will provide marketing help in return for computer technology know-how. This joint undertaking may enable AT&T to reestablish itself in the marketplace and obtain major contracts in the future.

The other major privatization move involved the 80-year-old Japan

Tobacco and Salt Public Corporation which became the Japan Tobacco, Inc., on April 1, 1985. As a result, beginning on that date, foreign tobacco products could be imported, ending the government monopoly which had existed since 1904. However, the new firm remained the sole domestic producer and processor of leaf tobacco, and became a "special corporation" under the government's jurisdiction. This placed limits on how it could act; its operating plans, for example, must be approved by MOF. Nonetheless, the corporation's board of directors is free to set the budget, and MOF does not get involved with any of the operational details.

According to the original privatization plans developed during the early 1980s, the entire monopoly was to be dismantled, including tobacco processing. However, vehement opposition from the tobacco *zoku* made this impossible, and thus Prime Minister Nakasone had to be satisfied with a partial restructuring of the industry. The new company did not have an easy start; by 1986 it faced stagnant demand, increased competition from abroad, and a surplus of workers. To resolve the problems, Japan Tobacco tried to diversify into new lines of business.

The third major privatization project was the denationalization of the Japan National Railroads (JNR) as of April 1, 1987, which also turned out to be a difficult undertaking. Long admired by the rest of the world for its advanced technology and excellent customer service, JNR was a debt-ridden, 227-line railroad system operating over 14,500 miles of track and employing approximately 330,000 people. Only a few of the lines, the *Shinkansen* (bullet trains) among them, earned a profit; the others incurred a daily operating loss estimated at over $40 million in 1986. The total FY 1985 losses were a record $9 billion up 12 percent from the FY 1984, although total revenue was up 5 percent during the same time period. The major reasons for such a dismal performance were the sudden jump in retirement allowance payments, and the heavy interest payments on the staggering $150 billion long-term debt.

To keep the virtually bankrupt system functioning over the years, the government had to provide a $4 billion annual subsidy with the remainder of the deficit financed through loans from the postal savings and insurance accounts, and by special bonds. In spite of such burdens, JNR's revenue increase of 5 percent in FY 1985 indicated that the railroad system had certain strengths. Through streamlining efforts by management and employees, some lines were doing reasonably well, whereas others were quite profitable. Revenues form the *Shinkansen* bullet-train services, for instance, reached about $10 billion in FY 1985, up 14 percent form FY 1984. Even the non-*Shinkansen* passenger lines increased their revenues by 2 percent in FY 1985 over the previous year.

Critics charge that JNR's financial troubles began with the pressures to expand the system in the 1960s and 1970s, when politicians used the project contracts to expand their influence among the voters. The contractors, the politicians, and the public benefitted from the expansion, but the JNR had to pay more than 30 percent of its revenues for the massive debt accumulated through the construction. Thus, critics argue, to divert attention from the real culprits, management and workers were accused of inefficiency and now have to pay the price for past political patronage through loss of employment, early retirements, retraining, and transfers. Such charges were especially vocalized by *Kokuro* (the National Railway Workers Union), which with 220,000 members was the militant vanguard of the divided Japanese trade union movement. Although a 1948 law prohibited strikes in the public sector, the *Kokuro* mobilized its supporters on the extreme left who engaged in a series of sabotage acts against the railroad in 1986, and threatened violence if the privatization bill moved ahead in the Diet. Furthermore, at the union's extraordinary convention in October 1986, *Kokuro's* newly elected chairman stated that he would fight privatization and that he would never agree to the plan of the former union head who wanted to sign a labor-management agreement with JNR to save jobs. This split the union, and after the convention, 13 *Kokuro* chapters that had supported the former leadership, established a new organization to compromise with the JNR so that some jobs could be saved. The demise of the once powerful union was further accelerated by the resignation of more than 10,000 JNR workers every month since April 1986.

The privatization of JNR was contained in eight bills submitted to the Diet. They called for the establishment of six regional passenger and one freight company; other measures included increased management flexibility and the ability to enter nontraditional lines of business, the erasing of JNR's massive debt through the sale of assets such as land, the redemption of bonds by the government, and most of all, the reemployment of redundant workers.

Since time was of the essence in the fall of 1986, the government incorporated only the major privatization measures into the bills and left the details to ministerial ordinances to be issued later. Nonetheless, to deal with the drastic labor cuts expected, the JNR established Human Resource Centers throughout the country in 1986 to employ redundant workers in various revenue-saving and cost-saving activities on a temporary basis. It also provided for the early retirement of some 20,000 workers, and promised to help those displaced and looking for jobs. Prime Minister Nakasone personally appealed to other public sector companies to employ 30,000 of the discharged employees, to JNR-affiliated enterprises to provide jobs for 21,000, and to the private sector to accept another 10,000.

The privatization of JNR and its division into several regional companies was not seen by the government as an immediate cure for the financial deterioration which took place over decades. Of the six regional passenger service lines, only the Tokai Company, which operates the highly profitable *Tokaido Shinkansen* between Tokyo and Osaka, is expected to generate immediate profits. All others are expected to lose money, at least for a while. The worst performers are likely to be the traditional money losers on the islands of Hokkaido, Shikoku, and Kyushu; in the past, these lines generated 7.2 percent of JNR's total revenue but accounted for 42.2 percent of its total loss.

In addition to the privatization of NTT, JTS, and JNR, the Transportation Ministry decided to also privatize Japan Airlines (JAL) beginning in 1987. This is expected to increase management flexibility, though the government will continue to be involved with the airline by providing guarantees for its bond issues. Furthermore, the 48 million shares presently held by the office of the Minister of Finance will eventually be sold to the public, but foreign ownership will be limited to one-third of the total.

As part of the deregulation of the airline industry, the Transport Policy Council has recommended that additional airlines be permitted to enter the field of regularly scheduled flights which were a virtual JAL monopoly in the past. Thus, All-Nippon-Airways (ANA) obtained permission to begin international flights between Japan and Guam as well as to and from the United States in 1986. Moreover, the Council proposed that the domestic airline business be opened to unrestricted competition, thus placing Japan's second major transportation mode under the free market system. Not surprisingly, during 1986 all airline companies submitted a variety of demands and requests concerning deregulation to the Transport Policy Study Council, the LDP's Special Committee on Measures for Civil Aviation, and most of all, to the *unyuzoku* or transportation *zoku*.

Increased Basic Research

According to Prime Minister Nakasone's vision, increased private sector vitality should be one of the major forces behind the internationalization of the Japanese economy. All the policy options explored so far, in some form or another, provide motivation for the private sector to devote its resources and energies to the task ahead. However, an additional policy option, not considered by the Maekawa Commission, increased research and development, could also be particularly important in this respect.

By 1986, Japan was already in the process of shifting from its traditional strategy of adopting the technologies developed in other countries to laying the foundations for its own long-term basic research program. According to MITI officials, the import of foreign technologies was helpful in catching up with the industrialized countries and in becoming a technology-intensive economy, but is no longer enough to sustain the nation through the new competition in, for example, electronics, biotechnology, optical engineering, and new materials.[12]

In contrast to widely held beliefs, post-World War II research and development received only a small amount of government funding in Japan. Over the years, less than 30 percent of the nation's total R&D was funded by the government. In comparison, the U.S. government and other industrialized Western nations provided between 45 and 55 percent of their nations' total research and development costs. Of course, the Japanese government's relatively small share was partially due to the lack of major defense-related research and development, which in the case of America and Western Europe played a major role. Table 6–2 shows a comparison of the sources and magnitudes of research and development expenditures in Japan and the United States over the last 15 years.

The promotion of increased basic research began in earnest with the Exploratory Research for Advanced Technology (ERATO) project in

TABLE 6–2. The sources and magnitudes of research and development expenditures in Japan and the United States in selected years

		R & D expenditures (U.S. $ million)	Percent of national income	Percent financed by public fund
Japan	1970	5,033[a]	1.96%	25.2%
	1980	19,721[a]	2.35	25.8
	1984	30,217[a]	2.99	20.8
USA	1970	26,134	2.89	57.0
	1980	35,213	2.68	47.1
	1984	95,925	2.94	46.6

[a] U.S. dollar figures are calculated at the 1984 annual exchange rates of the IMF, *International Financial Statistics*. U.S. $ 1.00 = Y 237.5.

Source: *Japan 1986, An International Comparison* (Tokyo: Keizai Koho Center, 1986), p. 26.

1981. The program is managed by the Research and Development Corporation of Japan which, in turn, is overseen by the government's Science and Technology Agency. The basic aim of the program is to promote scientific discovery through the funding of small groups of researchers who are engaged in interdisciplinary scientific investigations for a maximum of five years. However, while moderately successful, the program is not stimulating large-scale basic research; the private sector, for example, spends only about 3 percent of the total earmarked for basic research.

To promote basic research, the government, through MITI and the Ministry of Posts and Telecommunications (MPT), founded the Japan Key Technology Center in late 1985.[13] The center is expected to provide and manage a system of investments and loans to supply the needed "risk money." Japan Key-Tech, as it is known, does not own and operate any research and development (R&D) facilities; its major activities consist of arranging for capital investments in joint research and development activities between national and private sector research institutes. Moreover, it manages commissioned research and the Japan Trust International (an international research cooperation agency) as well as collects and disseminates research information.

Japan Key-Tech is supported by dividends generated by the government-held stock of the privatized former public corporations NTT and Japan Tobacco, Inc., and through funds provided by the Japan Development Bank, which is affiliated with MITI. Because MITI and MPT formed the center, basic research is promoted in areas which are somehow related to mining or manufacturing or telecommunications and broadcasting activities. MPT had a particularly strong reason to be associated with the center because it lost its research facitility as a consequence of the 1985 privatization of NTT.

Japan Key-Tech invests only in new research companies which are jointly established by two or more private companies for basic R&D projects. It invests up to 70 percent of the total funds; the remaining 30 percent must be provided by the joint investors. The projects are selected on the basis of the level of technology and potential profitability. Eventual intellectual property rights are held by the joint company and not the center.

By mid-1986 the center directly sponsored 25 projects. Eight of these focused on the development of software for information and communication systems in local areas, whereas the remaining 17 projects involved pure basic research. Of these, 10 were related to mining and industry, 2 were involved with new materials, 2 in biotechnology, and 5 in electronics. The seven others dealt with communication technology, while four focused on projects of the Advanced International Telecommunications Research Institute and involved such topics as automatic translation telephones, audiovisual mechanics, and optical telecommunications. All of the projects are scheduled to involve 7 to 10 years of research.

In addition to its direct investment assistance, the center also provides loans to individual private sector companies. The amount is usually about $3 million over a period of up to 10 years. Altogether, 60 projects have already been financed; of those, 34 are in mining and industry and 24 in telecommunications. The loans cover up to 70 percent of the total R&D cost and are made at an interest rate of 6.05 percent for 10 years, with payments beginning in the sixth year of the project. If the project is a success, the borrower must repay all the interest for the first five years together with the interest for the remaining repayment period. The loans are available to any company, including those established with foreign capital, as long as the research is done in Japan.

To diffuse basic research activities throughout the country, in May 1986 the Diet passed the Law for the Provisional Measures Relating to the Promotion of the Construction of Specific Facilities or the *Minkatsu* Law. as it is known. This measure is designed to encourage local governments and concerned business groups to use private sector capital to construct special facilities, such as regional R&D cores for joint research between business and academic groups, and between different industries to promote regional economic development. In this fashion the government wants to avoid the centralization of R&D activities in major metropolitan areas which could result in unbalanced growth, including major increases in urban land prices.

Concurrent to these public efforts are private sector moves to promote basic research. Out of competitive necessity and the desire to survive, heavy industrial companies such as shipbuilders and steel producers are shifting toward higher levels of technology during the second half of the 1980s. Pressured by declining demand throughout the world, the sharply appreciated yen, and the relentless competition by the Newly Industrialized Countries (NICs), these traditional mainstays of Japanese industry are showing impressive flexibility. While laying off workers for the first time ever, they are diversifying into such high-technology ventures as semiconductor materials and minicomputers. Nippon Steel, for example, established a wholly owned subsidiary (NSC Electronic Corporation) to produce silicon wafers, and also set up a joint venture with a new American manufacturer of minicomputers. Initially, Nippon Steel is only marketing the minicomputers but later plans to manufacture them under a licensing agreement. Among the shipbuilding companies, Mitsubishi Heavy Industries became involved in aerospace technology, nuclear energy equipment, and other high-technology ventures. Kawasaki Heavy Industries diversified into the building of geodetic satellites and, through a joint venture with another corporation, produces components for jet engines.

While Japan's move into basic research and high technology is necessary for the internationalization of the economy, it may also create a new set of trade conflicts with the United States. In a recent study, the Joint Economic Committee of Congress warned that the U.S. high-technology sector is losing in competition with Japan.[14] Others have pointed out that the Japanese are already ahead in consumer electronics, advanced materials and robotics, and are emerging as tough competitors in computers, telecommunications, home and office automation, biotechnology, and medical instruments. The potential significance of this development is illustrated by a 1986 survey of Japan's biotechnology industry which has shown that it expects the domestic market for biotechnology-based food and pharmaceutical products to grow by an average of 25 percent annually until the year 2000. This would increase the 1986 market size about 25 times.

At the same time, according to figures released by the Management and Coordination Agency in December 1986, Japan was still second in total technological research spending behind the United States in FY 1985 (ending in March 1986). While it thus surpassed the Soviet Union in total spending for the first time, it also lagged behind America in the spending per researcher which amounted to less than 60 percent of that of the United States.

However, while there is concern in Washington and throughout much of American industry about the emergence of Japanese high-technology competition, the recent R&D spending patterns of major American and Japanese corporations still show the United States ahead. In 1985, America's large Fortune 500 corporations have spent more on research and development in terms of both the absolute amounts and, more importantly, as a percentage of sales than their Japanese counterparts. Analysis of the data show that the average amount spent as a percentage of sales was 6.36 percent for the American companies and 5.27 for the Japanese. While this is no guarantee of continued American leadership in most of the high-tech industries, the dire warnings about a decline in U.S. high-tech capability may be somewhat exaggerated. Table 6—3 illustrates this conclusion.

Nonetheless, concerned about the possibility of a new round of U.S.– Japan trade conflicts, in 1986 the Ministry of Foreign Affairs commissioned the Gallup Company to conduct a survey on American attitudes toward Japan's increasing international competitiveness in high technology. Ac-

TABLE 6–3.   Research and development expenditures of Japanese and
American Fortune 500 corporations: 1985 (in millions of U.S. dollars)

Japanese corporations	R & D expenditures	R & D expenditures as a percentage of sales
Toyota Motors	1,140	4.8
Hitachi	1,071	5.3
Matsushita Electric	0,800	4.2
Toshiba	0,700	5.3
Nissan Motor	0,620	4.3
NEC	0,526	5.8
Honda Motor	0,439	4.1
Sony	0,399	7.9
Fujitsu	0,371	7.2
Mitsubishi Electric	0,307	3.8
American corporations		
General Motors	3,625	3.8
IBM	3,457	6.9
AT & T	2,210	6.3
Ford Motor	2,018	3.8
Dupont	1,144	3.9
ITT	1,085	9.1
General Electric	1,069	3.8
Eastman Kodak	0,976	9.2
United Technologies	0,916	6.1
Digital Equipment	0,717	10.7

Sources: Japanese figures from *Tokyo Business Today* (April 1986), p. 21; U.S. figures reprinted from June 23, 1986, issue of *Business Week* by special permission; © 1986 by McGraw-Hill, Inc.

cording to officials, the survey found that 58 percent of America's intellectuals and businessmen believe that such a development is in the interest of the United States, but this percentage was down eight points from 1985. At the same time, 29 percent saw Japan's efforts as a threat to the United States; this was a 6 percent increase over 1985. The challenge was seen as particularly grave in the area of computers and semiconductors; more than 50 percent of the respondents predicted that this would lead to major bilateral trade conflicts in the future.

Reduced Working Hours

One of the more controversial policy options to increase domestic demand and, thus, to promote the internationalization of the economy is the reduction of working hours to increase leisure time. This option is based on the proposition that the Japanese have lived under the threat of economic deprivation for such a long time that even today when they are well off, they do not know how to relax and enjoy life. Critics of the Japanese lifestyle point out that the word for leisure, *yoka*, means "excess time" which implies the misuse of time. Moreover, they argue that *reja*, as the English word "leisure" is pronounced, does not fit the experience of most Japanese, and thus is not understood. Most of all, they claim, many Japanese still do not feel confident that the nation's prosperity can be preserved without continued sacrifice and diligence, and believe that the free time they already have is enough.

There is evidence to support such views. In a 1986 survey by the Office of the Prime Minister, 56 percent of the respondents stated that they are satisfied with the leisure time currently available to them.[15] Although 41 percent wanted more free time, the percentage of those who were satisfied with the present arrangements increased by 3 percent over the last poll taken in 1982. Expectedly, more than half of those who wanted more free time were under 30 years of age, representing the new generation.

A current study by the Ministry of Labor confirms that young Japanese "salarymen" differ from their parents in that they are increasingly disenchanted with work.[16] According to the findings, about 33 percent of the workers under the age of 30 have already changed jobs, and about the same percentage plan to do so in the future. Moreover, 75 percent consider work simply as a means of making a living; work as a means to fulfill the purpose of life and as a civic duty was cited by only 10 percent of the respondents.

At the same time, views on the general importance of leisure activity appears to be undergoing a change among both the younger and older generations. A recent survey by the Office of the Prime Minister showed that in contrast to past years, when the procurement of housing was ahead of leisure, by 1985, 28 percent of the Japanese considered leisure activities more important than the provision of housing (25 percent) and securing food (15 percent).[17] Thus, leisure is now seen as a more important activity than the procurement of basic necessities of life by over a quarter of the population regardless of age. This seems to contradict the results of the 1986 poll concerning satisfaction with available leisure time, in which the younger and older generations expressed differing opinions. The discrepancy, however, is not a contradiction because the 1986 findings probably reflect a short-time response to the deflationary effects of the appreciation of the yen, whereas the 1985 results imply that a slow but steady society-wide change in basic attitudes is under way.

Meanwhile, international comparisons still show that of all industrialized nations, the Japanese work the hardest. A historical overview shows that Japanese diligence reached its peak in 1960 with 2,432 annual working hours, declined to 2,064 hours as a result of the first oil crisis in 1973, and then gradually rose again from 1974 through 1985. By 1985, the average annual working hours in Japan reached to 2,110 hours, whereas in the United States and Great Britain, workers spent 1,850 hours on the job, and in France only 1,650.[18]

Not surprisingly, the Japanese also put in the longest workweeks during the first half of the 1980s. Although only 22.1 percent of all companies employing 30 or more people maintained a six-day week and 77.1 percent some type of five-day work week, only 27 percent offered a real, two-day weekend on a continual basis. About 16.7 percent provided five-day weeks twice a month, 14.7 percent once a month, 10.9 percent every other weekend, 7.7 percent three times per month.[19] In comparison, the over-whelming majority of American and Western European workers enjoy real five-day workweeks on a continual basis.

Moreover the data indicate that during the early 1980s, Japanese workers also received fewer paid annual holidays (10) than Americans (19), British (23), and French (26). Of all Japanese employees with 20 or more years of service, 91 percent received 20 days or less annual vacation, only 5.1 percent received 21 to 26 days, that is, the average for all British and French workers, regardless of the number of years of service.

Although a basic societywide change in attitudes toward leisure is under way, the pace of change is slow. In 1986, for example, the average number of vacation days taken by workers in the manufacturing industries was 7.6 days, in other industries (mainly white-collar) only 5.1 days, amounting to an increase of 0.5 and 0.7 days, respectively, over 1985. This confirms the Labor Ministry's claim that only about 40–45 percent of all Japanese workers take all their annual paid leave entitlement, and that the majority continue to go back to work before they are required.

The Maekawa Commission recommended a reduction of the average annual working hours, and promoted the idea of longer vacations and a five-day workweek as a means of increasing leisure time, and thereby domestic demand for products and services. Such efforts are not new; in 1980, the Labor Ministry developed a Plan to Promote the Reduction of Working Hours which called for a decrease of average annual working hours to 2,000 by 1985. The plan was predicated primarily on the demographic changes engulfing Japan, that is, the evolution of the "aging society," and a projected increase in the workforce from 60 to 65 million between 1985 and 2000. It also considered the necessity to increase domestic demand to reduce international trade conflicts and to improve the quality of life. However, the plan failed because beginning with the 1973 energy crisis, labor productivity began to level off; 3 million redundant workers were carried by firms which instead of hiring new employees increased overtime when economic conditions improved. However, undaunted by its failure, the Ministry developed a second plan in 1985 which called for a reduction of average annual working hours to 2,000 by 1990. The plan envisions a revision of the 1947 Labor Standards Act which is based on an 8–hour day and a 48–hour workweek, because to achieve the 1990 goal, weekly work hours must be reduced from 48 to 45. Moreover, annual vacation days need to be increased from the current 6–20 to a 10–20 day range.

Revision of the 1947 Act is necessary, because Labor Ministry officials found that a decline in overtime does not significantly contribute to increased consumption. Only a shortening of the scheduled hours worked as mandated by the Act would significantly increase consumption expenditures because a permanent five-day workweek would trigger far more leisure activity than an uncertain and temporary reduction in overtime.

The Labor Ministry's new plan could provide a significant demand boost because leisure activity goods and services represent a major part of Japan's growing service market. According to MITI's Leisure Development Center, a government entity unique to Japan, in 1985 the leisure market amounted to over $300 billion or more than 20 percent of GNP. Moreover, the Center estimated that a general 40–hour or 5–day workweek could increase this market by a minimum of $20 billion or 6.6 percent annually.

In light of such expansive estimates, it is not surprising that in June 1986 the government termed the realization of reduced working hours and increased leisure time a "national task." Prime Minister Nakasone was also actively promoting the reduction of working hours, the introduction of the five-day workweek, and an increase in annual vacation time. To set a good example, he and Deputy Prime Minister Kanemaru took relatively long summer vacations. The Prime Minister took 20 days in four installments, and the Deputy Prime Minister vacationed for just over 20 days. Moreover, for the first time, there were no scheduled cabinet meetings between August 16 and 25, so that all other ministers could take some time off. This made it possible for government workers to take longer vacations than usual as well.

In addition, the government decided to adopt a five-day workweek for its employees during alternate weeks on an experimental basis for one year, beginning November 30, 1986. This was significant because for many years, the government maintained that it could not adopt a five-day workweek until other public service institutions such as banks did. Following the banks' first move in 1981, government employees got one Saturday a month off; when banks added another Saturday during the summer of 1986, the government followed, thereby sending a clear signal to the private sector that it meant what it said. To expedite matters, the Labor Ministry asked one of its advisory councils to develop a set of recommendations concerning the reduction of working hours.

The council concluded its discussions by early December 1986, and proposed a revision of the Labor Standards Act so that statutory working hours would be reduced from the current 48 hours to 40 hours in three stages. During these stages, working hours would be cut first to 46, then to 44, and ultimately to 40 hours per week. Companies would, however, be allowed to exceed the legal limit occasionally as long as they maintain an average of 40 hours per week over three-month periods. Moreover, the council recommended that small-sized and medium-sized firms with less than 300 employees be given a grace period of three years to switch to the new system, and that the minimum number of holidays be increased from the current 6 to 10 days in all organizations.

While the council did not set a timetable for the implementation of its recommendations, the Labor Ministry proposed introducing the 46–hour workweek as of April 1, 1988. Of course, the final shape of the revisions and the implementation timetable must be worked out by the LDP policy-formulating apparatus through the usual consensus-seeking process. The support of various interest groups, however, is not necessarily assured; many Japanese are not ready to change the traditional work ethic which has served them so well in the past. They are concerned that the *yamato damashii* or the Japanese spirit is declining and that the *shirake sedai* or the new sedate generation does not exhibit enough creative drive. Others, such as some senior business executives and even workers, are cool to the idea because it would change cost structures and established work patterns. The owners and managers of small-sized to medium-sized businesses are particularly concerned that the practice of reduced working hours and increased vacations is too costly. Their potential resistance is important because not only do they represent 99.4 percent of all business establishments and employ over 81 percent of all working people but they are also a key political base for the LDP, and thus, are influential.[20] Moreover, Ministry of Labor officials point out, not even all of the employees of small-sized and medium-sized businesses support the idea because they do not want to see their wages reduced. They are concerned because since the early 1970s, their wages have been declining relative to the wages of those working for large corporations.

The appreciation of the yen during 1986 and increasing competition from the Asian Pacific region's newly industrialized countries (NICs) have added to their concerns. Because of the stronger yen, many small-sized and medium-sized businesses are already in deep trouble; quite a few are on the verge of bankruptcy. If shorter working hours and longer vacations are enforced, critics of the recommendations argue, businesses will not only go under but the fierce competition coming from Taiwan and Korea will irreparably damage Japan's international competitiveness in the long run. Of course, some of these arguments are self-serving, but nonetheless, they cannot be ignored and will play a major role throughout the consensus formulation process.

The LDP's Labor Committee assigned the recommendations to its Subcommittee on Working Hours for further study in December 1986. While the subcommittee showed support for the proposal to revise the Act, it indicated that it may be better to first try a 44–hour workweek beginning three years after the revision, before switching to the 40–hour workweek. Moreover, the chairman of the subcommittee pointed out, small-sized to medium-sized enterprises should not be exempt from the proposed system because this would encourage them to postpone the changes.

Thus, by the beginning of 1987, the stage was set for the lengthy and difficult consensus seeking process concerning the revision of the 1947 Labor Standards Act. While the revision itself was a foregone conclusion, the details needed to be worked out against the backdrop of slower economic growth, increasing international competition, pressures from abroad, and conflicting domestic interests. Nonetheless, Labor Ministry officials were optimistic that their second plan, released in 1985, would become a reality by 1990, thereby increasing both domestic demand and the quality of life of the Japanese people.

Notes

1. The effective tax rate which includes both national and local taxes was calculated on the assumption that corporations reserve 30 percent of their pre-tax profits for dividend payments.
2. Because of rounding, the tax cut and increase do not add up to the same total.
3. All statistics are reported from *40 Years Since the End of World War II: On the Threshold of the Age of Maturity* (Tokyo: Economic Planning Agency, 1986), pp. 192–193.

4. *Urban Policies in Japan* (Paris: Organization for Economic Cooperation and Development, 1986).
5. Of the $23 billion reflationary package announced on September 19,1986, about $13 billion will be spent on public works in FY 1986.
6. OECD, *Urban Policies, op.cit.*, p. 75.
7. *The Journal of Commerce* (July 7, 1986), p. 4A.
8. Of the $23 billion reflationary package announced on September 19, 1986, about $4.5 billion is being spent on the improvement of home financing schemes.
9. *The Japan Economic Journal* (October 11, 1986), p. 1.
10. *The Japan Economic Journal* (June 7, 1986), p. 23.
11. *Business Week* (November 24, 1986), p. 102.
12. For a detailed discussion of these issues, see *Technological Innovation and the Changing Industrial Society* (Tokyo: Japan Committee for Economic Development (*Keizai Doyukai*), 1985).
13. The legal basis for the center, jointly formed by MITI and MPT, was provided by the 1985 Law for the Facilitation of Research in Fundamental Technologies.
14. *The U.S. Trade Position in High Technology: 1980—1986* (Washington, D.C.: The Joint Economic Committee of the United States Congress, October 1986).
15. *The Japan Times* (April 28, 1986), p. 2.
16. *The Japan Economic Journal* (August 9, 1986), p. 24.
17. *Survey on People's Life* (Tokyo: Office of the Prime Minister, 1985).
18. Ministry of Labor, internal documents; Tokyo, March 1986. The data refer to firms employing 30 or more persons. When comparing Japanese working hours with those of other nations it is, however, important to consider that the lower rate of absenteeism and the fewer days lost to strike in Japan affect the total.
19. Ministry of Labor, internal documents; Tokyo, March 1986.
20. *White Paper on Small and Medium Enterprises in Japan, 1985* (Tokyo: Ministry of International Trade and Industry, 1985), pp. 89—90.

7 THE INTERNATIONAL POLICY OPTIONS

Prime Minister Nakasone's blue-ribbon Economic Council recommended that Japan's record 1985 current account/GNP ratio of 3.7 percent, and the expected more than 4 percent 1986 ratio be reduced to around 1.5 to 2 percent by FY 1992. While this can partially be achieved through the implementation of the domestic policy options to increase demand, and thus imports, other measures such as increased foreign direct investment and foreign aid are also needed. To illustrate the point, the elimination of the 1986 current account surplus of $86 billion alone would have required a 33 percent domestic economic growth rate.

Foreign Direct Investment

In view of this, the Maekawa Commission recommended that Japan more than double its foreign direct investment as a percentage of Gross Domestic Product (GDP) by 1992, which would require an average annual growth rate of about 10 percent, a realistic expectation considering that during the first half of the 1980s, such investments were growing at an annual rate of about 14 percent. This, the Commission emphasized, would increase employment abroad and contribute to the economic growth of the developing nations. Moreover, in the long run, expanded foreign direct investment would be a more effective way to moderate the trade conflicts caused by the huge current and trade account surpluses than the various earlier market access measures. To this end, the Commission suggested that the government develop new tax, financial, and insurance incentives to encourage and protect Japanese direct investments throughout the developing world.

The Maekawa Commission's recommendations were supported by a report of the Mitsubishi Bank released in the fall of 1986. The report pointed out that Japanese corporations have already stepped up their direct investments abroad as a result of the rapid erosion of their export competitiveness due to the sharp appreciation of the yen. If this continues at the same pace as during the previous five years ending in FY 1985 (March 31, 1986), the accumulated total of such investments by 1990 may be twice as much as that by the end of FY 1985, or about $168 billion. This would reduce Japan's current account surplus by about $22 billion over the next few years.

During the first 20 years after World War II, Japan's accumulated foreign direct investment amounted to a paltry $6.7 billion, an annual average of about $330 million. By 1984, the sum increased to $72.4 billion and during the 1970s, the annual average ranged from over $2 billion in 1974 to almost $5 billion in 1979. Beginning in the early 1980s, the annual averages grew to $8−10 billion, reflecting Japan's newly acquired economic power.[1] Table 7−1 provides a summary overview of these developments.

Although the absolute amounts invested abroad increased on a yearly basis, foreign direct investment as a share of GNP represented only 3.6 percent in 1984 whereas the comparable level for the United States was 6.4, for the Federal Republic of Germany 7.3, and for the United Kingdom 17.2 percent, respectively.

Moreover, while by 1984 Japan's accumulated direct foreign investment amounted to $37.9 billion, or 6.9 percent of the world's total which moved Japan from fourth place in 1983 to third ahead of West Germany, the nation was still lagging behind the United States and the United Kingdom. Table 7−2 provides a comparison of the global shares of foreign direct investments of selected countries as of the end of 1984.

According to the prediction of a private advisory panel to the Economic Planning Agency, Japan's direct foreign investment is expected to rival that of the United States and of the United Kingdom by the year 2000, with the accumulated total estimated to reach $300 billion.[2] This would represent about 20 percent of total Japanese manufacturing capacity as against the current capacity abroad of only 2.4 percent, and assumes an average annual increase of almost 14 percent, the average growth rate in foreign direct investment achieved between 1978−1984.

TABLE 7−1.   Japan's foreign direct investments: FY 1951−FY 1985

Years	No. of cases	Amount[a] (U.S. $ millions)
1951−1972	6,411	6,773
1973	3,093	3,494
1974	1,912	2,396
1975	1,591	3,280
1976	1,652	3,462
1977	1,761	2,806
1978	2,393	4,598
1979	2,694	4,995
1980	2,442	4,693
1981	2,563	8,932
1982	2,549	7,703
1983	2,754	8,145
1984	2,499	10,155
1985	2,613	12,217
Total	36,927	83,649

[a] Figures are the accumulated value of approvals and notification.
Source: *Japan 1986: An International Comparison* (Tokyo: Keizai Koho Center, 1986), p. 56.

TABLE 7−2.   Foreign direct investments of selected countries: end of 1984

Country	Amount (U.S. $ billions)	Share (%)
USA	233.4	42.5
UK	85.3	15.5
Japan[a]	37.0	6.9
Germany, FR	36.6	6.7
Canada	31.3	5.7
Netherlands	31.2	5.7
Other	93.3	17.0
World, total	549.0	100.0

[a] Figure is for external assets and liabilities of Japan.
Source: *Japan 1986: An International Comparison* (Tokyo: Keizai Koho Center, 1986), p. 58.

Investment data released by JETRO in early 1987 indicates that such predictions are quite realistic. Spurred by the sharp increase in the value of the yen, foreign direct investment amounted to $12.5 billion during the first eight months of FY 1986, up 65 percent from the same period a year ago. Thus, four months before the end of FY 1986, the amount of foreign direct investment already exceeded the previous alltime high of $12.2 billion achieved in all of FY 1985 which, in turn, was up by 20.3 percent from FY 1984.

In the past, particularly during the 1960s and 1970s, slightly over 70 percent of all Japanese foreign direct investments were made in Latin America and Asia. Moreover, because during these years of rapid economic growth a stable supply of natural resources was important, the majority of investments were resource-related. To the extent that manufacturing investments were made, the motives for such investments were the protectionist import substitution policies of a number of countries, and in the case of the NICs of the Asian Pacific rim, the relatively high productivity and low wages of the labor force.

Beginning in the late 1970s, most investments in the developing nations went into manufacturing. The systematic resource and energy conservation efforts were successful, and thus, a stable supply of resources was no longer a dominant concern. At the same time, starting in the early 1980s, more manufacturing and service industry investments, such as in finance, were also made in the industrialized nations. This was partially due to the reduction in the relative wage differentials between Japan and these nations, and in the case of the United States and Western Europe, to the increasing protectionist attitudes and trade conflicts generated by the bilateral trade imbalances. Other reasons included the high rate of economic growth in America, particularly in the Southern and Western states which began around 1983, as well as the pre-1987 tax incentives such as the investment credits and Accelerated Cost Recovery System introduced by the Reagan Administration in 1981. As a consequence, by the mid-1980s, over one-third of total annual foreign direct investment was made in the United States. Table 7−3 illustrates the regional distribution of accumulated Japanese foreign direct investment as of the end of FY 1985.

Industrial patterns of foreign direct investment also began to change during the second half of the 1970s. Earlier, the textile and machinery industries, including machine tools, electric appliances, and transportation machinery, accounted for more than 20 percent of the total. By the early 1980s, however, the machinery industry alone increased its share to around 40 percent whereas the textile industry's share declined to less than 5 percent of the total.

TABLE 7−3. Japan's foreign direct investment by country: as of March 31, 1986

	No. of cases	Amount[a] (U.S. $ millions)
USA	12,525	25,290
Indonesia	1,381	8,423
Panama	2,374	6,440
Brazil	1,296	4,587
Australia	1,209	3,621
Hong Kong	2,405	2,931
UK	1,048	3,141
Liberia	637	2,455
Singapore	1,775	2,269
Canada	714	1,675
Korea, Rep. of	1,282	1,683
Saudi Arabia/Kuwait	4	1,268
Mexico	238	1,330
Netherlands	294	1,687
Total	36,927	83,649

[a] Figures are the accumulated value of approvals and notification.
Source: *Japan 1986: An International Comparison* (Tokyo: Keizai Koho Center, 1986), p. 56.

Due to the sharp appreciation of the yen and the general expansion of international finance, Japanese foreign direct investment underwent additional changes during 1985−1986. As part of the total increase of 20.3 percent over FY 1984, investments by financial and insurance companies jumped by 82.5 percent, and those by trading houses, channel of distribution intermediaries and advertising agencies by 28.9 percent. According to Ministry of Finance officials, this was mostly due to the revised Australian banking law which allowed foreign banks to establish subsidiaries, thus opening the way for the Bank of Tokyo and four other Japanese banks to move abroad. Another reason for the surge was the establishment of finance and insurance operations by manufacturers and trading companies that wanted to provide better services to their foreign marketing organizations.

In contrast, investments by manufacturing companies declined by 6.1 percent during 1985 1986, the second successive annual decrease caused chiefly by the retrenchment of textile, chemical, and metal firms, although investments by transportation equipment and electric appliance manufacturers, particularly in Europe and North America, increased. According to MITI officials, most manufacturers were uncertain about the unstable exchange rates, and wanted to wait until the dollar–yen relationship became more predictable.

The pressures on Japanese manufacturers to invest abroad increased throughout 1986, particularly as the yen appreciated to below 180 against the U.S. dollar, and it became clear that the trend would not be reversed. Moreover, nations resisting Japanese exports, particularly in the European Community, demanded local manufacture instead of exports. The capture of Congress by the Democrats in the fall 1986 elections also indicated that some form of protectionist legislation may be on its way in the United States by 1987. Thus, foreign direct investment gradually became not only economically feasible but politically necessary. According to the Long-Term Credit Bank of Japan, during the second half of 1986 more than 30 percent of all manufacturing companies entertained plans to move abroad.

The hard-hit consumer electronics industry was among the first to plan large-scale foreign investments during the second half of the 1980s. In late 1986 Toshiba Corporation, for example, announced a series of moves to reorganize and strengthen its global audiovisual products operations. Among other things, the plans call for the establishment of a new manufacturing plant in Mexico and the expansion of an existing operation in Singapore. Matsushita Electric Industrial Company will manufacture VCRs in Spain in response to the demands of the European Community to locally produce the products it sells in the Community. The company was also considering a plant in France and in Washington state. Sony Corporation built an audio-cassette tape manufacturing facility in northern Italy which is its fifth subsidiary in Europe. Sanyo Electric Company moved into Malaysia and set up an audio equipment manufacturing joint-venture with a West German subsidiary of ITT, an American company.

The current wave of Japanese foreign direct investment is not limited to medium-sized to large-sized firms. Investments by small to medium companies (less than 300 employees) amount to about 20–25 percent of the annual total. They are undertaken to either reduce their comparative disadvantage in labor-intensive production or to continue the subcontracting relationships with the large corporations that have moved abroad. According to the Small Business Administration Agency of MITI, between April and September 1986, it provided foreign direct investment consulting services to more than 130 small to medium firms, far more than ever before. Moreover, by the end of 1986, officials had advised more than 300 firms, a threefold increase over 1985. Most of the requests were for advice on investing in Korea, Taiwan, Singapore, and Thailand to take advantage of the lower labor costs. About 20 percent of the requests concerned moves to the United States to continue subcontracting relationships.

These trends have raised concerns about the "hollowing" of Japanese industry. According to MITI estimates, increased foreign direct investment may reduce domestic employment by about 560,000 jobs while generating more than 2 million new positions abroad by the year 2000. Of the new jobs, about 1,026,000 could be created in Indonesia, 840,000 in the United States, and 86,000 in the Republic of Korea. Some private sector economists, however, disagree with such estimates and believe that if the current investment trends continue, job losses could exceed the projected 560,000 and that more than 2.5 million new jobs may be generated abroad by the turn of the century. According to nonpublished estimates by the staff of a major private research organization, by the fall of 1986, of the slightly more than 14 million people employed in the manufacturing sector, about 900,000 were surplus workers. Their dismissal would increase the unemployment rate from 2.8 to over 4 percent.

Most of Japan's industrial captains believe that the boom to expand abroad is a lasting phenomenon. In a 1986 survey conducted by *The Japan Economic Journal*, 38 percent of the corporate heads surveyed believed that foreign direct investments will continue to grow over a long period of time even if the yen weakens somewhat.[3] Almost 60 percent believed that the boom will continue over the long run, although it may be subject to exchange rate swings. Thus, well over 90 percent of Japan's corporate leaders expect the trend to continue and only a very small minority thinks that it will end as soon as the yen exchange rate is "corrected," whatever that may mean.

With respect to the domestic impact of increased foreign direct investment, 71 percent of the industrial leaders believed that some "hollowing" of certain industries may occur; 5 percent argued that entire industries will be subject to such adverse effects whereas only 20 percent expected no hollowing at all. The industries most affected will be the automobile and electronic industries, textiles, and nonferrous metals and metal products, in this order. It is interesting to note that both the automobile and electronics industries have been among Japan's internationally most competitive industries since the mid-1970s, and they were the mainstay of the export drive of those years.

About 40 percent of the corporate leaders believed that the "hollowing" process will start during 1987–1990 while 10 percent did not expect it before 1990–1991. When queried about what the government should do to prevent the process, most argued for income, housing, and investment tax reductions, but only a few believed that additional interest rate reductions would be helpful. A number of respondents, however, wanted the government to promote investments in up-to-date manufacturing and information industries rather than in traditional public construction projects such as roads and bridges.

Members of the Maekawa Commission are not concerned about the possible hollowing of the Japanese economy.[4] They see the appreciation of the yen and the resulting foreign direct investment drive as an opportunity for the large Japanese *kaisha* to develop into multinational corporations, and thus, to take advantage of the international division of labor. They want to see increased investments not only in the United States and Western Europe but also in the developing countries and in the NICs of the Pacific Asian region. Capital outflows, they argue, promote the transfer of technology and management to the areas that need it, thereby contributing to Japan's official development assistance (ODA) program.

Concerned by the fairly widespread views that the Japanese economy is about to be hollowed out through foreign direct investment, MITI officials in the fall of 1986 released a report that contradicts most of the doomsday prediction.[5] The report rejects the view that the increase of such investment would result in major macroeconomic and microeconomic changes. With respect to the macroeffects, MITI argues that the economy is not going to be hollowed out. As a matter of fact, despite the growth in foreign direct investment, the ratio of manufactured output in Japan's real GNP increased to 32.9 percent during 1980–1984, compared with 29.6 percent during 1970–1974. Moreover, MITI officials pointed out that in spite of increased American foreign direct investment in manufacturing over the years, the ratio of manufacturing output to GNP in America remained about 20 percent for the last two decades.

Concerning the microeffects, MITI officials cited evidence that the job losses in the United States as well as in the Federal Republic of Germany over the years were mostly due to improvements in productivity rather than increased foreign direct investments. They also argued that over the five years between 1980–85, the Japanese economy generated 750,000 new jobs and that the high-tech and service industries are constantly creating new employment opportunities.

Projections by the EPA support MITI's conclusions.[6] Based on a multisectoral model of the economy designed to forecast industrial structures and employment trends by the year 2000, the EPA concluded that Japanese industry is going to shift from the production of large volumes of a limited number of mass-marketed products to a low-volume production of a wide variety high quality, that is, higher value-added products. At the same time, the EPA conceded while in 1980 employment in the secondary sector was 34.8 percent of the total, by the year 2000, this will be reduced to 30.1 percent. However, concurrently, employment in the teritary sector will grow from 54.5 percent in 1980 to 65 percent by the turn of the century. Along with the employment growth in the tertiary sector in general, the trend toward service rather than production employment by firms in the secondary sectors will also continue. The noticeably strong growth in business services if evidence of this, the EPA concluded.

In spite of such optimistic official views, unionized workers are very concerned about the potential job losses. In the summer of 1986, unemployment reached a record high of 2.9 percent and while it declined slightly to 2.8 percent by the fall of the same year, a trend was under way which was greatly disturbing in an economy where until recently, unemployment was not an issue. The Trade Union Council for Multinational Companies, a joint organization of trade unions in the automobile, textile, and steel industries, warned that the sharp appreciation of the yen will result in increased foreign direct investments with a corresponding loss in domestic employment. The organization, which was formed to increase employment and improve working conditions in foreign countries where Japanese manufacturing plants are located, has now turned its interests entirely to the domestic employment situation. Deeply concerned, the 600,000-member influential Confederation of Japanese Automobile Workers' Union, is also trying to find ways to cope with the possible hollowing out of its industry. Encouraged by this, the labor unions of the major electrical and electronics manufacturers have also begun exploring possible countermeasures against shifting production operations abroad.

Thus, while the appreciated yen has set in motion an increase in foreign direct investment, there is no consensus on what such an outflow of capital and jobs could mean in the long run. Views and predictions clash, and only time will tell whether hollowing will occur, what industries may be affected, and to what extent more foreign direct investment might raise a new set of domestic socioeconomic problems.

While aware of these concerns, the government is in favor of more investments abroad. To promote these capital outflows, the Export-Import Bank of Japan in October 1986 announced that it will lend funds directly to overseas joint ventures involving Japanese companies. When a firm borrows funds directly from the Bank, it is exempt from certain taxes on interest payments; therefore, joint ventures abroad can be financed at a lower cost. However, while this new policy may promote foreign direct investment in general, the management decision to move abroad is also influenced by other considerations which are unique to the region or country chosen, and these may hinder the flow of investments, at least in some parts of the world.

Investment Concerns in the United States

The United States has long been a major target for Japanese foreign direct investment. In FY 1979, for example, 26.9 percent of all investments were made in the United States, which increased to 33.1 percent in FY 1984 and then declined to just over 30 percent in FY 1985.[7] By comparison, in FY 1984 Asia received 16 percent, Europe 19.1 percent, Latin America 22.6 percent, and the Middle East and Africa 2.7 and 3.2 percent, respectively. This trend was expected to continue in 1986 when 47 out of the 76, or 62 percent, of direct investment projects of major corporations were planned for the United States.[8] Early 1987 reports confirmed such expectations. At the end of January JETRO announced that Japanese corporations invested more than $9 billion in American businesses, manufacturing plants and real estate in calendar 1986. This meant a 3.6 fold increase of private investment over calendar 1985 and represented the highest overall amount ever invested in the United States in a single year.

Japanese investments in the United States tend to involve wholly owned start-up operations. The major reason for this is that initially most projects are limited to final assembly and that, in general, Japanese investors want control so that they can introduce their management and production practices without major complications. In the case of acquisitions, only about one-third of the takeovers involve 100 percent control; most are joint ventures with enough control to install Japansse management and production methods. The most likely acquisition targets include auto parts firms, banking institutions, medical equipment manufacturers, machinery and tool producers, copier and appliance manufacturers.

A new feature of Japanese direct investment in the United States during the second half of the 1980s is the establishment and acquisition of research and development centers. Japanese companies in a number of industries want to obtain the most current technological information, and are concerned with the growing protectionist attitudes in U.S. government and industrial circles concerning the transfer of new know-how. Moreover, they also plan to provide the growing number of Japanese manufacturing operations with technical services, and believe that it is more effective to own a research facility where the most advanced technology is developed. Others take the position that sending employees to American universities to learn the know-how and then reassigning them to Japan to do their research work is costly and ineffective.

Although the sharply appreciated yen, the continual protectionist threats emanating from the U.S. Congress and the incentives provided by the various local governments combine into a strong incentive package, many Japanese companies find that setting up an operation in the world's largest and richest market is not as simple as it may seem. Identifying the proper location in a country which is about 25 times the size of Japan, is inhabited by many different ethnic groups and operates under laws and tax systems that change from state to state; it is a difficult undertaking. Moreover, personnel, distribution, and energy costs, the skill level of the local labor force, the complexity of parts procurement as well as the attitude of the local population to foreigners in general and the Japanese in particular must also be considered. Japanese executives with a lot of experience in the United States claim that new investors should operate on the assumption that "...the average American doesn't have any particular good feelings towards Japan."[9] While this may be somewhat of an exaggeration, the great publicity surrounding the bilateral trade conflicts and the excessive references to the "unfair" Japanese have undoubtedly had their impact on public opinion over the years.

In the view of many Japanese businessmen, America is the most risky country in which to invest.[10] They argue that the U.S. markets are extremely competitive and refer to a Department of Commerce report according to which in 1984 alone, $1.5 billion in capital was withdrawn despite $12.3 billion in new investments. Furthermore, they point out that the large and promising market is permeated by legal restrictions such as the antitrust laws and safety requirements which limit the range of competitive actions. For example, measures to ensure stable supplies, widely used in Japan, are prohibited, and acquisitions may also be problematic. Some Japanese point to the Justice Department's decision in November 1986 to review the proposed takeover of Fairchild Semiconductor Corporation by a unit of Fujitsu Ltd. The announcement was accompanied by growing opposition to the takeover by U.S. government agencies and some American companies. They were having second thoughts about the acquisition because of the possible technology transfer and competitive implications. When the takeover was rejected in the spring of 1987, Japanese government officials in Tokyo noted that the proposed merger would probably not have raised such concerns if Fairchild wanted to merge with a German or British company.

According to Japanese businessmen, many of their American manufacturing operations are also plagued by productivity problems, and by the American proclivity to resort to legal suits to resolve even minor disagreements. This has increased insurance costs to a level which most Japanese could not even imagine before investing in the United States.

Investing in America is further complicated by the immigration laws which are administered by understaffed and underfunded agencies. These laws were formulated 30 years ago, and thus do not reflect the rapidly changing requirements of foreign investors in the 1980s and beyond. For example, to obtain a Third Party Preference Category classification, which is required for a foreign executive to move into the United States permanently, the applicant must complete lengthy forms, go through interviews, and probably wait a long time. While the immigration laws as applied to expatriate executives may be modernized in the near future, they are currently seen by many Japanese investors as tall hurdles which make the proper staffing of new ventures during the critical start-up stages very difficult.

Investment Concerns in Western Europe

While modest in the 1960s and 1970s, Japanese foreign direct investment in Western Europe has continually increased during the early 1980s. Table 7–4 shows this trend.

Although there was a break in the trend in 1985, the appreciated yen and the increasing demands of particularly the European Community (EC) nations to produce locally for sale throughout the EC markets, are going to again increase such investments in the coming years.

According to a recent Keidanren survey, most Japanese investments in the European Community are made to insure increased sales throughout the region.[11] Other reasons mentioned were the collection of information,

TABLE 7–4.   Japanese foreign direct investment in Western Europe: FY 1981–FY 1985 (in percentage of totals)

Year	Percentage
FY 1981	8.9
FY 1982	11.4
FY 1983	12.2
FY 1984	19.1
FY 1985	13.0

Source: Ministry of Finance, Tokyo, March 1986; also, *Japan 1986: An International Comparison* (Tokyo: Keizai Koho Center, 1986), p. 57.

export substitution, skilled labor, the availability of economic aid, and the exploitation of technology. The Federal Republic of Germany and the United Kingdom are the countries favored most by Japanese investors, whereas Portugal and Greece are the least frequently chosen.

However, while the majority of Japanese investors consider Europe in general and the European Community in particular a good or at least reasonable place to invest, they express concerns about the general sluggishness of the economic climate and the foreign exchange risks they have to incur. Italy, France, the United Kingdom, and Belgium are seen as the countries where such problems are most frequently encountered. Another interesting, albeit understandable, concern of Japanese investors is the European educational system which does not provide Japanese language instruction for the children of the expatriate managers. This is found to be a problem in all of the EC countries.

The high cost of labor is a growing problem. Japanese investors are equally concerned about the cost of employing managers, mid-level staff, and workers; West Germany, the United Kingdom, and the Netherlands are most often mentioned in this respect. Furthermore, investors also have problems with the labor laws and management-union relations. The majority of companies report that they had to dismiss employees for a variety of disciplinary reasons and that such dismissals are often contested despite the fact that the employees in question violated the most basic disciplinary rules time and again.

The increasing use of investment performance requirements throughout the EC is another investment handicap. Particularly the local content requirements of the less developed EC nations create problems in terms of acceptable quality, delivery, price, and followup service. At present, the EC uses a rule of thumb that foreign-owned plants must obtain at least a 45 percent local-content in their manufacturing operations, although the United Kingdom and France are usually less demanding. According to a confidential document prepared by the EC staff and leaked to the mass-media in early 1987, the Europeans want to increase their local-content requirements. While such a measure might create more jobs and ease the competitive pressure on local competitors, it may very well reduce Japanese investments in the future. Other requirements are also increasing, such as compulsory exports, a reduction in the scale of production and a change in the nature of the business to avoid competition with local firms. Moreover, the Japanese investors are concerned that the acceptance of such performance requirements is an investment condition, although the negotiation of such demands is often done behind the scenes.

Finally, investors reported many problems in dealing with the European

Community's work permit system. The process is complicated and very lengthy, and creates serious difficulties particularly during the early stages of a venture when Japanese managers are needed to restructure or establish a new operation in accord with Japanese practices.

Investment Concerns in the Asian Pacific Region[12]

Japanese direct investment in the region grew at a rapid pace during recent years, increasing from 16 percent of the total in FY 1983 to 25.2 percent in FY 1984.[13] On a value basis, Indonesia received the most, followed by Hong Kong and Singapore, On the basis of the number of projects, Hong Kong led the list and was followed by Singapore and Taiwan.

On a value basis, the Association of Southeast Asian Nations (ASEAN) nations as a group received 31.1 percent of the total going into the region in FY 1981 and 18 percent in FY 1984. Analyzed by industry, more than half of the accumulated total investments throughout the region are in the nonmanufacturing sector, primarily in mining and financial services, whereas only a little over one-third are in the manufacturing sector, mainly iron and nonferrous metal, chemicals, and textile ventures. This pattern reflects past Japanese investment strategies which focused on serving local markets or producing for exports to third countries and the securing of raw material supplies.

However, while growing during the early 1980s, Japanese investments in the region declined 23 percent of the global total by the end of FY 1985. The ASEAN nations were particularly hard-hit; in FY 1985 they received only 7.7 percent of all investments going into the Asian Pacific region, less than half of the FY 1984 amount. The overall decline was due chiefly to the economic uncertainty caused by the sharp decline of oil rubber and tin exports, increasing protectionism in the target markets and the growing external debt. To deal with the uncertainty, governments introduced a series of investment performance requirements which had an unfavorable effect on the investment climate.

Expectedly, the rapid decline raised major concerns throughout the region in general and the ASEAN nations in particular. To reduce their dependence on commodity exports and to speed up economic development, governments ask for substantial manufacturing investments which would promote technology transfers, management expertise, employment, and most of all, would generate more competitive exports in the future. The nations of the region are looking to Tokyo for help because American investment is not as readily forthcoming as in the past; in 1985 it actually declined, and in 1986 it was stagnating.

The Japanese are ideally positioned to provide the needed investments. The yen has appreciated about 50 percent against its regional counterparts during 1985–1986, allowing Japanese companies to pick up assets for approximately half of what they would have had to pay earlier. Thus, in response to the yen's continued strength, Japanese manufacturing companies of all sizes have started to set up plants in Korea and Taiwan where labor costs are low and the local currency is linked to the dollar. In mid-1986, for example, the hourly compensation for production workers in U.S. dollars was $1.38 in Korea as opposed to $6.64 in Japan. Moreover, at the time when Japanese workers put in just over 40 hours per week, and the government was trying to convince the private sector to reduce the work week to stimulate domestic demand, the average number of hours worked in Korea was 54.5. Several manufacturers have also started discussions with the Thai Board of Investment concerning new projects, because in their view, the relatively inexpensive and skilled labor, plentiful resources, competitive tax incentives and satisfactory infrastructure make Thailand one of the best investment sites throughout the region.

However, while the outlook for new Japanese direct investments in some of these countries is promising, the prospects of the ASEAN countries as a group are still discouraging. According to a 1986 survey of the *Keizai Doyukai*, an association of Japanese businessmen, interest in ASEAN investments is sagging because of complicated red tape and unfavorable economic conditions.[14] The specific concerns include cumbersome profit transfer requirements, in some cases high wages, high inflation rates, the difficulties of importing spare parts and materials, and foreign exchange fluctuations.

To entice foreign investors in general and Japanese investors in particular, governments of the region are beginning to introduce measures to lift restrictions, cut taxes, and generally to improve incentives. On October 1, 1986, for example, Malaysia relaxed its rules so that foreign investors can now own up to 100 percent of export-oriented projects. In early November of the same year, the Indonesian government allowed expatriates to become directors and financial managers of joint ventures with a minimum of $10 million in equity, of which at least 75 percent comes from foreign sources. Moreover, the government eased visa restrictions for business travellers. However, while these are steps in the right direction, only time will tell to what extent they motivate Japanese companies to increase investments throughout the region.

Japan's political ties to the ASEAN group are important; thus, the

Nakasone government was disturbed by the declining investments and the displeasure expressed by some nations over trade relations. To reduce the displeasure, the Japanese invited individual ASEAN heads of state to Tokyo during late 1986 to explore matters of mutual concern. In addition, MITI together with the Japan External Trade Organization (JETRO) developed special programs to encourage Japanese companies to invest in the ASEAN nations.

Specifically, MITI intends to provide official development assistance funding on a wider basis, set up an ASEAN investment promotion company, create an industrial technology transfer center and establish a new training institute for engineers from developing countries in general, particularly the ASEAN nations. The new investment firm will be capitalized at about $130 million provided by both public and private sources. In a sense, the new firm is an expansion of the existing Japan-ASEAN Investment Company capitalized at $10 million and created with the backing of the Keidanren. The new firm will invest in and provide financing for joint ventures in the ASEAN nations as well as fund wholly owned Japanese direct investments. In turn, MITI hopes that the ASEAN nations will liberalize foreign investment rules which currently discourage Japanese investors.

JETRO's program, the "Join Scheme," is a foreign direct investment cooperation plan. It covers all ASEAN nations except oil-rich Brunei, and promotes direct investments by small and medium-sized Japanese manufacturers. JETRO aids companies in undertaking feasibility studies, helps to search for prospective local partners, and consults with the ASEAN governments on behalf of the investors. The plan gives priority to manufacturing companies which intend to export most of their joint-venture output, apply a high value-added manufacturing process, and could aid the host economy in a number of additional ways.

Such measures are promising. However, good intentions notwithstanding, their effectiveness may be limited as long as the various investment disincentives in the host nations remain. Moreover, more direct investment in developing countries in general and the ASEAN nations in particular requires large amounts of low-interest, long-term capital backed by appropriate insurance to reduce the perceived high risks to an acceptable level.[15]

These issues were brought into sharp focus when Prime Minister Nakasone returned from his visit to the People's Republic of China in November 1986. Although Japan is the third largest investor in China after Hong Kong and the United States, Chinese officials told the Prime Minister that if Japan is sincere about assisting China's fledgling economy, it should significantly expand investments.

A large-scale expansion of investments, however, may not be possible, at least within the foreseeable future. In the fall of 1986 and in early 1987 MITI and MOF officials reported that Japanese companies are very hesitant about investments in China, including technical assistance projects and joint ventures. This is so because they do not believe that the Chinese fully observe international trade customs and properly appreciate the technologies offered. Japanese businessmen are particularly concerned about the Chinese practice of considering technology as just another commodity, not paying internationally accepted prices and demanding the most advanced technology regardless of their ability to effectively absorb and apply it. Moreover, they object to the short duration of joint-venture contracts, the problems of getting the necessary information for feasibility studies, the lengthy approvals, the difficulties involved in procuring local materials for plant construction, the often vague wage and related labor standards and the uncertainties about being able to sell the goods produced in China's domestic market as well as the repatriation of the earnings from such sales. Although in the fall of 1986 the Chinese government announced new measures which include lower taxes, reduced charges for labor, land, raw materials as well as greater freedom for the hiring and firing of labor, the questions of domestic sales and earnings repatriation were not addressed. Thus, Japanese companies may continue their cautious attitudes toward investing in the People's Republic of China for some time to come.

Nonetheless, Prime Minister Nakasone instructed the MITI minister to facilitate Japanese investments. He also asked the minister to determine how the revision of the export insurance system could be used to such an end. Revisions could be helpful because the present insurance arrangements are designed to assist Japanese companies to cover risk of war, civil conflict, and nationalization, considerations which are not applicable to stable countries such as China. The necessary changes include coverage for slow foreign sales as well as sharp price increases in locally procured parts, risks about which Japanese investors in China have expressed concern.

Official Development Assistance

Japan's foreign aid program, known as Official Development Assistance (ODA), is about 30 years old and has its origins in postwar reparations to the Southeast Asian countries.[16] Indonesia and the Philippines were among the first to receive substantial payments in the late 1950s, lasting until about 1965 when the formal aid programs began.

Throughout the second half of the 1960s, ODA programs provided primarily tied-aid which had to be spent on the purchase of Japanese goods. Later, in the aftermath of the 1973 oil crisis, financial aid was given primarily to resource-rich developing countries and nations situated on important shipping routes. Beginning in the early 1980s, the focus of aid programs changed again, and more emphasis was put on the reduction of poverty and the support of those developing countries which are important to the worldwide strategic concerns of the Western alliance. Currently, ODA is focused on rural and agricultural development, the creation of new and renewable energy sources, human resources, and the promotion of small- and medium-sized businesses.

In comparison to other industrialized nations, after a relatively slow start in the early 1970s, Japanese foreign aid grew at an average rate of 10.5 percent between 1978 and 1984, increasing the share of such aid in GNP from 0.24 percent during the mid-1970s to 0.34 percent in 1984. Table 7–5 provides a summary overview of Japan's foreign aid contributions in comparison to other major industrialized nations over a 10-year period.

However, even though in absolute terms Japan is among the top donor nations in the world behind the United States, Ameica devotes 6.5 percent of its GNP to the combination of defense and foreign aid, whereas the comparable figure for Japan is only 1.5 percent.

To strengthen foreign aid programs, the Japanese government decided to double the funding. It first called for an increase from $1.4 billion in 1977 to $2.8 billion in 1981, and then decided to again double ODA during the 1981–1985 period. The first time it achieved the goal, however, the second time funding fell short of the objective set; the amount spent was 16 percent less than targeted. As a consequence, ODA accounted for only 0.29 percent of GNP in 1985 as opposed to the high of 0.34 in 1984, and so Japan was still far off the 0.7 percent which the OECD recommends as a target ratio to its member nations.

The reason for the shortfall during the 1981–1985 period was that in 1985 alone, ODA was down by 12 percent from the previous year due chiefly to a sharp drop in contributions to multilateral agencies which reflected the cyclical nature of such contributions rather than a change in policy. The funding of mulitateral institutions declined by 34.4 percent in 1985 because Japan made special contributions to the International Development Agency (IDA), and subscribed to a special replenishment of World Bank in 1984. Additional reasons for the shortfall of ODA included the average decline inthe value of the yen of about 15 percent beginning in 1981 and lasting through the fall of 1985, and the deteriorating economies of the developing countries that delayed the implementation of several aid projects.

TABLE 7–5. International comparison of official development assistance to developing nations and multilateral agencies: net disbursements, 1973–1984 (in millions of U.S. $)

	1973–1975 average	1982	1983	1984	Annual growth rate of ODA[a] 1978/79– 1983/84	Share of GNP(%) 1973–1975	1983	1984	Share of total (%) 1973–1975	1983	1984
USA	3,497	8,202	8,081	8,711	3.1%	0.24	0.24	0.24	30.4	29.3	30.4
Japan	1,095	3,023	3,761	4,319	10.5	0.24	0.32	0.35	9.5	13.6	15.1
France	1,723	4,034	3,815	3,788	6.9	0.61	0.74	0.77	15.0	13.8	13.2
Germany, FR	1,408	3,152	3,176	2,782	3.9	0.37	0.48	0.45	12.2	11.5	9.7
Canada	703	1,197	1,429	1,625	0.8	0.48	0.45	0.50	6.1	5.2	5.7
UK	780	1,800	1,610	1,418	-6.1	0.03	0.35	0.33	6.8	5.8	4.9
Netherlands	455	1,472	1,195	1,268	2.6	0.64	0.91	1.02	3.9	4.3	4.4
Italy	197	811	834	1,133	21.8	0.11	0.24	0.33	1.7	3.0	3.9
Australia	429	882	753	777	0.2	0.56	0.49	0.46	3.7	2.7	2.7
Sweden	414	987	754	741	-0.3	0.68	0.84	0.80	3.6	2.7	2.6
DAC, total	11,519	27,731	27,560	28,686	4.1	0.33	0.36	0.36	100.0	100.0	100.0

[a] At constant prices and exchange rates.

Source: *Japan 1986: An International Comparison* (Tokyo: Keizai Koho Center, 1986), p. 55.

Of all ODA during 1981–1985, about 71.0 percent went to the Asian Pacific region, in particular the ASEAN countries of Indonesia, Thailand, Malaysia, and the Philippines.[17] On an individual country basis, at first Indonesia led the way, but was replaced by the People's Republic of China in 1982, a position it still holds. The ASEAN member nations have alternated in the second, third, and fourth positions over the years, never falling lower than fifth place. The distribution of ODA has reflected Japan's desire to maintain satisfactory political relations throughout the region, and recently, to complement long-term Western strategic interests as illustrated by the aid given to the People's Republic of China.

Japanese ODA is criticized by the recipient countries for a number of reasons. Objections are expressed to the perceived strategy of using foreign aid to promote Japanese business interest. Recipients complain that the policy of granting aid on a request basis only, allows Japanese business firms to lobby governments for project requests which only they can fulfill. The large average yen loan share of aid packages, the relatively high interest rates, and tough repayment schedules have also been criticized. This developed into a particularly bitter complaint on the part of the ASEAN nations when the yen suddenly appreciated in 1985–1986, thereby dramatically increasing the repayment burden. As Japan's current account and global trade surpluses reached new heights during the same years, such criticism became even more strident not only throughout the developing countries, but also in the industrialized world. Foe and friend alike expected Japan to use its newly amassed wealth to be more generous and flexible with its aid programs.

Although the Japanese public supports ODA, criticism of foreign aid has also increased at home recently.[18] In addition to echoing some of the concerns expressed by the recipient nations, domestic critics of ODA complained about the misuse of funds, the inefficient coordination of grants, loans and technical assistance among the Overseas Economic Cooperation Fund, the Japan International Cooperation Agency, and the Export-Import Bank of Japan. In 1986 when evidence began surfacing that Japanese firms and members of the aid bureaucracy were involved in payoff schemes in the Philippines under the now defunct Marcos regime, the generally loose followup procedures became another topic of discussion. After the new Aquino government cancelled four projects arranged earlier as part of an aid-package because the arrangement involved too many of Marcos' close allies, embarrassment and concern over foreign aid reached new heights in Tokyo.[19]

In response to growing criticism, Minister of Foreign Affairs Shintaro Abe established the Advisory Committee on the Effective Implementation of ODA in April 1985. A few months later, in December, the 16—member committee submitted its final report listing a number of specific recommendations. They included the use of more untied yen loans, increased yen loans to nations settled by external debts, the introduction of an international cooperation tax, and the development of alternate sources of ODA funding. The committee also argued for an international development institute to train Japanese aid specialists and for an overhaul of the existing institutions involved in assistance efforts. Finally, it emphasized the need to educate the Japanese public about the role of ODA and called for the development of uniquely Japanese aid policies.

While the advisory committee was still discussing ways to improve both the quantity and quality of ODA, in September 1985 the Nakasone government approved the third medium-term plan calling for the doubling of aid between FY 1986 and the end of FY 1992. The new plan envisions the spending of more than $40 billion through an increase in grants and technical assistance aid, broader commitments to international financial institutions, and better disbursal of yen loans. Japan's aid/GNP ratio is expected to increase to 0.42 percent by the end of 1992, a substantial increase over the more modest ratios of recent years. In addition, the plan calls for improvements in the general administration and followup of assistance projects.

It is a reflection of the government's commitment to increase aid that the FY 1986 budget, which was overshadowed by the Nakasone government's fiscal austerity policy, included a 7 percent ODA increase over FY 1985. Although historically defense and aid have always been exempted from cuts, there were heated discussions over how much should be spent on aid in FY 1986. The Ministry of Foreign Affairs asked for a 10.4 percent raise whereas MOF argued for only a 5.3 percent increase. The 7 percent, therefore, represents a reasonable compromise, particularly since the MOF could point to the appreciated yen as a convincing reason for a more modest increase. However, the strong appreciation of the yen was reflected in the austere FY 1987 budget wherein ODA received only a 5.8 percent increase over FY 1986, although the Ministry of Foreign Affairs requested a 7.8 percent increase. Based on the strong appreciation of the yen, the 5.8 percent represent a 9.4 percent increase in dollar terms, according to officials in Tokyo.

The Japanese government's commitment to the improvement of ODA was also underlined by the decision to adopt a more flexible yen loan policy in the summer of 1986. In the past, yen loans were earmarked for the purchase of materials from abroad. Funds for labor, fuel, and other domestically procured goods and services had to be obtained separately.

Under the new flexible policy, up to 30 percent of the yen loans may be spent on domestic procurement; additional funds for the same purpose will be extended to projects already under way. Thus, Japanese yen loans are turning into "financial assistance" rather than just a loan. This change in policy is particularly important to the nations of the Asian Pacific region in general and the ASEAN countries in particular which have most bitterly criticized the inflexibility and "tied" nature of the past yen loans.

Moreover, amid the difficult 1986–1987 OECD negotiations concerning the redefinition of official development assistance loans during which the United States strongly criticized Japanese ODA policies, the Japanese government announced in December 1986 that it would provide two loans totaling $6.2 billion to the World Bank and the International Monetary Fund for aid to developing nations, and that the loans would not be tied to the purchase of Japanese products.

The New 'Uruguay round' GATT Negotiations

The General Agreement on Tariffs and Trade (GATT), established in 1948, is at a critical juncture today. Slow world economic growth, the energy crises of 1973 and 1979, the indebtedness of the developing nations and the increasing number of bilateral trade conflicts have fostered a new version of economic nationalism that endangers the trade system.

As a major economic power, Japan must accept its share of the responsibility for the strengthening of the GATT. The system is important, because it is the only institution that stands between a relatively free and competitive global marketplace and an economic chaos characterized by bilateral debates and solutions. As the history of U.S.–Japan trade relations shows, bilateral bickering cannot resolve any of the major problems faced by the world community. At best, it leads to a temporary truce which may satisfy short-term politicial interests of the feuding nations, but it does not resolve any of the underlying economic issues in a mutually acceptable manner. While there is no guarantee that a strengthened GATT would necessarily enable the world's nations to come to lasting multilateral agreements, it would provide a more effective platform on which to try.[20]

Japan is vitally interested in the maintenance of an open, flexible, and strong world trade system; thus, it was an early and consistent supporter of the American effort to launch the new round of talks. Prime Minister Nakasone first proposed the new round on the occasion of President Reagan's visit to Japan in November 1983. Recognizing the dangers surrounding the world trade system the Prime Minister referred to the process of trade liberalization as "pushing a cart uphill; if we pause too long, the cart will fall backward."

The Japanese delegation to the agenda-setting Punta del Este talks in September 1986, was carrying a set of proposals which were similar to those championed by the United States. However, Japan not only agreed with the United States to put agriculture and services on the agenda but also tried to include some of the major concerns of the developing countries. More specifically, it wanted to see negotiations in nine sectors, including the establishment of a medium-term framework for the liberalization of textile-trade, measures to promote exports of tropical products, greater market access for farm goods, better rules on safeguard means for emergency import controls, improvement of the dispute settlement procedures, and the reduction or elimination of restrictions on services. In addition to proposing a full agenda, Japan also wanted to play a major role in the formation of the informal agreements which are so important during official multilateral negotiations. This is in stark contrast to past negotiations when Japan stayed on the sidelines.

The Punta del Este discussions were difficult for Japan whose current-account and trade-account surpluses were strongly criticized. The European Community wanted a resolution calling for the better distribution of world trade benefits which was designed to prepare the ground for major Japanese concessions during the new round of talks. But, with the support of the United States, the Japanese managed to prevent the inclusion of the resolution in the closing statement. Nonetheless, when the MITI Minister returned to Tokyo, he warned that Japan must stimulate domestic demand on a short-term basis and promote industrial structural changes on a medium-term and a long-term basis to pacify trading partners who are very upset about the surpluses.

The inclusion of agriculture on the agenda of the new round of talks, was surrounded by a great deal of controversy. The European Community strongly opposed the discussions of farm subsidies which represent the basis of its Common Agricultural Policy (CAP) and is, thus, a politically sensitive subject. However, the United States, 14 agricultural exporting nations, and Japan eventually managed to have the Europeans accept a resolution calling for the gradual reduction of agricultural subsidies and the expansion of GATT rules to farm products.

The participating nations also agreed to discuss both general and sector-specific rules in services. Some nations, particularly India and Brazil, wanted negotiations to be conducted outside the GATT framework on a separate track. However, the United States, supported by Japan, insisted that all negotiations be conducted under the aegis of a single Trade Negotiating Committee. Thus, the discussion of services will be part of the overall talks carried out under the rules and procedures of the GATT.

While there was agreement on the agenda, as Aho and Aronson have also pointed out, one of the major underlying problems of the new round of talks will be the question of "fair" versus "unfair" trade practices which have played such a central role in Japan's international trade relations, particularly with the United States.[21] Unless there is a clarification of these terms, or even better, nations stay away from their use, it is hard to see how any new agreements on specific technical issues could be effective in the long run.

The heavy external debt of many of the developing countries will also pose a problem to the successful conclusion of the talks. While the resolution of the debt problem is critical to world trade, it is not within the purview of the trade ministers who will be negotiating, but is under the control of a small group of central bankers and finance ministers from the industrialized nations. It is possible that unless they can resolve the debt-problem in the near future, the agreements achieved through the Uruguay round will be consistently observed only by the highly industrialized nations.

Thus, the world will have to wait until the talks are finished in four years to find out whether the various nations have made a real commitment to improve the international trade system. Particularly since the United States, burdened by a $200 billion fiscal and over $150 billion trade deficit, is not likely to be able to exert the kind of decisive leadership it did in the past.

As a consequence, Japan will have to play a major role, although it can expect to come under great pressure during the negotiations. The most difficult part of the talks will be the discussion of agricultural policies. Changes in the price-support system touch on powerful political interests, and may, thus, create a great deal of domestic controversy. At the same time, a multilateral agricultural agreement may be the most beneficial long-term outcome of the new Gatt talks for the internationalization of the Japanese economy as conceived by the Maekawa Commission.

Notes

1. If nondirect or portfolio investments are also included, the total increases to $50–60 billion annually.
2. *The Japan Times* (March 26, 1986), p. 9.

3. *The Japan Economic Journal* (June 7, 1986), p. 1.
4. Shoichi Akazawa, Chairman of the Japanese External Trade Organization (JETRO); Tokyo, March 1986.
5. *The Japan Times* (October 14, 1986), p. 5.
6. Internal documents, Economic Planning Agency (Tokyo: May 1986). The primary sector includes agriculture, forestry, and fisheries; the secondary sector is manufacturing, mining, and construction, while the tertiary sector is comprised of the service industries, government, and utilities.
7. Ministry of Finance sources (Tokyo, March 1986).
8. For a list of these projects, see appendix G.
9. *The Japan Economic Journal* (October 25, 1986), p. 13; also, *Business Week* (July 14, 1986), pp. 53–54.
10. *The Japan Economic Journal* (July 5, 1986), p. 13.
11. "Problems Experienced by Japanese Companies Investing in the EC: Keidanren Survey," *Keidanren Review* (February 1986), pp. 8–11. These findings were confirmed by a JETRO survey. See *Japanese Manufacturing Companies Operating in Europe* (Tokyo: Japan External Trade Organization, 1986).
12. In addition to Japan, the region includes the NICs of Southeast Asia (Hong Kong, Taiwan, Korea and Singapore, also known as the "four tigers"), as well as Indonesia, Malaysia, the Philippines, Thailand and the People's Republic of China. The former four together with Singapore and Brunei are members of the Association of Southeast Asian Nations (ASEAN).
13. *Japan: An International Comparison* (Tokyo: Keizai Koho Center, 1985 and 1986 issues, respectively) pp. 57, 57; and *Japan and the World in Statistics: 1986* (Tokyo: The Tokyo Chamber of Commerce and Industry, 1986), pp. 88–89.
14. *The Japan Times* (March 12, 1986), p. 3.
15. Saburo Okita, "Japan is Advised to Diversify Investments to Aid Developing Nations' Economic Growth," *The Japan Economic Journal* (August 30, 1986), p. 7.
16. William L. Brooks and Robert M. Orr, Jr., "Japan's Foreign Economic Assistance," *Asian Survey* (March 1985), pp. 322–340.
17. Ministry of Foreign Affairs (Tokyo, March 1986).
18. See, among others, "Needed: More Active Economic Cooperation" (Tokyo: Keizai Koho Center, June 28, 1986). This *Keidanren* statement was submitted to Prime Minister Nakasone in April 1985.
19. *The Daily Yomiuri* (March 28, 1986), p. 5.
20. For a discussion of the issues surrounding the new round of talks, see C. Michael Aho and Jonathan Davis Aronson. *Trade Talks: America Better Listen* (New York: Council on Foreign Relations, 1986).
21. C. Michael Aho and Jonathan D. Aronsone, *Trade Talks, op.cit.*, p. 25.

Afterword

Although from the outside the process may seem slow and uncertain at times, the internationalization of the Japanese economy is under way. The sharp appreciation of the yen unleashed a set of market forces which cannot be turned back. Some of these forces are deflationary in the short-term to medium-term, and therefore, by depressing demand, they may work against internationalization. Others, such as increased foreign direct investment due to a stronger yen, however, may promote the process. Whatever the case may be, in unison with market forces, a step-by-step implementation of the Action Program and of the Maekawa Commission's domestic and international policy recommendations will inevitably change Japan's domestic economic landscape and global role. By the summer of 1987, MITI completed a five-year plan "aimed at the restructuring of Japan's economy through higher economic growth, domestic expansion and decrease of exports." The plan is scheduled to start in FY 1988. Moreover, Japan's exports had decreased 1.2 percent while imports increased 12.5 percent in volume terms in 1986, setting the stage for the changes.

This will not be esay, however. By the end of 1986, and the beginning of 1987, the signs of an economic slowdown were unmistakable. Corporate earnings were down, unemployment reached the 3 percent mark, and business confidence appeared to be sagging despite the fall 1986 Comprehensive Economic Measures and reduction of the official discount rate.[1]

Most private forecasters doubt that the annual 4 percent real economic growth envisioned by the government to continue through 1990 and believed to be necessary for an uninterrupted internationalization process could be achieved. In the short run, for example, the Bank of Tokyo predicted a modest 2.7 percent growth in real terms for FY 1987. The bank cited an expected drop in overseas demand for Japanese products stemming from the yen's rise in value as the major reason for the projected slow economic growth. While more optimistic than the Bank of Tokyo, even the government reduced its expectations and set a 3.5 percent growth target for FY 1987. Domestic demand would account for about 3.9 percent of growth, against exports' contribution estimated at 0.5 percent. To achieve this, the government announced the possibility of additional special economic stimuli of $34 billion of direct government spending during 1987.

However, what actually happens in FY 1987 and beyond depends on what the combined effect of the fall 1986 and 1987 reflationary packages, the successive discount rate reductions, reformed personal and corporate income tax system, increased infrastructure and housing investments, privatization and continuing austere government budgets will be on domestic demand. The outlook is hazy, because the spring 1987 tug-of-war over the yen-dollar exchange rate and the satiated Japanese consumer — whose consumption contributes more than 60 percent to Gross Domestic Product — represent uncertainities which are difficult to evaluate. Particularly, since by late spring the controversy surrounding the tax reform raised the possibility that some aspects of the reform would have to be changed. This, together with the declining popularity of Prime Minister Nakasone, the lackluster performance of LDP candidates in the local elections, both caused by the tax reform controversy, and the $300 million U.S. tariffs imposed on Japanese electronic products, added to the spring 1987 uncertainty.

Nonetheless, the Japanese government is confident that the uncertainty will only be temporary and that once the short-term economic adjustments, necessitated by the sharply appreciated yen, are mastered and the policy stimuli take effect, the economy will move back into a steady growth path. Part of this optimism is based on the fall 1986 and spring 1987 agreements between Japan and the United States to coordinate exchange rate policies, among others. Japanese officials believe that in spite of the conflicting statements coming out of Washington and the rapidly depreciating dollar in early 1987, U.S. officials do not want an appreciation of the yen to the point where it would choke off exports and, thereby, create a serious recession in Japan.

By reaching an agreement, however fragile, both the Japanese and the American governments have transcended political posturing to satisfy narrow domestic interests and, thus, showed a measure of long overdue statesmanship. Although no reference was made to "target zones," the acceptance of an exchange rate of somewhere around 150 yen to the dollar, for all practical purposes established such a range. Of course, it is not easy to manage such agreements. The coordination of economic policies and of exchange market interventions are complicated matters and subject to domestic political pressures. Nevertheless, the effort to stabilize the exchange rate must be made, otherwise the situation can quickly get out of control. The tug-of-war that went on early 1987 and the statements by U.S. officials and politicians that the yen must appreciate much more than it already had, are prescriptions for serious worldwide economic problems. According to the forecasts of some private Japanese research institutes, an appreciation of the yen to 140 to the dollar would reduce Japanese economic growth to 1.2 percent in FY 1987 and beyond. This is not in the interest of Japan nor can it be in the interest of the United States and the rest of the world.

Japan's successive reductions of the discount rate indicated that the stimulation of domestic growth is a major policy objective of the government. Together with the exchange rate agreement the reductions imply that the United States and Japan may be willing to act as a "Group of Two" to create a more stable world economy, if necessary.

The two nations together account for 70 percent of the GNP of the major industrialized nations and around 40 percent of global GNP; thus their close cooperation could be a decisive factor in the future. This is not to say that they can ignore the other industrialized nations, but it does imply that if necessary, they may be inclined in the future to coordinate economic policies through bilateral rather than multilateral consultations with the Western European nations. Of course, joint policy efforts by the G-5 nations (United States, Japan, the Federal Republic of Germany, the United Kingdom and France), would be preferable. However, while problematic, American–Japanese co-leadership would still be better for the world-economy than a split or no leadership at all.

Whether this means the beginning of a historic "special relationship" between the United States and Japan to the detriment of America's "special relationship" with Western Europe remains to be seen. Suffice it to say that the agreement with Japan is an unmistakable move on the part of the United States to become more involved with the Asian Pacific region, a development long predicted by some observers. However, for the new partnership to work, Japan must resolve its intensifying trade problems with the European Community. Japanese exports to the EC have increased 53 percent in dollar terms in 1986 alone, and the EC's trade deficit with Japan has doubled in eight years to almost $14 billion in 1985, and surpassing $16 billion in 1986. The Europeans believe that hit by the high yen against the dollar, Japan has shifted its exports from the United States to Western Europe because the European currencies have fallen only half as far as the dollar. They also think that Japan has continually snubbed them in favor of the United States. Thus, if left unattended, the imbalances could develop into festering trade conflicts similar to those Japan has experienced with the United States in recent years. Such deep and continual disagreements with Europe could make close economic cooperation with America very difficult, if not impossible.

From the Japanese point of view, the agreement with America marks the assumption for unequivocal responsibility for global economic developments. Both nations recognize that as major economic powers they share a large part of the responsibility for the future of the world economy and, must, therefore cooperate.

Undoubtedly, the new role of Japan will change the nature of future U.S.–Japan economic relations. While committed to free trade as shown by their stance in the new GATT round, the Japanese will no longer passively endure unilateral American pressure in the course of bilateral economic and trade discussions. Fortified by the newly won economic power, the emerging generation of Japanese political and economic leaders, unaffected by guilt feelings about World War II, will act with more self-confidence than their elders did in the past. While on occasion such self-assurance combined with economic clout may be seen as arrogance by the rest of the world, a more assertive Japan taking on a co-leadership role is necessary for the coordinated management of a highly interdependent world economy.

Bold Japanese economic leadership in tandem with the United States is of particular importance in the new GATT Uruguay round over the next four years. The inclusion of agriculture in the agenda will be a severe test of Japan's commitment to the internationalization of its economy. While agreements can only be reached if the United States and the European Community are also willing to make economic and political sacrifices, the world's attention will be focused on Japan to see how willingly and to what extent it will revise its agricultural policies.

In the meanwhile, the United States must get its own economic house in order through the reduction of the huge fiscal deficits and through significant improvements in the international competitiveness of its industries. In spite of its weakening economic performance during the last two decades, America still represents an economic force second to none. The Reagan Administration's increasing recognition that the nation's economic problems are chiefly caused by low productivity and the resulting decline in international competitiveness is a hopeful sign for the future. Although some Washington skeptics argue that this is a diversionary tactic designed to moderate protectionist sentiments in the new Democrat-controlled Congress, the Administration's new focus is on the mark and cannot be ignored even by the most dyed-in-the-wool protectionists for too long.

In view of the changing global economic conditions, the 100th Congress must rethink its approach to international economic relations in general and to U.S.–Japanese bilateral trade relations in particular. Japan-bashing is not a policy but an emotional outlet which does not help correct fundamental economic problems, although it makes good newspaper headlines. As the fall 1986 report of the Office of the USTR on foreign trade barriers illustrates, Japan can no longer be accused of maintaining a bilateral trade surplus through protectionism, as other nations are much more active in keeping imports out of their markets[2]. Congress also needs to recognize that the sharp appreciation of the yen against the dollar will not solve the trade problems by itself because the dollar depreciation was far more limited against the currencies of the NICs in general and of the Asian Pacific Rim nations in particular which have become major trading partners of the United States. Members of Congress should also consider the arguments of the President's Council of Economic Advisers concerning the reasons for the U.S. trade imbalances. In their January 1987 report to Congress the Council pointed out that the trade imbalances are caused mostly by macroeconomic phenomena and not by "unfair" foreign trade practices.

Furthermore, dire predictions of future U.S.-Japan relations must not be allowed to become self-fulfilling prophecies.[3] As the spring 1987 arguments have shown disagreements will continue, but there is no reason why the two nations could not come to an understanding of what needs to be done by both sides to avoid further worsening of relations. As the latest poll of the *Asahi Shimbun* newspaper indicates, despite the various forms of bilateral economic conflicts between the two nations, relations as measured by the sentiments of the two peoples remain on solid ground.[4] The survey showed that 64 percent of the American and 48 percent of the Japanese respondents believed that relations between the two nations are good. There was almost no change in the attitude of the Americans from the previous survey in 1982, whereas the Japanese views have improved since the last survey when only 32 percent believed this to be the case. Moreover, 45 percent of the American and 56 percent of the Japanese respondents believed that the good relations between the two nations will continue as long as both governments act responsibly. While national policies cannot be formulated on the basis of public survey results, neither can the governments of democratic societies ignore the views of the public.

Japan's new economic role will be particularly important in the rapidly growing Asian Pacific region which is in the process of becoming a major global economic and trade center. According to predictions, if the present economic trends continue, by the turn of the century the region may account for about 25 percent of global production as compared to the North American continent's share of a little under 30 percent.[5] A particularly important aspect of this trend is that most countries of the Asian Pacific region want to improve their international competitiveness through the application of the dynamic concept of comparative advantage, just as Japan did earlier. This will undoubtedly create new trade tensions throughout the world.

The handwriting is on the wall. By the mid-1980s, for example, the export/GNP ratio of the Republic of Korea reached 35 percent, that of Taiwan 53 percent, and that of Hong Kong 89 percent. Moreover, Korea's world export share increased from 0.6 percent in 1973 to 1.5 percent in 1984, Taiwan's from 0.8 to 1.6 percent, and Hong Kong's share from 0.9 to 1.5 percent. The success of the Korean car manufacturer Hyundai in the competitive American market is a good illustration of the rapidly increasing international competitiveness of these nations. Not surprisingly, this is already causing concern in Washington, London, and the chanceries of continental Europe and Tokyo.

However, Japan's concern must be tempered by its responsibility for the economic development of these nations. Japan must promote and accelerate their economic growth through more concessionary development assistance, inceased foreign direct investment, and manufactured imports. Inasmuch as a substantial part of such imports are, for example, parts and components for consumer electronic products and office equipment purchased with as stronger yen, this promotes the horizontal international division of labor throughout the region with Japan as its center. However, such a process has its limits too; robotics and other technological developments are already gradually depriving the region's nations of their major economic advantage — skilled, low-cost labor.

According to unofficial predictions, Japan's net external assets (external assets-external debts) are likely to reach \$1 trillion by 1995, a level which will make it the chief supplier of capital to the world. It is therefore important that both the Japanese government and the private sector find new, imaginative ways to invest this capital, not only in the industrialized nations but most of all in the developing countries badly in need of help. Only through such enlightened economic policies can Japan truly internationalize its economy and fulfill its new global role.

To what extent the internationalization process will reduce Japan's current and trade account surpluses cannot be answered with certainty. The goal of reducing the current account/GNP ratio from 3.7 percent in 1985 and more than 4 percent in 1986 (amounting to \$86 billion), to about 1.5−2.0 percent by the early 1990s, as recommended by Prime Minister Nakasone's Economic Council, is necessary for a more balanced global economy. But this alone cannot be the objective of the internationalization process, even though many abroad believe so. The Japanese can be expected to fully embrace the idea only if it also leads to a substantial improvement in their quality of life.

Notes

1. Japan defines unemployed workers as those who receive unemployment insurance. Layed-off workers are excluded because they receive part of their wages. According to MITI sources, if Japan's unemployment rate were calculated like America's rate, it would have been over 5 percent by the end of 1986.
2. *National Trade Estimate: 1986 Report on Foreign Trade Barriers* (Washington, D.C.: Office of the United States Trade Representative, 1986).
3. See, for example, Thomas K. McCraw, editor, *America versus Japan: A Comparative Study* (Boston: Harvard Business School, 1986). The authors of this collection of articles explore the reason of "why the United States and Japan may be on a collision course for world economic leadership."
4. *Asahi Evening News* (December 8, 1986), p. 1.
5. For a discussion of the evolution and potential future of the region, see *Economic Changes in the Asian Pacific Rim: Policy Prospectus,* (Washington, D.C.: Congressional Research Service, August 1986).

Bibliography

Articles

Bergsten, C. Fred. "What to Do About the U.S.-Japan Economic Conflict." *Foreign Affairs* (Summer 1982): 1059−1075.

Brooks, William L., and Orr, Robert M., Jr. "Japan's Foreign Economic Assistance." *Asian Survey* (March 1985): 322−340.

"Bureaucrats' Rebellion Against Nakasone." *The Oriental Economist*, July 1985, p. 12.

"Business Fads: What's In and Out." *Business Week*, 20 January 1986, pp. 52−61.

"Can Japan Go Direct?" *Tokyo Business Today*, October 1986, p. 28.

Cline, John M. "Inter-MNC Arrangements: Shaping the Options for U.S. Trade Policy." *The Washington Quarterly* (Fall 1985): 57−71.

Culbertson John. "Control Imports Through Bilateral Pacts." *The New York Times*, 11 August 1985, p. F3.

−−−−. "Free Trade Is Impoverishing the West." *The New York Times*, 28 July 1985, p. F3.

"Importing a Lower Standard of Living." *The New York Times*, 17 August 1986, p. F3.

"The Dangers of Neonationalism." *Tokyo Business Today*, November 1986, pp. 22−26.

Federal Reserve Board of New York, "Japan's Intangible Barriers to Trade in Manufactures." *Quarterly Review* (Winter 1985−86): 11−18.

"The Hollow Corporation." *Business Week*, 3 March 1986, pp. 57−81.

Hosomi, Takashi. "The Ugly Japanese." *Tokyo Business Today*, March 1986, p. 8.

Ishizuka, Masahiko. "New Self-Assertion, But Whither." *The Japan Economic Journal*, 11 October 1986, p. 6.

"Japan Under Nakasone: Image of National Pride?" *The New York Times*, 26 September 1986, p. A13.

Kato, Susumu. "Three Scenarios for Economic Policy." *Economic Eye*, September 1986, pp. 19–22.

Komiya, Ryutaro. "Industrial Policy's Generation Gap." *Economic Eye*, March 1986, pp. 22–24.

Little, Jane Sneddon. "Intra-Firm Trade and U.S. Protectionism: Thoughts Based on a Small Survey." *New England Economic Review* (January/February 1986):

"Living Standards: A Self-Admiring Portrait." *The Japan Times*, 18 March 1986, p. 14.

Manoochehrix, G.H. "Suppliers and the Just-in-Time Concept." *Journal of Purchasing and Materials Management* (Winter 1984): 18.

Matsuzawa, Takuji. "Keidanren's Viewpoint on Government Spending and Future Administrative and Fiscal Reform." *Keindanren Review* (October 1985): 3.

Ohara, Susumu. "An Island Unto Itself: The Roots of Japan's International Isolation." *Speaking of Japan*, May 1986, pp. 18–21.

Ohmae, Kenichi. "Rising Yen But No Falling Trade Gap." *The Wall Street Journal*, 1 July 1986, p. 26.

Okawara, Yoshio. "Constructive Approaches Are What We Need." *Tokyo Business Today*, November 1986, p. 10.

Okita, Saburo. "Japan Is Advised to Diversify Investments to Aid Developing Nations' Economic Growth." *The Japan Economic Journal*, 30 August 1986, p. 7.

"Problems Experienced by Japanese Companies Investing in the EC: Keidanren Survey." *Keidanren Review* (February 1986): 8–11.

Rowan, Carl T. "The Real Issue Nakasone Raised." *The Washington Post*, 7 October 1986, p. A17.

Sato, Seizaburo, and Matsuzaki, Tetsuhisa. "Policy Leadership by the Liberal Democrats." *Economic Eye*, December 1984, pp. 25–32.

Saxonhouse, Gary R. "The Micro- and Macroeconomics of Foreign Sales to Japan." In *Trade Policy in the 1980s*, pp. 259–304. Edited by William R. Cline. Washington, D.C.: Institute for International Economics, 1983.

Scott, Bruce R. "National Strategies: Key to International Competition." In *U.S. Competitiveness in the World Economy*. Edited by Bruce R. Scott and George C. Lodge. Boston: Harvard Business School Press, 1985.

Thayer, Nathaniel B. "Nakasone Is Not a Racist." *The Washington Post*, 30 September 1986, p. A15.

"Thoughts on August 15." *Asahi Shimbun* (Tokyo), 16 August 1986, p. 9.

White, Theodore. "The Danger of Japan." *The New York Times Magazine*, 28 July 1985, pp. 18–22+.

Asahi Evening News (Tokyo), 25 April; 22 May; 23 July; 13, 16 September; 8, 20 December 1986.

Asahi Shimbun (Tokyo), 20 May, 2 August 1986.

Business Week, 8 April 1985; 5 May, 14 July, 24 November 1986.

The Daily Yomiuri (Tokyo), 28 March 1986, p. 5.

The Japan Economic Journal, 18 January; 22, 29 March; 12 April; 3 May; 7 June; 5

July; 9, 30 August; 6, 13 September; 11, 18, 25 October; 1, 15 November; 13 December 1986.
The Japan Times, 7, 12, 26 March; 24, 28 April; 28 July; 28 August; 14 October 1986.
The Journal of Commerce (New York), 7 July 1986.
The New York Times, 1 September 1985; 18 January, 3 May 1986.
The Wall Street Journal, 23 October, 13 December 1985; 29 August 1986.
The Washington Post, 31 July 1985, 15 September 1986.

Books

Abegglen, James C., and Stalk, George, Jr. *Kaisha: The Japanese Corporation.* New York: Basic Books, Inc., 1985.
Aho, Michael, and Aronson, Jonnathan Davis. *Trade Talks: America Better Listen.* New York: Council on Foreign Relations, 1986.
Bergsten, C. Fred, and Cline, William R. *The United States-Japan Economic Problem.* Washington, D.C.: Institute for International Economics, 1985.
Destler, I. M.; Fukui, Haruhiro; and Sato, Hideo. *The Textile Wrangle: Conflicts in Japanese-American Relations 1969–1971.* Ithaca, N.Y.: Cornell University Press, 1979.
Destler, I. M., and Sato, Hideo. *Coping with U.S.-Japanese Economic Conflicts.* Lexington, Mass.: D.C. Heath, 1982.
Higashi, Chikara. *Japanese Trade Policy Formulation.* New York: Praeger Publishers, 1983.
Johnson, Chalmers. *MITI and the Japanese Miracle.* Stanford, Calif.: Stanford University Press, 1982.
Ogura, Kazuo. *U.S.-Japan Economic Conflict.* Tokyo: Nihon Keizai Shimbun, 1982.
Ohmae, Kenichi. *Triad Power: The Coming Shape of Global Competition.* New York: Free Press, 1985.
McCraw, Thomas K., ed. *America versus Japan: A Comparative Study.* Boston: Harvard Business School, 1986.
Mouer, Ross, and Sugimoto, Yoshio. *Images of Japanese Society.* London: KPI Limited, 1986.
Pepper, Thomas; Janow, Merit E.; and Wheeler, Jimmy W. *The Competition: Dealing With Japan.* New York: Praeger Publishers, 1985.
Porter, Michael E., ed. *Competition in Global Industries.* Boston: Harvard Business School Press, 1986.
Rosecrance, Richard. *The Rise of the Trading State.* New York: Basic Books, Inc., 1986.
Vogel, Ezra F. *Japan as Number One.* Cambridge: Harvard University Press, 1979.
Wolf, Marvin. *The Japanese Conspiracy.* New York: Empire Books, 1983.

Studies

Japan Committee for Economic Development (Keizai Doyukai). *Technological Innovation and the Changing Industrial Society*. Tokyo: Japan Committee for Economic Development, 1985.
Japan External Trade Organization. *Japanese Manufacturing Companies Operating in Europe*. Tokyo: Japan External Trade Organization, 1986.
Organization for Economic Cooperation and Development. *Costs and Benefits of Protection*. Paris: Organization for Economic Cooperation and Development, 1985.

Special Reports

Organization for Economic Cooperation and Development. *Japan*. Paris: Organization for Economic Cooperation and Development, 1985.
——. *Urban Policies in Japan*. Paris: Organization for Economic Cooperation and Development, 1986.
U.S.-Japan Trade Study Group. *Progress Report: 1984*. Tokyo: U.S.-Japan Trade Study Group, 1984.
U.S.-Japan Trade Study Group. *TSG Progress Report 1986*. Tokyo: U.S.-Japan Trade Study Group, September 1986.
Advisory Committee for External Economic Issues. *Report of the Advisory Committee for External Economic Issues*. Tokyo: 9 April 1985.
The Report of the Advisory Group on Economic Structural Adjustment for International Harmony. Tokyo: Advisory Group on Economic Structural Adjustment for International Harmony, 7 April 1986.

Statistical Summaries

Keizai Koho Center. *Japan: An International Comparison*. Tokyo: Keizai Koho Center, 1985.
——. *Japan: An International Comparison*. Tokyo: Keizai Koho Center, 1986.
——. *Japan 1985, An International Comparison*. Tokyo: Keizai Koho Center, 1985.
Tokyo Chamber of Commerce and Industry. *Japan and the World in Statistics: 1986*. Tokyo: Tokyo Chamber of Commerce and Industry, 1986.
World Bank. *1983 World Bank Atlas*. Washington, D.C.: The World Bank, 1983.

Statements

Keizai Koho Center. *How Can Japan Contribute to a Healthy World Economy*.

Tokyo: Keizai Koho Center, March 1986.

——. "Needed: More Active Economic Cooperation." Tokyo: Keizai Koho Center, 28 June 1986.

Government Sources

United States

Congressional Budget Office. "The Effects of Targeted Import Surcharges." Staff Working Paper. Washington, D.C.: Congressional Budget Office, 1985.

Congressional Research Service. *Economic Changes in the Asian Pacific Rim: Policy Prospectus.* Washington, D.C.: Congressional Research Service, August 1986.

General Accounting Office. *United States-Japan Trade; Issues and Problems.* Washington, D.C.: Government Accounting Office, 1979.

Office of the United States Trade Representative. *The Japanese Government, External Economic Measures: The U.S. Government's Assessment of Their Implementation and Impact.* Washington, D.C.: Office of the United States Trade Representative, 1984.

Office of the United States Trade Representative. *National Trade Estimate: 1986 Report on Foreign Trade Barriers.* Washington, D.C.: Office of the United States Trade Representative, 1986.

U.S. Congress. Joint Economic Committee. *Industrial Policy Movement in the United States: Is It the Answer?.* Washington, D.C.: U.S. Government Printing Office, 1984.

U.S. Congress. Joint Economic Committee. *The U.S. Trade Position in High Technology: 1980–1986.* Washington, D.C.: Joint Economic Committee, October 1986.

U.S. Department of Commerce. Office of Business Analysis. *Trade Ripples Across U.S. Industries.* Working Paper. Washington, D.C.: U.S. Department of Commerce, 1986.

U.S. Department of State. *U.S.-Japan Joint Report on Sectoral Discussions,* by George Shulz and Shintaro Abe. Washington, D.C.: U.S. Department of State, 10 January 1986.

U.S. President. *Economic Report of the President.* Washington, D.C.: Government Printing Office, 1986.

U.S. President. *Economic Report of the President.* Washington, D.C.: U.S. Government Printing Office, 1987.

Vogt, Donna U. "Japanese Import Barriers to U.S. Agricultural Exports." Report No. 85–153 ENR. Washington, D.C.: Congressional Research Service, Library of Congress, 1986.

Japan

Economic Planning Agency. *Economic Survey of Japan (1984–1985)*. Tokyo: Economic Planning Agency, 1985.

——. *40 Years Since the End of World War II: On the Threshold of the Age of Maturity*. Tokyo: Economic Planning Agency, 1986.

——. Internal Working Papers. Tokyo: n.p., March 1986.

——. Internal Working Papers. Tokyo: n.p., May 1986.

——. *Outlook and Guidelines for the Economy and Society in the 1980s*. Tokyo: Economic Planning Agency, August 1983.

——. *White Paper on National Life: FY 1986*. Tokyo: Economic Planning Agency, 1986.

Economic Planning Agency, Economic Council, Long Term Outlook Committee. *Japan in the Year 2000*. Tokyo: The Japan Times Ltd., 1983.

Fair Trade Commission. Internal Documents. Tokyo: n.p., March 1986.

Japanese Government-Ruling Parties Joint Headquarters for the Promotion of External Economic Measures, *The Action Program for Improved Market Access* (Tokyo: 1985).

Ministry of International Trade and Industry. *Japan In the Global Community: Its Role and Contributions on the Eve of the Twenty-First Century*. Report of Roundtable Discussions on "Japan in the Global Community." Tokyo: Ministry of International Trade and Industry, April 1986.

Ministry of International Trade and Industry. *White Paper on Small and Medium Enterprises in Japan, 1985*. Tokyo: Ministry of International Trade and Industry, 1985.

Ministry of International Trade and Industry, Industrial Structure Council. *The Vision of MITI Policies in the 1980s*. Tokyo: Ministry of International Trade and Industry, March 1980.

Ministry of International Trade and Industry, Industrial Structure Council, Co-ordination Committee, Planning Subcommittee. *An Outlook for Japan's Industrial Society Towards the 21st Century*. Interim Report Focusing on International Perspective. Tokyo: Ministry of International Trade and Industry, February 1986. Internal Documents. Tokyo: n.p., May 1986.

Ministry of Labor. Internal Documents. Tokyo: n.p., March 1986.

Office of the Prime Minister. *Survey on National Attitudes on Living Standards*. Tokyo: Office of the Prime Minister, 1986.

Office of the Prime Minister. *Survey on People's Life*. Tokyo: Office of the Prime Minister, 1985.

Appendix A
List of Cartels Authorized by the Fair Trade Commission (as of April 30, 1986)

Name of Law	Purpose of Cartel	No. of Cases
Law to Prohibit Private Monopoly and to Secure Fair Transactions	Depression Cartel (Article 24-3)	0
	Rationalization Cartel (Article 24-4)	0
Law on Organizing Associations of Small and Medium Size Companies	Coordination clause on stable business	226
	Coordination clause on rationalization of business	0
	Subtotal	226
Export Import Transactions Law	Export transations agreement	41
	Export domestic transaction agreement	13
	Import transaction agreement	2
	Trade league	3
	Subtotal	59
Law of Temporary Measures for Improvement of Designated Industrial Structures	Coordinated action of scrapping facilities	6
Law of Temporary Measures to Stabilize Fertilizer Prices	Agreement on price between producers and sellers	3
Law on Fishing Union to Coordinate Fishing Production	Coordination clause	4
Law on Promotion of Export Oriented Fishing Industry	Coordination clause	4
Law of Special Measures to Restructure Fishing Industry	Reduction of no. of ships	0
Domestic Sea Transportation Union Law	Coordination clause	4
Law on Normalization of Management of Environmental Sanitation Business	Normalization clause	116
Total		422

Source: Fair Trade Commission (Tokyo: June 1986).

Appendix B
The Repetitive Pattern of
U.S.—Japan Trade Conflicts

While minor trade skirmishes went on most of the time, the first event in a major U.S.—Japan trade conflict usually involved the publication of trade data in the United States showing the nation's deteriorating global trade balance in general, and worsening bilateral trade balance with Japan in particular. Extensive treatment of these disputes by the mass media usually ignored the complex underlying causes, and this was normally accompanied by equally questionable statements and speeches by those members of Congress whose districts encompassed the most affected industries. The gradually more aggressive and protectionist rhetoric was eventually joined by those other members of Congress who found it politically expedient to do so. Since they all knew that any President would veto a strongly protectionist bill, they enjoyed what is known in Washington parlance as a "free ride"; members of Congress received the benefits of political posturing without the possibility of incurring any cost to themselves or to the nation. Simultaneously, the Administration was compelled to find ways to satisfy Congressional demands without relenting too much to the special interest groups; the Administration had to juggle its free trade stance and protect America's international trade obligations while maintaining good relations with its most important ally in the Far East. If Congressional elections were on the horizon, such maneuvers, difficult even under the best of circumstances, called for a great deal of political savvy and visible White House actions. One of the ways to achieve these ends was either to continue existing negotiations or to initiate a new round of talks with the Japanese, who at this point were usually relying on their Washington lobbyists for insights into unfolding events and cues on how to react. The narrowly defined American negotiation demands were usually accompanied by tough Administration statements issued partially to pressure the

238

Japanese and partially to appease the Congressional critics who blamed the Administration for not doing enough for America's farmers and manufacturers.

Throughout all this, the Japanese mass media representatives in Washington filed their exaggerated reports about the increasingly ugly mood in America and the Congressional activities shaping punitive legislation directed against Japan. They embellished the basic theme that the large, but now inefficient, America was again intimidating the small, but efficient, Japan with whatever illustrative stories they could find. Amid emotionally charged atmospheres, the negotiations, interspersed with Congressional hearings, disagreements along party lines, clashes among interest groups, and the usual give-and-take between Congress and the Administration, proceeded at a snail's pace. Delays were caused by the Japanese who had no proactive negotiation strategy and were usually engaged in consensus-building across several ministries, interest groups, and some key Liberal Democratic Party politicians who wanted to make the most of any difficulty the Prime Minister faced to strengthen their domestic political base for the time when their chance to take the government helm would arrive. The delayed Japanese responses to the forceful American demands were usually defensive and, more often than not, took the form of a "package" of market access measures. The Americans, exhausted by the long negotiations and irritated by what they saw as deceptive Japanese strategies, were additionally frustrated by the packages which could not possibly reduce the trade imbalances, no matter how unrealistic such expectations were in the first place, Americans regularly accused the Japanese of "doing too little, too late." The Japanese, upset by the outright rejection of what they considered to be their best efforts, were indignant, and felt misunderstood and unappreciated.   To the Japanese the sentiments about the unreasonable and aggressive Americans were proved all over again.

Eventually some sort of accommodation was reached. More often than not, the accommodation involved Japanese concessions, and this usually enabled both sides to take a respite. However, it was just a matter of time before the entire major conflict cycle repeated itself. The only difference might have been a change in the Administration, a slightly realigned Congress, or maybe a new Prime Minister in Tokyo; regardless, attitudes and approaches remained the same.

Appendix C
An Outline of the Decisions by the Ministerial Conference for Economic Measures

	External Economic Measures (Dec. 16, 1981)	Market Opening Measures (May 28, 1982)	On the Promotion of Immediate External Economic Measures (Jan. 13, 1983)	Comprehensive Economic Measures (Oct. 21, 1983)	External Economic Measures (Apr. 27, 1984)	External Economic Measures (Dec. 14, 1984)
1. Reduction of tariff rates. Relaxation of import restrictions (Reduction of tariff rates).	• Advanced implementation of scheduled reduction of tariff rates in the Tokyo round Agreements (across the board by two years). • Reduction of tariff rates on whisky, etc.	• Elimination or reduction of tariff rates on 215 items.	• Elimination or reduction of tariff rates on 86 items.	• Elimination or reduction of tariff rates on 44 items. • Advanced implementation of the scheduled reduction of tariff rates in the Tokyo round agreements (Industrial products). • Increase in the total ceiling quotas for industrial products by approximately 50% under the Generalized	• Elimination or reduction of tariff rates on 76 items. • Advanced implementation of the scheduled reduction of tariff rates in the Tokyo round agreements (taking into account the advanced implementation by other industrial countries, by one year for agricultural forestry and fishery products	• Advanced implementation of the scheduled reduction of tariff rates in the Tokyo round agreement, (Among agricultural, forestry, and fishery products, items of special interest to developing countries are to be advanced by (cont'd)

System of Preferences (GSP).

by two years for industrial products).
- Expansion of tariff-exempt items under the Agreement on Trade in Civil Aircraft.

two years, other products by one year; industrial products by two years.)
- Elimination of tariff on certain items (11 item).
- Increase in the total ceiling quotas for industrial products under the Generalized System of Preferences (GSP).
- Reduction of the number of Selected Products (SP) items under the GSP.
- Reduction of Exceptions to the Special GSP Treatment for Least-Developed Countries.

External Economic Measures (Dec. 16, 1981)	Market Opening Measures (May 28, 1982)	On the Promotion of Immediate External Economic Measures (Jan. 13, 1983)	Comprehensive Economic Measures (Oct. 21, 1983)	External Economic Measures (Apr. 27, 1984)	External Economic Measures (Dec. 14, 1984)
(Relaxation of import restrictions).					
• Review of import restrictions, report of the results.	• Increase in the quantities of import quotas or setting of the minimum amount of import quotas on four items, including herring and prepared or preserved pork.	• Relaxation of import restrictions on six items, including dried leguminous vegetables and groundnuts.	• Implementation of necessary measures on the basis of the results of consultations with other countries.	• Increase in the import of high-quality beef and oranges, etc. • Import liberalization and increase in the import quotas on some other items, etc.	
2. Improvements in standards and certification systems and import testing procedures, etc.	• Reviewing the procedures for domestic testing, etc., and putting together specific measures for their improvement by January 1982. For those	• Positive and active use of the OTO. Immediate improvement with respect to wild rice, metal bats, etc. • Smooth implementation of improvements	• Improvements in standards and certification systems (establishment of the Standards and Certification System Liaison and Coordinating Headquarter.	• Vigorous promotion of the activities of the OTO. • Steady implementation of improvements of standards and certification systems.	• Positive utilization of foreign testing organizations. • Acceptance of foreign test data and internationalization of Japanese standards. • Simplification	

and speeding up of certification procedures.

which require legal amendments, the necessary amendments are to be submitted to the next Ordinary Session of the Diet
• Administering import testing procedures, etc., appropriately.

in the customs clarance procedures, etc.
• Ensuring the transparency in the formulation of standards (participation of interested foreign parties in drafting process).

Further improvements of import testing procedures.
• Setting-up an OTO Advisory Council.
• Strengthening the functions of OTO (instituting a new system allowing the filing of complaints by proxy).
• Strengthening administrative inspection.
• Ministerial-level responsiveness. complaints by proxy).
• Strengthening administrative inspection.
• Ministerial-level responsiveness.

3. Import promotion.

• Dispatch of import

• Improvement of the

• Necessary improvement of

• Strengthening the import

• Implementation of programs to

External Economic Measures (Dec. 16, 1981)	Market Opening Measures (May 28, 1982)	On the Promotion of Immediate External Economic Measures (Jan. 13, 1983)	Comprehensive Economic Measures (Oct. 21, 1983)	External Economic Measures (Apr. 27, 1984)	External Economic Measures (Dec. 14, 1984)
missions, holding of product exhibitions, etc.	distribution system and business practices (study at the Manufactured Imports Promotion Committee of the Trade Conference, and strict enforcement of the Anti-monopoly Act, etc.). • Procurement by government agencies and organizations in	the distribution system and business practices. Further utilization of the business consultant service system. • Procurement by government agencies and organizations in	promotion function of Japan External Trade Organization (JETRO). • Improvement of the distribution system for imported goods. • Carrying out measures for import promotion (designation of a month to promote imported goods, etc.) • Promotion in the procurement of imported goods	promote market penetration of specific foreign manufactured goods • Support for exhibitions of foreign manufactured goods such as the German Exhibition '84 and the French Exhibition.	

accordance with the Agreement on Government Procurement.

by the government and other related entities.

accordance with the Agreement on Government Procurement. Implementation of necessary measures to facilitate participation of foreign companies in the NTT procurement.

- Liberalization of cigarettes importation, improvements in the distribution for imported cigarettes (Submission of the bills to reform tobacco monopoly system).

- Improvements in the distribution for imported cigarettes.

- The expansion of the number of retailers handling imported cigarettes.

- Gradual expansion of the number of retailers handling imported cigaretts who wish.

- Promoting imports through loans of Export-Import Bank of Japan.
- Promotion of yen

- Foreign Currency Loan for Urgent Imports.

- Foreign Currency Loan for Urgent Imports.

External Economic Measures (Dec. 16, 1981)	Market Opening Measures (May 28, 1982)	On the Promotion of Immediate External Economic Measures (Jan. 13, 1983)	Comprehensive Economic Measures (Oct. 21, 1983)	External Economic Measures (Apr. 27, 1984)	External Economic Measures (Dec. 14, 1984)
			denomunated short-term import finance.		
• Increase of the government oil stockpile by approximately 1.5 million kiloliters in FY 1982. • Implementation of necessary measures for promoting private stockpile of rare metals.	• Closer contact between governments for indirect support for the promotion of exports of Alaskan oil and Western coal from the United States.			• Enhancement of Japan's cooperative relationship with the energy-supplying countries (including followup measures of Joint Policy Statement announced by Japan — U.S. Energy Working Group). • Communications satellites, etc. — Necessary measures	

4. Market-opening in the high-technology

| | • Implementation of measures to relax regulations on | | | | |

sector, etc.

the use of telecommunication network for data processing.

- Commitment to free trade principles in trade in high-technology areas, promotion of international cooperation for research and development, consideration for the participation of foreign-owned Japanese firms in projects supported by the government.
- Establishment of Japan–U.S. Working Group on High-Technology
- Positive consideration of

will be taken to open the way for private firms to purchase foreign-made communications satellites.

— The way will be opened for the Nippon Telegraph and Telephone Corporation (NTT) to purchase communications satellites, either in Japan or from abroad on its own judgment, while ensuring consistency with the

External Economic Measures (Dec. 16, 1981)	Market Opening Measures (May 28, 1982)	On the Promotion of Immediate External Economic Measures (Jan. 13, 1983)	Comprehensive Economic Measures (Oct. 21, 1983)	External Economic Measures (Apr. 27, 1984)	External Economic Measures (Dec. 14, 1984)
	joint research and joint development of technology.			space development policy. — The way will be opened for the government and its related agencies to purchase either in Japan or from abroad those satellites which are not necessary for the autonomous development of technology under the	

space development policy.

- Telecommunication business.
  — Due application of law.

  — Consideration for fair competition concerning the new NTT business activities.

- Software protection.
  — Further interagency coordination.

- Review of the Real Demand Rule in Forward Exchange Transactions.
- Study toward establishment of the yen-denominated

5. Liberalization of Financial anc Capital Markets, etc.

- Continuation to firmly sustain the national treatment for the entry by and operations of foreign banks, insurance companies, and

External Economic Measures (Dec. 16, 1981)	Market Opening Measures (May 28, 1982)	On the Promotion of Immediate External Economic Measures (Jan. 13, 1983)	Comprehensive Economic Measures (Oct. 21, 1983)	External Economic Measures (Apr. 27, 1984)	External Economic Measures (Dec. 14, 1984)
	securities companies. • A request will be made to the associations concerned to set up an office providing information with respect to the entry by and operations of foreign banks, insurance companies, and securities companies. • Further facilitating foreign borrowers financing in the Japanese financial market.		banker's acceptance market. • Promotion of smoother exchange of capital. • Continuation to firmly sustain the national treatment for the entry by and operations of foreign banks, insurance companies, and securities companies, and promotion of the provision of information with regard to the Japanese financial and capital markets.		

6. Others	Positive promotion of industrial cooperation with the EC countries, etc., in mutual investment, technological exchange and	Encouraging industrial cooperation between the countries concerned on mutual investment, technological exchange, and	Encouraging industrial cooperation between the countries concerned on mutual investment, technological exchange, and	• Issuance of government-guaranteed overseas bonds in the U.S. market. • Arrangement of the legal framework for instruments such as public bonds denominated in foreign currencies, etc. • Promotion of the liberalization of financial and capital markets and the internationalization of the yen. • Improved system of information dissemination for international investment. • Strengthening the OTO system for

joint technology research and development cooperation in the markets of third countries, etc.

- Making efforts in full implementation of the medium-term target for Official Development Assistance (ODA).
- Usage of foreign grown grains in implementing the KR Food Aid budget.

cooperation in the markets of third countries, etc.

- Making efforts in full implementation of medium-term target for Official Development Assistance (ODA).
- Active pursuance of food aid using foreign products (the KR Food Aid Program, etc.).
- Making efforts in the expediting of

dealing with complaints regarding inward direct investments.
- Support for investment promotion missions.
- Procedural improvements to promote inward direct investment in Japan.
- Efforts for further improvement in effective as well as efficient promotion of economic cooperation.

cooperation in the markets of third countries, etc.

- Making efforts to have an appropriate

solution materialized as early as possible on the question of foreign lawyers' activities in Japan.

negotiations between the Japan Federation of Bar Association and the American Bar Association (ABA) on the question of foreign lawyer's activities in Japan.

- Constructive contribution to the formulation of international rules for trade in services in the GATT.
- Avoidance of excessive concentration exports of specific products.

- Avoidance of excessive concentration of exports of specific products.

- Avoidance of excessive concentration exports of specific products.

- Moderate exports in specific products.
- Appropriate financial cooperation with international financial institutions such as the DMF and IBRO.

Source "Report of the Advisory Committee for External Economic Issues" (Tokyo: April 9, 1985).

Appendix D
Select List of 1985 Legislative Actions affecting U.S.–Japan Trade Relations, 99th Congress

Continued automobile export restraints by Japan tied to U.S. access to Japanese domestic markets. Introduced 2/20/85.

Extension of Japanese voluntary restraint agreement on automobiles. Introduced 3/21/85.

President urged to respond to Japanese trade practices adversely affecting U.S. interstate commerce. Introduced 4/2/85.

Retaliation against Japan. Approved by House, 394–19, 4/2/85; placed on Senate legislative calendar 4/4/85.

Japanese trade practices and U.S.–Japan security relations linked. Introduced 7/31/85.

Automobile imports limited to 15 percent of U.S. market. Introduced 2/7/85.

Continues voluntary automobile export restraints until end of 1985. Introduced 2/7/85.

Import surcharge. Introduced 2/19/85.

Domestic content requirements for automobiles sold in the United States. Introduced 2/28/85.

Japanese auto import quotas. Introduced 4/4/85.

Response to unfair foreign trade practices. Introduced 7/18/85.

Trade Emergency and Export Promotion Act including 25 percent import surcharge. Introduced 7/18/85.

Amendment to Trade Act of 1974 to insure reciprocal trade opportunities. Introduced 6/24/85.

Retaliation against barriers to U.S. telecommunications products. Introduced 7/31/85.

Nonbinding resolution calling for retaliation against Japan for failure to open domestic markets. Approved by Senate, 92–0, 3/28/85; approved by Finance Committee as legislation, 12–4, 4/2/85.

Urges reduction of Japanese trade barriers. Introduced 2/27/85.

Calls Japanese market opening measures inadequate. Introduced 8/1/85.

254

Quantitative restrictions on imports of Japanese telecommunications products. Introduced 3/20/85.

Surcharge on all imports from Japan. Introduced 3/28/85.

U.S. export promotion through elimination of Japanese nontariff barriers. Introduced 3/28/85.

Blanket import surcharge on goods from Japan and other countries with major bilateral trade deficits. Introduced 4/16/85.

Telecommunications Trade Act of 1985. Reciprocal telecommunications market access bill. Introduced 4/17/85.

Japanese Technical Literature Act of 1985 to improve availability of science and engineering materials. Introduced 5/6/85.

Presidential action against unfair Japanese trade practices. Filed by Finance Committee 7/9/85.

Trade Emergency and Export Promotion Act including 25 percent import surcharge (Senate version). Introduced 7/17/85.

Fair Foreign Trade Practices Act. Modifies Section 301 of 1974 Trade Act by giving U.S. Trade Representative most authority currently held by President. Introduced 7/19/85.

Comprehensive Trade Law Reform Act (TRAC). Strengthens antidumping, countervailing duty provisions, and transfers Presidential authority to central Administration Introduced 7/25/85.

Appendix E
Summary of Action Program Details

More specifically, according to the report, tariffs were reduced by an average of 20 percent on 1,849 items as of January 1, 1986. Four wine tariffs were reduced one year in advance in April 1986; the review of the Generalized System of Preferences (GSP), which provides special treatment for certain developing countries, would be completed by April 1, 1987, at which time fundamental changes will be introduced.

Based on the principle of "limiting government intervention to a necessary minimum" and "consumer selection and responsibility to the fullest extent," 88 standards and a number of certification procedures were changed during the first year. Specific timetables for the approval and certification of 276 products were also announced. In contrast to the open-ended process of the past, the relevant ministries must provide an explanation if they cannot complete the certification processess within the specified time.

Electrical appliance safety standards have also been changed to conform to the guidelines of the International Electro-Technical Commission. Altogether, 40 standards applied to household electrical appliances and 17 applied to lighting equipment were affected. Comprehensive licensing standards for seven categories of cosmetics were also introduced. New import procedures for cars and trucks were established so that foreign manufacturers can now submit their own test data.

The Japanese also decided to accept foreign test data when considering applications for the Japan Industrial Standards (JIS) product certification. Fifty-seven foreign factories, including two Americans, have been authorized to submit such data. MITI has also given permission to Underwriter's Laboratories, Inc. (UL), of the United States to act as a designated JIS testing organization for other American manufacturers.

Moreover, 71 electric appliances no longer need to be certified by the Japanese authorities. Manufacturers may submit their own certification to prove that products meet required standards. The items include fans, coffee mills, lawn mowers, and sewing machines, among others. Accordingly, the new policy reduces the market introduction time of such products to about three months for domestic and to about four months for foreign manufacturers, both of whom in the past had to wait much longer for certification.

The Japanese government increased the transparency of standards development and revision through the publication of the structures of advisory councils and standards committees and their meeting schedules. Beginning in the spring of 1985, representatives of foreign interests have already participated in or attended meetings of the Japanese Industrial Standards Committee and of the Telecommunications Advisory Council.

In its final parts, the report referred to the various steps taken to liberalize the financial markets, and cited the legislation allowing foreign lawyers to practice in Japan as additional achievements.

On November 27, 1986, the Action Program Promotion Committee released an updated version of the First-Year Report which reviewed the progress of the implementation of all measures through September 1986, including the number of arrests connected with the counterfeiting of products. The updated report concluded that program implementation is on schedule and that the commitments made by the Japanese government are being fulfilled.

Appendix F
The 1985 Cabinet Directive concerning
the Detregulation of Urban Housing Construction

Big Item	*Middle Item*	*Small Item*
Rationalization of procedure and burden	a. Collection of excess burden	(a) Collection of excess guideline on land reclamation for housing purpose
		(b) Decision of flexible lasting greenery area in forest development permission relating to private forest targetted by regional forest development plan in an area covered by urbanization.
	b. Simplification and speed up of procedure	(a) Simplification and speedup of procedure for development permission judgment
		(b) Simplification and speedup of land conversion
		(c) Speedup of buried cultural asset investigation
		(d) Speedup of building confirmation procedure
		(e) Speedup of procedure regarding land transaction, etc.
Revision of city planning for the promotion of intensive use and building restriction	a. Revision of land use	(a) Collect change in classification from the first type in the center of big cities
		(b) Selection of rational shade restriction corresponding to revised land use

Big Item	Middle Item	Small Item
	b. Deregulation of volmetric regulation for the promotion of good redevelopment	(a) Increase in volume by the flexible implementation of special area and total designing system
		(b) Relaxation of regulation on water recycling system and area airconditioning
		(c) Promotion of excellent city redevelopment enterprise by private sector
Revision of city planning for scheduled development	a. Revision of line drawing for classification (deviation of area covered by urbanization and area adjusted under urbanization)	(a) Early completion of revision of line drawing for classification.
		(b) Functional use of line drawing system by the use of reserved population frame
	b. Promotion of area development in area adjusted under urbanization	(a) Deregulation of development permission scale condition
		(b) Promotion of investigation for a large-scale residential land development promotion in the area adjusted under urbanization of big city area
	c. Collective execution of land readjustment business	
Revision of restrictions for the promotion of effective use of land	a. Abolition of land-rent and house-rent control law	
	b. Revision of rent-land and rent-house law	
	c. Use of land credit	

Source: *The Economic White Paper 1986, Japan (Tokyo: Economic Planning Agency, 1986)*, p. 191.

Appendix G
Planned Major Foreign Direct Investment Projects-1986

Company Name	Country of Investment	Amount of Investment	Production Plans	Product
Toyota Motor	USA	100% subsidiary. $800 million	Yearly production of 200,000 Camry cars from 1988	Compact passenger cars
	Canada	100% subsidiary. CAN $400 million	Yearly production of 50,000 Corolla from 1988	Compact passenger cars
	Taiwan	Joint venture with Kuo Zui Motors. 22% Capital participation. ¥ 10 billion	Yearly production of 40,000 Corona from 1988	Compact passenger cars and others
	Taiwan	Joint venture with Fung Yong Co. 80% capital participation. ¥ 6 billion	Operation set for 1988	Components for vehicular stamping machines
Suzuki Motor	Canada	Fifty-fifty joint venture with U.S. GM. Capitaliztion unknown	Production begins 1989	Compact passengers cars and others
Mazda Motor	USA	100% subsidiary. ¥ 110 billion	Production begins fall 1987	Compact passenger cars
Fuji Heavy Industries	USA	Joint venture with Isuzu. 51% capital participation. Approx. ¥ 20 billion	Production begins 1989	Compact passengers cars
	Taiwan	—	Negotiations for joint venture production underway	Compact passenger cars
Isuzu Motors	USA	Joint venture with Fuji Heavy Industries. 49% capital participation. Approx. ¥ 20 billion	Production begins 1989	Compact passenger cars

Company	Country	Ownership	Status	Products
Nippondenso	Korea	Joint venture. Undetermined	Begin 1988 with yearly 100,000 production of vehicular airconditioners, 200,000 production of vehicular heaters	Automobile airconditioners and heaters
	Taiwan	Joint venture. Undetermined	Operation set for 1988	Automotive components
	USA	100% subsidiary. ¥ 20 billion	Pilot production began June 1986. Full production from 1989	Airconditioners, heaters, radiators
Tokai Rika	USA	100% subsidiary. Undetermined	Operation set for 1988	Automotive switches
Toyoda Gosei	USA	Joint venture, 80% capital participation. ¥ 1 billion.	Operation set for spring 1987	Steering wheels; small, precision, resin automotive components
Aisin Seiki	USA	100% subsidiary. Undetermined	Operation set for spring 1988. Present sales company to become production company	Components for automotive stamping machines
Pacific Industrial	USA	Undetermined	Operation set for 1987. Advanced up one year from 1988	Automobile tire valves, valve cores
Tokai Rubber Industries	USA	100% subsidiary. ¥ 700 million at beginning	Operation set for March 1987. mass production in 1988	Anti-shock rubber products
Fuji Seiko	USA		About 1988	Cemented carbide tools
Kinguawa Rubber Industrial	USA	Joint venture. 40% capital participation. ¥ 1.2 billion	About summer 1986	Automobile-use rubber parts
NHK spring	USA		Joint venture with GM to be decided this fall	Springs, sheet
	USA		Joint venture with Barnes Group to be decided this fall	Springs
Ichikoh Industries	USA		Under consideration to be decided in near future	Mirrors

Company Name	Country of Investment	Amount of Investment	Production Plans	Product
Iidosha Denki Kogyo	USA	100% subsidiary. ¥ 600 million	Yearly production of 120,000 from February 1987	Wipers
Toyo Radiator	USA, Europe	Joint venture, under consideration	Under consideration	Heat exchangers
Akebono Brake Industry	USA	Joint venture, 50% capital participation	—	Automobile brakes, etc.
Topy Industries	USA	100% subsidiary. $10 million	Present monthly production at 200,000 units	Automobile wheels
NIFCO	Korea	Joint venture, 57% capital participation. W 228 million	Monthly production of ¥ 10 million by end of 1986	Automobile-use fasteners
	Taiwan	Joint venture, 45% capital participation. NT $675	Monthly production of ¥ 2 to 3 million by end of 1986	Automobile-use fasteners
Matsushita Electric Industrial	USA	100% subsidiary of Matsushita-Kotobuki Electronics. $20 million	Operation for color TVs by fall 1986 VTR production to reach 20,000 by end of 1986.	Color TVs, VTRs
	USA	Fifty-fifty joint venture with Matsushita Communication Industrial. Investment of ¥ 3.6 billion by 1990	Operation set for May 1987	Car audio systems
	W. Germany	100% subsidiary. ¥ 2 billion gross investment	Operation by fiscal 1986	Mechanisms for VHS video equipment
	W. Germany	Fifty-fifty joint venture with Matsushita Electronic Components. ¥ 1 billion	Operation by end of 1986	Electronic components
Tokyo Sanyo Electric	Taiwan	—	Production begins first of 1987	Linear ICs
Toshiba	France	100% subsidiary. ¥ 4 billion	Production by end of 1986. First fiscal year production at	Plain paper copiers.

Company	Country	Investment	Operation	Products
	W. Germany	100% subsidiary. ¥ 4 billion within 3 years	100,000 units and at 200,000 by after 3 years Operation by March 1987 with yearly production at 120,000 and to reach 400,000 after 3 years	VTRs
	USA	100% subsidiary. ¥ 8 billion	Operation from fall 1986	Medical-use communication equipment
	USA	Joint venture with US Westing-house. ¥ 20 billion.	Operation by end of 1986 with first fiscal year production at 1 million units and 1.6 million by fiscal 1989	Braun tubes
Hitachi	USA	100% subsidiary. ¥ 10 billion within 5 years	Operation by April 1987 with sales targeted for first fiscal year at ¥ 5 billion.	Magnetic disk equipment and peripherals
	USA	100% subsidiary. Undetermined	Operation by June 1986 with monthly production of 50,000 units	Automotive electronic components
	USA	100% subsidiary.	Operation by May 1986 with yearly production of 100,000 units	VTRs
Mitsubishi Electric	USA	Branch factory of U.S. subsidiary. ¥ 3 billion	Yearly production set at 300,000 color TVs and 60,000 mobile telephone units	Color TVs, mobile telephones
Tokyo Electric	W. Germany	100% subsidiary. ¥ 1.5 billion	Monthly production set at 1,000 to 1,500 units beginning fall 1986	Typewriters
Sony	Austria	¥ 6 billion	Production begins by summer 1987 with production of 1 million CD software	CD software
	France	100% subsidiary. Several tens of millions of francs	Production of CD players set to 10,000 by end of 1986 and 8 mm VTRs at 5,000	CD players, VTRs

Company Name	Country of Investment	Amount of Investment	Production Plans	Product
Victor	USA	IVC U.S. subsidiary. ¥ 9 billion	Completion in 1987 with monthly production of video tape set at 1 million and that of CD software at 10 million	Video tape, CD software
Nippon Columbia	USA		Operation set for January 1987 with year CD production of 12 million	CDs
Clarion	USA	100% subsidiary of U.S. sales company. $2.9 million	Production set to start in January or February 1987 with monthly production of car audio systems of 10,000	Car audio systems
Pioneer Electronic	USA	100% subsidiary of U.S. sales company. ¥ 2.15 billion	Operation set from fall 1986 with output of 10,000 units	Car stereo systems
	Spain	Joint venture, 80% capital participation. Capitalized at ¥ 150 million	Production begins July 1986	Amplifiers
Canon	USA	100% subsidiary, ¥ 30 billion in 5 years	Operation set from spring of 1987, with output of 5,000 units	PPCs, OA equipment
Graphtec	USA	¥ 300 million	Operations set from first of 1987	Recorders
Brother Industries	USA	—	—	Electronic typewriters
TDK	USA	—	Production at videotape plant in Georgia to begin from end of 1986	Capacitors and other electronic components
Mitsumi Electric	SE Asia	—	Presently conducting a feasibility study for a seventh	—

Company	Region	Investment details	Operation timing	Products
			plant following those in Taiwan, Korea, and Malaysia	
Alps Electric	USA	Joint venture with subsidiary. 40% capital participation. $6 million	Operation to begin first of 1987	Car audio systems
Hirose Electric	USA	—	—	Connectors
CMK	Europe	—	—	Printed substrates
Asahi Glass	USA	Joint venture with U.S. PPG, 80% capital participation. $12 million	Operation set for 1987	Safety glass for vehicles
	USA	Joint venture with US PPG and others, 60% capital participation. $900,000	Operation set from April 1986	Assembly of safety glass for vehicles
	India	Joint venture with local capital, 20% capital participation. Rs2.2 million	Operation set from October 1986	Safety glass for vehicles
	Singapore	100% subsidiary. S$2 million	Operation set from 1987	Glass bulbs for Braun tubes
	Taiwan	100% subsidiary	Operation set from February 1987	Glass bulbs for Braun tubes
	Indonesia	Joint venture with local capital, 70% capital participation. ¥ 47 billion	Operation set from last half of 1988	Soda, PVC
Sanyo Shokal	USA	Joint venture, 75% capital participation. $3 million	Operation set from April 1987	Apparel
Bridgestone	USA	—	Undetermined	Automotive tires
Nippon Oil	USA	Joint venture, 32.5% capital participation		Oil
Nippon Pigment	USA	100% subsidiary	Second plant being planned	ABS, PP compounds
Nihon Parkerizing	China	Joint venture, 45% capital participation. ¥ 74 million	Operation set from May 1986	Antirust agents
Shin-etsu Chemical	Canada	Joint venture, 70% capital participation. ¥ 10 million	—	Rare-earth metals

Company Name	Country of Investment	Amount of Investment	Production Plans	Product
Pokka	USA		Presently being investigated, possible action after 1987	Beverages
	Canada			Instant tea liquid
Q.P.	USA	Fifty-fifty joint venture, Approx. ¥ 1 billion	U.S. incorporated Q & B Foods' new plant to be finished within 1986	Dressing, mayonnaise
Ajinomoto	Thailand	Joint venture, 70% capital participation. B330 million	Plant with yearly production of 2,000 tons to be completed fall 1986	Feedstuff-use lysine
	USA	Joint venture, 50% capital participation. $35 million	Plant with yearly production of 6,000 tons to be completed fall 1986	Feedstuff-use lysine
Yamanouchi Pharmaceutical	Ireland	100% subsidiary. ¥ 4 billion	Bulk production of peptic ulcer agents Gaster to begin in 1988	Peptic ulcer agents
Toyoda Machine Works	USA	$5 million	KD production by U.S. sales company to begin fall 1986	Machining centers, NC lathes

Source: *Tokyo Business Today* (September 1986), pp. 56–59.

About the Authors

Dr. Chikara Higashi is a member of the Japanese Diet since 1983. He is also the Founding President of the Research and Exploration Center for International Affairs in Tokyo and the President of the Japanese branch of Temple University. Prior to entering politics, he was a career official in the Ministry of Finance where he advanced to the position of Special Adviser to the Minister. Dr. Higashi is a graduate of Tokyo University and received his doctorate from the School of Government and Business Administration of The George Washington University. He is the author of several books in Japanese on various domestic issues, of a number of English and Japanese articles, and, in English, *Japanese Trade Policy Formulation*, published by Praeger in 1983.

Dr. G. Peter Lauter is a professor of international business at the School of Government and Business Administration of The George Washington University in Washington, D.C. He is the author of two books and a number of scholarly articles on various aspects of international business. He served as a consultant to U.S. government agencies and to private business firms in the United States and abroad. Dr. Lauter is a senior associate of the Research and Exploration Center for International Affairs in Tokyo. He holds a Ph.D. from the Graduate School of Management of the University of California at Los Angeles.

Index